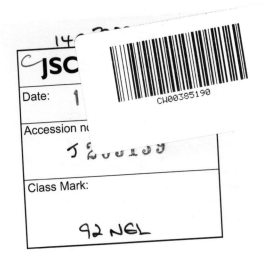

Admiral Lord Nelson

Admiral Lord Nelson

Context and Legacy

Edited by
David Cannadine

First published 2005 by
PALGRAVE MACMILLAN
Houndmills, Basingstoke, Hampshire RG21 6XS and
175 Fifth Avenue, New York, N.Y. 10010
Companies and representatives throughout the world

PALGRAVE MACMILLAN is the global academic imprint of the
Palgrave Macmillan division of St Martin's Press LLC and of
Palgrave Macmillan Ltd.
Macmillan® is a registered trademark in the United States,
United Kingdom and other countries. Palgrave is a registered
trademark in the European Union and other countries.

ISBN-13: 978–1–4039–3906–7 hardback
ISBN-10: 1–4039–3906–3 hardback

This book is printed on paper suitable for recycling and made
from fully managed and sustained forest sources. Logging,
pulping and manufacturing processes are expected to conform to
the environmental regulations of the country of origin.

A catalogue record for this book is available from the British
Library.

A catalogue record for this book is available from the
Library of Congress

Printed and bound in Great Britain by
CPI Antony Rowe, Chippenham and Eastbourne

Contents

Notes on Contributors

David Cannadine is Queen Elizabeth the Queen Mother Professor of British History at the Institute of Historical Research, University of London, where he was previously Director. Among his many publications are *The Decline and Fall of the British Aristocracy, G.M. Trevelyan: A Life in History, The Rise and Fall of Class in Britain,* and *Ornamentalism: How the British Saw their Empire.* He is also the editor of *What is History Now?* and *History and the Media.*

Martyn Downer was born in 1966 and educated at Stowe and at Edinburgh University where he studied history. In 1993, after some years working in the art and antiques business in London, Martyn joined Sotheby's auctioneers where he subsequently became a director and head of the jewellery department. He lives in rural Hertfordshire with his wife, who is a painter, and his three young children. In 2003 Martyn left Sotheby's to pursue a career as a full time writer. *Nelson's Purse* (Bantam Press, 2004) is his first book. He is currently working on an account of life inside the Court of Queen Victoria.

John B. Hattendorf is the Ernest J. King Professor of Maritime History and Chairman of the Maritime History Department at the US Naval War College, Newport, Rhode Island. He holds degrees in history from Kenyon College, Brown University, and the University of Oxford, where he earned his D.Phil. at Pembroke College in 1973–79. He has taught at the National University of Singapore and has been visiting scholar at the German Armed Forces Military History Research Office. The author or editor of more than thirty books and numerous articles, his scholarship in the field of maritime history has been recognised with the award of an honorary doctorate of humane letters, the Caird Medal of the National Maritime Museum, Greenwich, and the K. Jack Bauer Award from the North American Society for Oceanic History.

Holger Hoock is a British Academy Postdoctoral Fellow in the Faculty of History and at Selwyn College, Cambridge. A Fellow of the Royal Historical Society, he is also a research curator for the exhibition 'Nelson and Napoleon' at the National Maritime Museum (2005). His publications include *The King's Artists: The Royal Academy of Arts and the Politics of British Culture, 1760–1840* (Clarendon Press, 2003), proxime accessit in the RHS Whitfield Prize 2003, and essays on artists' dinner culture, the history of collecting, and the history of national commemoration.

John MacKenzie is Professor Emeritus of Imperial History at Lancaster University, and also holds honorary professorships at the Universities of St

Andrews, Aberdeen and Stirling. He is the general editor of the Manchester University Press 'Studies in Imperialism' series and has written extensively on the popular culture of imperialism, including the role of mythic heroes. He is currently interested in the dissemination of the culture of empire around the 'British World'.

Nicholas A.M. Rodger has had a diverse career, initially in the Public Record Office, later attached to the National Maritime Museum, and now as Professor of Naval History at the University of Exeter. He has published two of three volumes of *A Naval History of Britain: The Safeguard of the Sea* (HarperCollins, 1997) and *The Command of the Ocean* (Allen Lane, 2004).

Colin White is Deputy Director of the Royal Naval Museum in Portsmouth, and is currently serving on secondment at the National Maritime Museum. He has written and broadcast widely on Nelson and the Navy of his times. *The Nelson Letters Project*, of which Colin is director, has located over 1,300 unpublished letters written by Nelson and he will be publishing the results of his research in two ground-breaking books this year – *Nelson: The New Letters* (Boydell and Brewer: forthcoming April 2005) and *Nelson the Admiral* (Sutton and the Royal Naval Museum: forthcoming August 2005).

Kate Williams began researching her biography of Emma Hamilton in 2001. The book will be published by Random House in the US and UK in 2006. Kate studied a BA at Oxford, an MA in eighteenth-century writing and society at Queen Mary, University of London and a D.Phil. at Oxford in eighteenth-century culture. She lectures regularly on Emma Hamilton, as well as on Nelson, and she has consulted and appeared on television programmes about Emma and Nelson.

Kathleen Wilson is Professor of History at the State University of New York at Stony Brook. She writes on masculinity, popular politics and the culture of empire in eighteenth-century Britain and its extended domains. Her most recent books are *The Island Race: Englishness, Empire and Gender in the 18th century* (Routledge, 2003), and *A New Imperial History: Culture, Identity and Modernity in Britain and the Empire, 1660–1840* (Cambridge University Press, 2004). She is currently at work on a study of British theatre and the colonial order, 1720–1840, in sites that range across the Atlantic and Pacific worlds.

List of Illustrations

Figures

Colour plates

17. Pendants and brooches made to commemorate Nelson after the Nile and after Trafalgar.

18. 'Dresses à La Nile respectfully dedicated to the Fashion Mongers of the day'. A print from October 1798 gently pokes fun at the British craze for wearing Nelson fashions.

19. *Emma Lady Hamilton as A Bacchante* Louise Elizabeth Vigée-Le Brun, 1790–91. Beautiful, artistic, glamorous, and compelling, Lady Hamilton recurred again and again in eighteenth-century novels as the desirable, talented, and often virtuous heroine.

20. *Rear-Admiral Lord Nelson* Lemuel Francis Abbott, 1800.

21. Emma Hamilton as Britannia, crowning the brows of the hero. Thomas Baxter, 1806.

22. Lieutenant Nelson boarding an American prize. Richard Westall, 1806.

23. *Victory at Trafalgar* J.M.W. Turner, 1822–24.

24. *England's Pride and Glory* Thomas Davidson, c.1890.

25. Nelson's 'Trafalgar' coat.

26. *Funeral procession of the late Lord Viscount Nelson, from the Admiralty to St Paul's, London, 9th January 1806* M. Merigot after Augustus Charles Pugin, 1 April 1806.

27. *Interment of the Remains of the late Lord Viscount Nelson, in the Cathedral of St Paul, London on the 9th January 1806* Frederick Christian Lewis after Augustus Charles Pugin, 1 April 1806.

28. *Nelson's Tomb, Crypt of Saint Paul* Anonymous, date unknown.

29. *The Death of Lord Nelson* Benjamin West, 1806.

30. *The Sailor's Monument to the Memory of Lord Nelson* William Holland, 1806.

31. *Greenwich Pensioners at the Tomb of Nelson* H. Macbeth-Raeburn after Sir John Everett Millais, date unknown.

32. *The United Service* Andrew Morton, 1845.

Acknowledgements

The publishers wish to thank the following for the use of images in the book:

John Flaxman, *Monument to Lord Nelson* (1808–18), and Thomas Banks R.A., *Monument to Captain Burgess, St Paul's Cathedral, London* (1798–1802) appear courtesy of the Conway Library, Courtauld Institute of Art, London

Benjamin West, *The Death of Lord Nelson* (1807) appears courtesy of the Walker Art Gallery, Liverpool

John Bacon, *Monument to Major-General Dundas for St Paul's Cathedral, London,* Design drawing, c.1798 appears courtesy of the National Archives

Benjamin West, *Sketch for a Monument to Lord Nelson* (1807) appears courtesy of Yale Center for British Art, New Haven, CT

All other pictures appear courtesy of the National Maritime Museum, Greenwich

Admiral Lord Nelson

Introduction

'England expects every man will do his duty.' 'Thank God I have done my duty.' With these stirring words – the first his signal to the British fleet on the eve of the Battle of Trafalgar, the second his last recorded utterance as he expired on the deck of the aptly-named HMS *Victory* – Horatio, Viscount Nelson created and crafted his own story-book ending to his own story-book life on 21 October 1805. For his death came at his supreme moment of triumph, his annihilation made possible his apotheosis, and Nelson was launched on his new career of posthumous fame, national glory and global heroism which continues to flourish, to fluctuate, and to renew itself, down to our own day. Thus did a mere mortal man become 'the immortal memory' – perpetuated in countless biographies, in shrines and relics and statues and rituals, in the Trafalgar Day toast, in Trafalgar Square itself, and much more besides. In 2002, Nelson was the only military figure voted into the top ten of the BBC's 'Great Britons', and the two hundredth anniversary of his death witnesses another upsurge of interest, analysis, reflection and retrospection.

One reason why the heroic Nelson has endured so long is that for one hundred and fifty years after his death, Britain continued to be a great maritime and a great imperial power, and his dutiful professionalism, mastery of strategy and tactics, and matchless leadership remained not only resonant and relevant, but also instructive and inspiring. At the same time, Nelson was so complex and so protean a character that there were many other reasons for admiring him, which means that there was (and is) a Nelson to suit almost every taste: the son of an obscure country parson, who raised himself to fame and glory by his own efforts and abilities; the fearless fighter and courageous champion, who was indifferent to his own physical danger; the wise commander and humane captain, who loathed the carnage and waste and destruction of war; the insubordinate officer who was as devoted to his men as they were to him; the ardent, romantic, Byronic lover, with a complex private life; the wounded and disabled figure who triumphed over every obstacle and adversity; and so on. Only the primest of moralists (among them Gladstone) have been indifferent to Nelson's many merits or immune to his undoubted charms.

The essays gathered together in this book are offered as a further contribution to the constant process of Nelsonian re-evaluation, and also as a new examination of Nelson's continuing appeal: hence the 'context' and the 'legacy' of the title. With so many Nelsons now on offer, and with many of them stressing the personal, the private and the emotional, it is important to remember that he lived primarily for duty, for the Navy and for the sea. N.A.M. Rodger's opening chapter emphatically makes these points as, in a complementary manner does Martyn Downer, with his examination of Nelson's networks of all-male friendships. In a sense, there was nothing particularly unusual about all of this: Nelson operated in an ordinary professional environment, but transformed and transcended it because of his extraordinary talents and accomplishments. As a result, and as Kathleen Wilson demonstrates, he was both a quintessentially aggressive, masculine and patriotic male, in the tradition of a long line of national naval heroes, yet also the wounded embodiment of a very different version of manliness; and this, in turn, may help us understand Nelson's wide appeal to late eighteenth and early nineteenth century women which Kate Williams describes.

His outstanding naval victories; his remarkable range of public interest and attention as both a fighting man and a vulnerable man; the triumph and tragedy of Trafalgar: all this helps explain Nelson's unrivalled resonance and popularity in life, as well as the cult which developed (and still abides) after his death. But this is not the whole story of his astonishing and sustained apotheosis. For Nelson's legacy was an appropriately complex amalgam of sentiment and spontaneity, deliberation and calculation. In life, as Colin White points out, Nelson himself had carefully cultivated and manipulated his own image, and in death his relics were safeguarded, his biography carefully crafted, and the rituals of Trafalgar Day self-consciously created; and at the same time, as Holger Hoock reminds us, the elaborate memorial ensemble in St Paul's Cathedral was constructed for similar purposes. Thus securely established, the cult of Nelson spread across the whole of nineteenth-century Britain, to the Empire beyond and even, according to John MacKenzie, as far as Japan; while, as John B. Hattendorf explains, his exploits afloat were studied at the highest level by naval personnel in Europe and Asia and in North and South America.

These contributions also serve to remind us that the centenary of Trafalgar was celebrated in circumstances very dissimilar from those of 1805, just as 2005 in turn is very different again from 1905. By the early twentieth century, the steel-and-shell technology of dreadnoughts was wholly different from the canvas and cannon of Nelson's age of fighting sail, and Britain's enemy was no longer France, which had recently become an ally, but Imperial Germany. Hence, perhaps, the rather muted centenary observances, for fear of offending the French. During the First World War, a full-scale battle between the British and the German navies was eagerly anticipated. But while the British wanted another Trafalgar, all they got was Jutland; and while they hoped for another Nelson, they got Jellicoe instead. To be sure, the German Fleet never left harbour again, and would eventually surrender; but the sort of Nelsonian, knock-out victory which had been hoped for never materialised. By the inter-war years, Britannia was obliged to share the waves with other navies, as was tacitly acknowledged with the founding of the National Maritime Museum at Greenwich in 1934. From the outset, Nelson himself was the star exhibit, as in many ways he still is.

One hundred years further on, and in the year of the two hundredth anniversary of Trafalgar, the picture is very different again. The Royal Navy may be efficient, but it is also exiguous; Britain's once far-flung seaborne empire has vanished; and even the royal yacht has been given up. To be sure, rival navies had once again confronted each other in the North Sea and the Mediterranean during the Second World War, but most of the fighting was done on the eastern front, or in the Pacific, where aircraft carriers had superseded battleships as the most significant means of projecting force by sea. In the era of decolonisation, of naval downsizing, and of the guided missile and the hydrogen bomb, Nelson's world seemed ever more remote: a place of escapism and nostalgia, of fiction rather than fact, as exemplified in the novels of C.S. Forester, Alexander Kent, Dudley Pope and Patrick O'Brian. As a result, the Nelson who appeals to most Britons today is not the dutiful professional and the victorious admiral, but someone seeking fulfilment in his private life, and who is also an example and inspiration to the disabled. But as this book serves to remind us, there have been many varied and different Nelsons during the intervening two hundred years, and who can know in which new or old guises he may reappear before his third centenary in 2105?

The following chapters originated from lectures delivered in the Beveridge Hall of the University of London in October 2004, and they were generously supported by a grant from the Linbury Trust, which helped to make the occasions especially memorable. The lectures were jointly sponsored by the National Maritime Museum and the Institute of Historical Research, and I am most grateful to their respective Directors, Roy Clare and David Bates, for their help, encouragement and support. At the Museum, special thanks are owed to Margarette Lincoln, Nigel Rigby, Janet Norton and Rachel Giles; and at the Institute to Helen Cornish, Felicity Jones and Richard Butler. Once again, it has been a pleasure to work with the publishing team at Palgrave: Sam Burridge,

Luciana O'Flaherty, Michael Strang and Dan Bunyard. Ray Addicott and Chase Publishing Services have seen the book through the press with their customary speed and skill and sureness of touch. I am especially grateful to the contributors for converting their original lectures into publishable essays, and for meeting a very tight deadline with exemplary professionalism and good cheer. Like Nelson, they have done more than their duty, and I thank them all.

David Cannadine
New Year's Day 2005
Norfolk

Part One
Context

1
Nelson and the British Navy: Seamanship, Leadership, Originality

N.A.M. Rodger

There was much about Nelson's career which was not at all unusual. As the son of a country clergyman, he came from that wide social range from the lesser gentry to the middle classes which provided the Royal Navy with so many of its officers. He might be compared with his contemporaries on the flag list St Vincent, Duncan, Cornwallis, Keith, Gardner, Gambier, Collingwood, and the brothers Bridport and Hood; St Vincent's father was a provincial barrister, Duncan's Provost of Dundee, Gardner's an army officer, Gambier's lieutenant-governor of the Bahamas, Collingwood's a merchant, and the Hoods' another clergyman. Cornwallis and Keith were younger sons of peers, but in Keith's case his father was both poor and Jacobite. Only Cornwallis – ironically the only one of the ten who was never ennobled – could be said to have come from a privileged home. Nelson's career benefitted from the powerful patronage of his uncle Captain Maurice Suckling, Controller of the Navy from 1775 to 1778, who helped him to his first lieutenant's commission at the age of eighteen, but such interest was a common feature of successful careers. St Vincent's uncle Sir Thomas Parker was Chief Baron of the Exchequer; Cornwallis was the son and nephew of peers close to Sir Robert Walpole; Keith, who had no notable patron early in his career, became a friend of the Prince of Wales; Gambier had two uncles on the flag list; and the Hood brothers were connected to the Pitt–Grenville cousinhood. Only Duncan, Gardner and Collingwood seem to have had no other backers than those they had earned by their own service.

Having reached captain's rank at the age of twenty-one (from which all promotions to flag rank were made by seniority), Nelson had moved as quickly as possible to becoming an admiral, which he did in 1797 at the age of thirty-eight, but this too was far from unprecedented. Barrington, with a brother on the Admiralty Board, was a captain at eighteen and an admiral at thirty-nine; Keppel, son of an earl, was a captain at nineteen (less than five months after his first commission as lieutenant), a commander-in-chief at twenty-three, and an admiral at thirty-seven. Moreover the speed with which Nelson's career advanced can be explained to a considerable extent by the luck of a suitable date of birth. He belonged to a fortunate generation, of which over one tenth became admirals. He was promoted from lieutenant to captain between 1777 and 1779, exactly the years of maximum demand for officers as the American War of Independence broke out, and twenty years later the French Revolutionary War came at the right moment for him to distinguish himself as a commodore and confirm his suitability for flag rank. None of this would have been possible if he had lacked talent, but little of it was unusual by the standards of other talented and lucky officers.[1]

I

Nelson's education was equally typical of senior officers of his day. Like him, most of them had left school at around twelve or thirteen. A generation or two earlier, there had been admirals like Russell, Norris, Henry Medley, Thomas Pye and John Elliot who never mastered even simple English spelling. Lord Howe never learnt to express himself intelligibly, in speech or writing. Against such a background Nelson's fluent pen shows to good effect, and his ignorance of foreign languages and the wider world was not out of the ordinary. Nevertheless we have to acknowledge that Nelson's career survived some serious political misjudgements. As a young frigate captain stationed in the West Indies in the aftermath of the American War of Independence, his enthusiastic efforts to enforce the Navigation Acts in circumstances unforeseen when the acts were originally passed had done real damage to British economic, political and diplomatic interests, and incurred the wrath both of his commander-in-chief and of the civil authorities. Though he had the letter of the law on his side, and though in the end the government was embarrassed into supporting him, it is hard to avoid the conclusion that he was out of his depth. His stubborn independence of mind and confidence in his own judgement would have been more admirable if he had been less ignorant and more prudent. Moreover it is not as easy as his admirers would wish to praise his disinterested motives, for he stood to make, and tried to make, a lot of money by seizing American merchantmen for trading in breach of the law.

Much less than this was needed to set a black mark against an officer's name, and this was not the only episode which cast doubt on young Captain Nelson's judgement. In November 1786, when he was temporarily the senior officer on the station, George III's son Captain Prince William Henry of the frigate *Pegasus* arrived in the Leeward Islands. The prince's disciplinarian enthusiasm, untempered by moderation or experience, soon put him at odds with the older officer who had been appointed as his First Lieutenant. An uncritical enthusiast for the royal house, Nelson unhesitatingly backed the prince, against the common opinion of other officers on the station. What was worse, he began to imitate the prince's disciplinarian excesses himself. As a result of this affair two observers concluded that he was not to be trusted with independent responsibility: Lord Howe at the Admiralty, and George III, who viewed his son's faults of character with a dispassionate, not to say jaundiced eye. Soon afterwards Nelson's ship was paid off, and he entered on five years of half pay. When the rest of the Navy mobilised in the face of the Nootka Sound crisis of 1790, he was not offered a ship. This was the first and only period of his life in which he lived for any length of time with his wife Frances, whom he had married in the West Indies in 1787.

Nelson's grounded, if not shipwrecked, career was refloated by the outbreak of the French Revolutionary War in 1793. In an age when navies were demobilised in peacetime, there was always a serious shortage of officers with recent sea experience on the outbreak of a war. Even so, Nelson was given only the *Agamemnon*, one of the smallest class of ship of the line, and he was not considered for any sort of independent command. As part of the Mediterranean squadron, he was under the immediate eye of his commander-in-chief, Lord Hood. It was no sort of disgrace – the majority of line-of-battleships were always in the major squadrons – but it was the sort of situation where officers were put whose judgement was not altogether trustworthy. Bold, sanguine and aggressive, Hood was Nelson's kind of admiral. Himself a less than safe pair of hands in matters of strategy and diplomacy, who had no time for the immobility of the British army of the day, Hood soon identified in Nelson the qualities which the new kind of warfare demanded. It was evident to both of them that the era of civilised restraint in war was over. In the face of murderous fanatics who had abolished religion and overthrown civil society, who massacred prisoners and threw away their own men's lives in senseless slaughter, the only response was an uncompromising determination to conquer. Unlike the American war, this was not a civil war in which political judgement would have been as important as military. Though the French Revolution had some British sympathisers, the great majority of the nation agreed with Nelson that moderation in war against such enemies was futile. Moreover, as the armies of Revolutionary France spread across Europe, this war took on for Britain the character of a desperate struggle for survival.

These were the circumstances in which Nelson first had the chance to shine professionally. In January 1794 Hood entrusted Nelson with the blockade of Corsica, and cooperation with the Corsican patriots under Pasquale Paoli who were trying to throw off French rule. Cooperation with the British army was more difficult, but in spite of General David Dundas's refusal to support it, Hood undertook the siege of Bastia with the squadron's marines alone. Nelson landed to take command on 4 April, and in eight weeks Bastia surrendered. In June, this time in conjunction with the army, Nelson was once again ashore besieging Calvi, which surrendered on 10 August. It was during this siege that he received the wound which cost him the sight of his right eye. In the next year, with the Mediterranean Fleet temporarily under the command of Vice-Admiral William Hotham, naval warfare reverted to an older style. In March 1795 the French fleet (seventeen ships of the line) made a sortie from Toulon in the hope of retaking Corsica. The British intercepted them and in the course of a straggling engagement on 13–14 March, took two ships from the fleeing enemy. The *Agamemnon* was faster than the rest of the fleet, and Nelson had the leading share in the success, but he was thoroughly dissatisfied with Hotham's caution, and believed a decisive victory could have been achieved. 'My disposition can't bear tame and slow measures. Sure I am, had I commanded our fleet on the 14th, that either the whole French Fleet would have graced my triumph, or I should have been in a confounded scrape.'[2] On 14 July a similar affair took place, in which another French ship was taken, but to Nelson's disgust Hotham again recalled his headmost ships as the French closed their own coast.

Nelson was now put in command of a small detached squadron supporting the Austrian army and blockading Genoa, nominally neutral but increasingly French-controlled. Nelson imposed the blockade on his own initiative, well understanding the risk of being disowned by government and ruined by private lawsuits: 'Political courage in an officer abroad is as highly necessary as military courage', he wrote.[3] He had shown political courage before, of course – to very bad effect – but in his first independent command for eight years, he was beginning to show that his judgement had matured.

In January 1796 the new commander-in-chief, Sir John Jervis, arrived on the station. Jervis in his way was as much a stranger to civilised moderation as any French revolutionary. He and Nelson took to one another at once; in April Jervis appointed him a commodore, in June he hoisted his broad pendant in the *Captain*, 74, and in August Jervis (stretching his authority) made him an established commodore with a flag-captain – in all but name an acting rear-admiral. Meanwhile the strategic situation was deteriorating rapidly, as the French armies under General Bonaparte continued their advance across northern Italy, and Spain was forced into the war on the side of France. The position of the Mediterranean Fleet was now precarious. In the autumn the government took the decision to abandon Corsica and withdraw the fleet from the Mediterranean. In practice slow communications obliged Jervis and Sir Gilbert Elliot, the Viceroy of Corsica, to take many critical decisions themselves, guessing ministers' intentions. The evacuation of Corsica in the face of advancing French troops was perilous, and it was largely thanks to Nelson's determination that Elliot, the entire garrison and nearly all their stores were safely retrieved from Bastia in October and landed on Elba, now the last British refuge in the Mediterranean, while the fleet withdrew to Gibraltar.

On 15 December Nelson with two frigates alone was sent back on a perilous rescue mission. On the way they met two Spanish frigates and Nelson in the *Minerve* captured the *Santa Sabina*, after a very severe fight. Next day the appearance of a Spanish fleet forced Nelson to abandon his prize, but the two frigates escaped to reach Porto Ferrajo on Christmas Day. There Nelson came around the gun-deck of the other frigate, the *Blanche*, shaking hands with the men and congratulating them on their performance in action. There was more to this episode than simply a successful action. The *Blanche* had been an unhappy ship for some time and she had just lost her long-serving captain, court-martialled for sodomy. The men were disturbed, ashamed of the disgrace cast on their ship, divided by the captain's activities. By reaching out to them at this moment, Nelson was implicitly extending his sympathy. Soon afterwards these same men mutinied rather than receive a new captain, 'bearing the name of such a tarter by his own ships crew'. This was a real and dangerous mutiny, not just a strike or demonstration. The men were armed and on the verge of firing on their officers, but when Nelson came on board he was able to win them over with a few words. He already had their trust.[4] Very few if any British admirals had Nelson's instinctive ability to win the sympathy of people of every social background. In an age of revolution it was a quality as essential, and very much rarer, than purely military skill, and it was soon to be very much in demand.

Sailing from Elba on 29 January 1797 with Elliot and the naval stores, Nelson rejoined Jervis on 13 February and returned to the *Captain*. These three years in the Mediterranean had demonstrated some of Nelson's professional qualities: his outstanding physical courage combined with coolness under fire, his aggressive determination to attack the enemy whenever possible, his indifference to convention and his outstanding tactical judgement. His reputation in the Navy was now largely restored, but he was as yet unknown to the public at large. Next day, 14 February, that changed. With fifteen ships of the line Jervis met and attacked a Spanish fleet which was reckoned at twenty-seven ships of the line, though in fact some of the ships were transports, and there were only twenty-two Spanish battleships present. The British were well aware of the poor efficiency of their late allies, and Jervis rightly judged that 'the circumstances of the war in these seas, required a considerable degree of enterprise'.[5] Jervis deftly cut between the two Spanish forces, then tacked in succession to attack the main body from the rear. This tactic of 'rolling up' an ill-formed enemy from the rear was something of a British speciality, which had brought victory to Anson, Hawke and Rodney. Initially it went well, but a bold counter-attack by part of the Spanish force held up Jervis and the centre of his fleet, leaving the leading ships unsupported. At this moment the Spanish commander-in-chief signalled to his leading ships to bear up and attack the British rear, a manoeuvre which might well have retrieved his situation if it had been smartly carried out.

Seeing the risk, Jervis ordered Rear-Admiral Charles Thompson with his rear division to tack in order to frustrate the Spanish move. Thompson did nothing, but Nelson (fourth from the rear) wore out of line and cut across to join the head of the British line, to leeward of the Spaniards, thus blocking their move. With part of the British to leeward of the Spanish main body and others coming up to windward, a fierce battle developed, in the course of which the *Captain* was considerably damaged. She was in action with the *San Nicolas* and *San Josef* when Collingwood in the *Excellent* came up on the other side of them and fired with such effect that the Spanish ships collided in confusion. Seeing the opportunity, and with his own ship now almost unmanageable, Nelson ran aboard the *San Nicolas*, and himself led one of the two boarding parties. There was bloody fighting, but it was soon over. The much bigger *San Josef*, however, was still alongside, though heavily pounded by another British ship from the other side. Before the Spaniards could rally, Nelson led the boarders onward and took her too: 'and on the quarterdeck of a Spanish first-rate, extravagant as the story may seem, did I receive the swords of the vanquished Spaniards; which as I received I gave to William Fearney, one of my bargemen, who put them with the greatest sang-froid under his arm'.[6] At the end of the day the Spanish fleet was decisively defeated, losing four prizes, though the great four-decker *Santissima Trinidad*, the ambition of every British captain, narrowly escaped.

The victory was the fruit of teamwork. Nelson greatly contributed by wearing out of line, but it is going much too far to call this 'disobedience', or to make him solely responsible for the success of the day. Jervis had previously ordered him to use his initiative in such a case, and he acted in accordance with the admiral's tactical intentions. Nelson's boarding party was the most spectacular moment of the day. To board an undefeated enemy was a bloody and desperate move; for a flag officer to lead in person, and take not one but two ships bigger than his own, had no precedent, even though the ships in question had first been battered for two hours by a total of five British ships. Nelson emerged from the battle a public hero, and his 'patent bridge for boarding first-rates', as the press called it, instantly captured the public imagination. This glamorous heroism, easily understood by laymen, eclipsed in the public mind the efficient teamwork and gallantry of his brother officers. Nelson's career was now public property, and his new fame provided some sort of guarantee that he could not be set aside again. Having reached the top of the captains' list, he was promoted rear-admiral as soon as the battle was over and made a knight of the Bath for it.

After the Battle of St Vincent the Spanish fleet stayed in Cadiz, while Jervis (now Earl St Vincent) established a blockade, and considered means of forcing the Spanish fleet to sea. To this end he made his blockade as tight and aggressive as possible. An inshore squadron under Nelson's command was anchored at the mouth of the harbour, so close that they could easily distinguish the ladies of Cadiz walking on the ramparts. Then in May and June 1797 the mutinies at Spithead and the Nore paralysed the Navy in home waters and threatened disaster. In St Vincent's ships discipline was tight and morale was high, so in the aftermath of the mutinies, many of the most disaffected ships were sent to join the Mediterranean Fleet. When the *Theseus* arrived 'in great disorder', her captain was removed, Nelson, his flag-captain Ralph Willett Miller and several of his favourite officers turned over to her. Within a fortnight a note was left on the quarterdeck from the ship's company: 'Success attend Admiral Nelson God bless Captain Miller we thank them for the officers they have placed over us. We are happy and comfortable and will shed every drop of blood in our veins to support them, and the name of the *Theseus* shall be immortalised as high as *Captain*'s ship's company.'[7] There was only one Nelson, however, and many troubled ship's companies. St Vincent showed no mercy and no spirit of compromise towards mutinous men or idle officers, but he well understood that inactivity had been one of the springs of discontent in the Channel Fleet, and he made sure that his fleet was not inactive.

On the night of 3–4 July, an attempt was made to bombard Cadiz by night from a bomb-vessel, protected by ship's boats. A few days before, some British boats had shown marked reluctance to come to close quarters with the Spanish gunboats. When they counter-attacked this time, Nelson in person led the British boats in his barge. There was desperate hand-to-hand fighting, in which Nelson's life was saved by his coxswain John Sykes, who put out his own arm to receive a cutlass blow aimed at Nelson's head. Nelson mentioned Sykes in his dispatch (an almost unheard-of honour for a rating) and got him promoted. Once again Nelson had shown extraordinary personal courage, and had risked his life in circumstances where no flag-officer would normally be found. With morale and discipline tottering throughout the Navy, there was an acute need of senior officers ready to lead from the front – but only Nelson responded to it. Other admirals reacted in the obvious way, by reinforcing the machinery of formal discipline and stressing their power and authority, but only Nelson threw propriety to the winds to inspire junior officers and men by sharing their perils. He was also lucky in reaching flag-rank just as the great mutinies traversed the Navy and terrified admirals and politicians alike, for his instinctive human sympathy and complete lack of pretension – unorthodox qualities which might in ordinary times have done him harm – were now exactly what the Navy needed.

St Vincent then dispatched Nelson on another operation; a raid on Santa Cruz, Tenerife, in the Canary Islands, which promised to gain a good prize, occupy the men and dishearten the Spaniards. Two landing attempts on 22 July only succeeded in alerting the defences, but then a deserter's information persuaded the captains to make another attempt, and Nelson consented. This time the plan was for a direct frontal assault of the town in darkness, relying on speed to overwhelm the strong defences. Everyone knew it was very risky, and Nelson insisted on leading in person. The attack was driven off with heavy casualties, including Nelson himself, who was badly wounded as he stepped ashore. Having had his right arm amputated, Nelson did not rejoin St Vincent off Cadiz until April 1798, by which time the strategic situation was again critical. A very large expedition was known to be preparing at Toulon for an unknown destination. Austria, driven out of the war at the peace of Campo Formio in October 1797, would not re-enter without a British fleet in the Mediterranean to guard her southern flank and protect her protégé, the Kingdom of the Two Sicilies. In these circumstances St Vincent was ordered to detach a small force on reconnaissance into the Mediterranean. As soon as Nelson joined he was sent towards Toulon with three ships of the line and four frigates. In England the government had at last made up its mind to risk stationing a proper fleet in the Mediterranean again, leaving home waters with no margin whatever in the face of threatened invasion. On 24 May St Vincent received a reinforcement of eight sail of the line, and the same day he detached ten to join Nelson.

II

Meanwhile Nelson had met disaster. His new flag-captain, Captain Edward Berry, had won Nelson's heart by his gallantry in battle, but he had never commanded a big ship before, and experience was to prove him an indifferent seaman and a poor manager of men. In the early hours of 21 May the *Vanguard* was completely dismasted in a gale; only fine seamanship by Captain Alexander Ball of the *Alexander* got the flagship in tow and saved her from driving on the coast of Sardinia. Since the other ships in company did not suffer severely, the *Vanguard*'s accident must be attributed to bad seamanship, and it came at the worst possible moment. This was the very day when the French expedition which Nelson was supposed to be watching sailed from Toulon, and as a consequence it escaped undetected. Not until two months later did he catch up with the French squadron on the coast of Egypt. The sequel was the crushing victory of the Nile – but if the *Vanguard* had not been crippled an equivalent victory would probably have happened sooner, when Bonaparte and his army were still afloat, with incalculable benefits to the British war-effort, and not only to Britain. With Bonaparte and his insatiable ambitions eliminated, Europe might have been spared another fifteen years of destructive war, and France might never have been driven from the ranks of the great powers. It was a momentous night, a real crux in history which might have had very different results if the flagship had only taken the same seamanlike precautions as the other ships in company. The obvious person to blame is Berry, but this does not wholly absolve Nelson, for an admiral of his day was expected to interfere as necessary in the management of his flagship. In fact there is much evidence that Nelson was not a particularly good seaman by the very high standards of the Navy of his day. He succeeded in spite of the fact that he was not outstandingly good at basic seamanship, the standard by which all British sea officers measured themselves. He was lucky yet again that this disaster occurred soon after he had reached flag rank, when it was too late for it to blast his career, and just before the stunning victory which put him on a pedestal of fame for all time.

This was the Battle of the Nile, fought on 1 August 1798 when Nelson finally located the French fleet, lying in Aboukir Bay on the coast of Egypt after disembarking Bonaparte's army. The wind was blowing into the bay, and Nelson, accepting the risks of fighting in shoal water and gathering darkness, ordered an immediate attack, with his ships forming a rough line as they stood in. Rounding the island of Aboukir which marked the southern entrance of the bay, they hauled up to reach the head of the line. Captain Thomas Foley of the *Goliath*, the leading ship, observing the French ships lying at single anchor, correctly deduced that they must have enough deep water ahead and inshore to swing, and so crossed the head of the enemy line and came down the inshore side, where the French had not even cleared for action. The next three ships did the same, while Nelson and the rest of the fleet took the outside berth. Vice-Admiral Brueys had stationed his weakest ships at the head of his line on the assumption that it could not easily be attacked: instead they received an overwhelming onslaught without the rest of the fleet to leeward being able to help them. The British worked methodically down the line until they came to the flagship, the 120-gun *l'Orient*, usually reckoned the largest warship in the world. She seriously damaged the *Bellerophon* which was driven out of action, but then caught fire herself. Late that evening she blew up with an explosion which stunned both French and British and brought all fighting to a halt for some time. The action subsequently resumed, but all through the night the French rear division, under Rear-Admiral Villeneuve, made no attempt to come to their comrades' assistance. Next morning, when most of the British ships were too much damaged to follow, Villeneuve made his escape with two ships of the line and two frigates. He left behind eleven battleships and two frigates taken or sunk, by a squadron of thirteen ships of the line (one of which ran aground and did not get into action) and one 50-gun 4th Rate. 'Victory is certainly not a name strong enough for such a scene', Nelson wrote to his wife.[8] Nelson's reward was a peerage, though he and many others thought a barony scarcely an adequate recognition.

Contemporaries asked, and historians continue to ask, how Nelson had been able to achieve this unprecedented victory, fought at night when an admiral had even fewer chances than usual in an eighteenth-century naval battle to keep his squadron under direct control. He himself attributed it to the fact that 'I had the happiness to command a Band of Brothers',[9] and Berry referred to

> his practice during the whole of the cruise, whenever the weather and the circumstances would permit, to have his captains on board the *Vanguard* where he would fully develop to them his own ideas of the different and best modes of attack ... With the masterly ideas of their admiral therefore on the subject of naval tactics, every one of the captains of his squadron was most thoroughly acquainted.[10]

Yet in reality this squadron was assembled at sea less than two months before the battle, and spent almost all the intervening time under way. In such circumstances, how could the admiral talk to his captains? In late eighteenth-century conditions, when disengaging gear was unknown and davits were only just coming into use, putting a boat in the water in a seaway was a hazardous operation, and in fact only a few of Nelson's captains seem to have been often on board the flagship. Foley of the *Goliath*, who led the fleet into battle and took the most crucial decision on his own initiative, seems to have visited but once, and only while the fleet watered at Syracuse in July can there have been any opportunity for Nelson to assemble all the captains together.[11] If Nelson commanded a 'band of brothers', he had had hardly any time to mould them to his way of thinking.

Wounded in action, Nelson recuperated from the minor head injury at the court of the Two Sicilies at Naples. There he was inevitably involved in strategy and diplomacy, and naturally guided in them by the British minister Sir William Hamilton. After twenty-four years in post Hamilton had been completely captured, not so much by Neapolitan views, as by those of Queen Maria Carolina, the real head of her husband's government, which were extremely unpopular among informed Neapolitans. Ignorant alike of local politics and foreign languages, Nelson suspected nothing of this, and enthusiastically backed an aggressive policy which provoked the French conquest of Naples, and wrecked Britain's nascent coalition against Napoleon. In fairness to Nelson he was ordered to support Britain's ally, and to be guided by Hamilton, but when everything has been said to excuse his conduct in this episode it remains an outstanding example of what could go wrong when admirals with scarcely a primary education were promoted to handle great affairs of war and state.

Having evacuated the Neapolitan royal family to Sicily at the end of December, Nelson spent nearly all of 1799 living ashore with the court at Palermo. Exhausted, overworked and unwell, uncomfortable at the disastrous results of his meddling in foreign affairs, resentful of the Admiralty for what seemed to be its slighting treatment, and at his wife for the fewness of her letters, Nelson badly needed emotional support, and from Lady Hamilton alone he received it. Vivacious and uninhibited even by the relaxed standards of the Bourbon court, she threw herself, and drew him, into an extravagant social round. By February their relationship had passed beyond dalliance. As an intimate of Queen Maria Carolina, Emma Hamilton became the means by which the queen in effect gained control of Nelson's squadron. When the French Brest fleet escaped in May and entered the Mediterranean, presenting a grave threat to the whole allied position in that theatre, Nelson thrice refused direct orders from Keith, the commander-in-chief, to rejoin the main fleet, on the grounds that the protection of Naples was more important than anything else. For this he was subsequently reproved by the Admiralty. No other officer would have got off so lightly, for he was in no position to judge of the strategic situation, and his refusal to concentrate as ordered left the fleet open to defeat in detail. At the same time Nelson was deeply involved in the internal affairs of the Two Sicilies. Royalist rebellion, assisted by Russian and Turkish troops and British ships, had overthrown the French puppet republic in Naples, and Nelson, once more guided by the Hamiltons, played a part in the restoration of royal authority which subsequently allowed his enemies to represent him as bloodthirsty and vindictive. Other officers, no better educated than he but shrewder, saw the dangers of being drawn into local politics, and lamented that Nelson had in effect abandoned the sea.

By the summer of 1800 Lord Spencer, the First Lord of the Admiralty, had lost all patience and virtually ordered Nelson to give up his command. When he reached England in November he was still the hero of the Nile with the public, but his professional reputation, among ministers and admirals who knew what had been going on in the Mediterranean, was in ruins. They had not forgotten his extraordinary talents as a sea commander, and St Vincent, who became First Lord of the Admiralty in February 1801, was determined to get him to sea again, out of the arms of Lady Hamilton – but after such spectacularly bad strategic and political judgement there could be no question of giving him the independent command to which his rank (he was promoted vice-admiral on 1 January 1801) might otherwise have entitled him.

Nelson was therefore appointed second-in-command of a fleet for the Baltic, under Vice-Admiral Sir Hyde Parker. Their task was to frustrate the Armed Neutrality, a dangerous combination of Denmark, Sweden and Russia acting under the Tsar's direction, and effectively in French interests, which threatened to shut off the supply of timber and naval stores on which the Royal Navy depended. Parker did not go out of his way to discuss his plans with Nelson, nor did he consult the several Baltic experts who had been attached to his fleet, although the situation was delicate and he needed all the intelligence he could get. War had not been declared and diplomatic negotiations continued; if fighting was necessary, Parker had to decide whom to attack, and how. Nelson wanted to ignore the Danish fleet, which was in no condition to put to sea, and strike straight at that part of the Russian fleet which was laid up in Reval, while the remainder was still frozen in Kronstadt. This would have been the boldest and safest course, tackling the real core of the alliance rather than the reluctant Danes and Swedes, but it was too bold for Parker. After much hesitation, he agreed to risk the passage of the Sound, where the much-feared Danish batteries did them no damage, and the Swedes did not fire at all. On 30 March they anchored in sight of Copenhagen.

The month lost by Parker's idling had allowed the Danes to put the defences of Copenhagen into a formidable condition, but fortunately for the British they had moored their ships along rather than across the channels leading towards the city, so that they could be attacked one after the other as at the Nile. Moreover the line along the King's Deep in front of the city was strongest at the key point off the dockyard where the Tre Kroner fort marked the angle of the two channels, and weakest at its further, southern end. Nelson saw that that end could be attacked by a fleet which came up the Hollands Deep, rounded the end of the Middle Ground shoal and came back down the King's Deep. It would not even be necessary to subdue the strongest part of the defences in order to get bomb vessels within range of the city and force a negotiation with the Danes. On 1 April Nelson was detached to attack with twelve smaller ships of the line, while Parker with the bigger ships waited offshore. That evening he anchored at the southern end of the Middle Ground. At dawn the next morning, with a favourable southerly wind, the British ships weighed anchor to attack. Almost at once things miscarried. Without reliable charts or pilots, the British thought the deepest part of the channel was further from the Danish ships than it was, and kept too far to seaward. One ship grounded before the action began, and two more grounded on the farther side of the channel, at very long range. The remaining nine fought at the relatively long range of a cable (240 yards), reducing the effectiveness of their gunnery, though subsequent sounding showed that they could have run right alongside the Danish line, and even doubled it, as at the Nile. The Danish defences were stronger than anticipated, their guns were served with great gallantry, and the result was a slow and hard-fought victory, with several ships suffering severely before the superiority of British gunnery began to tell.

At this point Parker, still four miles away, hoisted the signal of recall, made 'general' (i.e. directed to each ship individually). Had the signal been obeyed it would have transformed victory into catastrophe, for Nelson's ships could only have withdrawn across the face of the undefeated northern defences, in front of which several of them subsequently ran aground when attempting this move after the cease-fire. Angry and agitated at his superior's folly, Nelson turned to his flag-captain and said 'You know, Foley, I have only one eye – and I have a right to be blind sometimes ...', and, putting the telescope to his blind eye, 'I really do not see the signal'. Fortunately Nelson's captains, seeing that he had not repeated Parker's signal, copied him in disobeying the commander-in-chief. To save further slaughter, Nelson sent a message with a Danish-speaking officer proposing a truce. Virtually ignoring Parker, Nelson now negotiated in person with the Crown Prince, effective head of the Danish government. In these discussions Nelson's uncomplicated approach to diplomacy showed to best effect. Language was not a problem, since both the Crown Prince and his naval ADC spoke English. Domestic politics were not involved, and the international situation was essentially simple: fear of Russia had forced Denmark into the Armed Neutrality, and fear of Britain had to force her out of it. Nelson wanted a truce of sixteen weeks, sufficient to sail up the Baltic and deal with the Russian fleet. The Danes eventually agreed to fourteen, having heard (some time before the British did) of the murder of Tsar Paul and correctly guessing that Russian policy might change.

After the battle Nelson, physically and emotionally exhausted, and convinced that further fighting was unlikely, was preparing to return to England on sick leave when on 5 May Parker received orders to hand over his command to Nelson and himself return to England. The arrival of unofficial accounts of the battle soon after Parker's dispatches had convinced ministers that he had to be replaced at once, and revived their confidence in Nelson. The prospect of command and activity revived Nelson himself, as it always did. On the 6th he took command, and next day he sailed for Reval. There he found the new Russian government conciliatory, and with no further need of fighting in the Baltic, he returned to England, landing at Yarmouth on 1 July. Copenhagen raised Nelson to a viscountcy, and wiped the disastrous effects of Lady Hamilton from his reputation. His friends, especially St Vincent at the Admiralty, intended to prevent him falling into the same situation again by keeping him busy. On 27 July he was appointed to command the local anti-invasion forces in the Channel. The appointment of a vice-admiral to what was essentially a captain's command was justified by the necessity of quieting public alarm, but it is difficult to believe that this was the sole motive. However, he undertook his new command with his customary energy. On the night of 15 August he organised a boat attack on French invasion craft moored at the mouth of Boulogne harbour, but the enemy were forewarned, and the attack was driven off with loss. By this time peace negotiations were under way, and on 1 October an armistice with France was signed.

III

The Peace of Amiens provided Nelson with nineteen months of rest. As Franco-British diplomatic relations worsened again in May 1803 he was re-appointed to the Mediterranean command, and in July he joined the fleet already off Toulon. His function there was to protect Malta and Gibraltar, to keep in check the French Mediterranean squadron, and above all to prevent it escaping through the Straits to participate in Napoleon's invasion schemes. With the *Grande Armée* assembling around Boulogne, it was essential that the French squadrons be prevented from uniting and coming up the Channel. It was very difficult to mount a close blockade of Toulon, in the face of frequent offshore gales in winter, and the mountains behind the port from which the blockaders could be seen far out to sea. Nelson was insistent that he never meant to blockade the place, but to watch it from a distance, far enough to tempt the French out, near enough to catch them when they came. To this end he often used an anchorage in the Maddalena Islands off the northern end of Sardinia, where water and fresh provisions were plentiful. Throughout the eighteen weary months of observation, usually at sea, far from a base, for long periods acutely short of naval stores, Nelson devoted great care to keeping his ships in repair and his men supplied with fresh food. Always careful of morale, he deliberately varied his cruising grounds to provide new sights and experiences, visiting from ship to ship was allowed whenever the weather permitted boatwork, and the men were encouraged to music, dancing and theatricals.

This routine went on all through 1804. By the end of the year Nelson was unwell and hoping for leave, but then Napoleon crowned himself as Emperor, Spain entered the war as a French ally, sharply worsening the situation of the Mediterranean squadron, and on 19 January 1805, at Maddalena, Nelson heard that the French fleet had sailed from Toulon, eluding his frigates. Once again he had to endure a frustrating search with little information, until after a month he discovered that the French had been driven back to port by gales. On 4 April, off Majorca, he learnt that the Toulon fleet was at sea again. This time Villeneuve, warned by a neutral merchantman of Nelson's whereabouts, succeeded in getting out of the Mediterranean without being intercepted, and in the face of persistent headwinds it was not until the beginning of May that Nelson was able to get through the Straits in pursuit. The problem now was to guess where in the world Villeneuve, and the Spanish ships he had collected from Cadiz, might be bound. An obvious possibility was to the northward, to join the other French squadrons, enter the Channel in overwhelming force, and cover Napoleon's invasion. This was the greatest risk, to counter which the standing practice of British admirals in such a situation was to fall back on the Western Approaches and join the Channel Fleet. Sir John Orde, commanding the squadron off Cadiz, had done so already, and Nelson was preparing to follow suit when, off Cape St Vincent, he learnt from a Portuguese warship that Villeneuve's ships had steered westward, across the Atlantic.

Nelson had now to take a difficult strategic decision. He had to assume that no other British admiral yet knew the movements of the Toulon fleet. If he did not pursue and mark it, untold damage might be done to British interests in the West or even East Indies. On the other hand the French plan might be (and in fact was) a feint, designed to lure as many British ships as possible away from European waters before the invasion. Information might have reached the Admiralty and caused them to detach other squadrons, fatally weakening the Channel Fleet at the critical moment. Weighing these factors, Nelson decided to follow Villeneuve across the Atlantic. After only a brief pause to water and revictual, his squadron (which had been at sea more or less continuously for twenty-two months) set out westward, eleven ships of the line pursuing eighteen. Although he did not know it, at almost the same moment his old friend Collingwood had been detached with a squadron from the Channel Fleet under orders to do the same thing, unless he heard that Nelson had gone before him, but learning of Nelson's movements, he took Orde's place off Cadiz instead.

Nelson left the Portuguese coast on 11 May, only three days before Villeneuve reached Martinique. His orders were to wait there for the Brest squadron, which was to escape and join him before they returned in overwhelming force to sweep away whatever British squadrons had not been decoyed away from the Channel. Nelson reached Barbados on 4 June, and in spite of being delayed by false intelligence was only 150 miles behind when Villeneuve sailed for home on 10 June. Not knowing Villeneuve's destination, he steered for Cadiz to return to his station, but he also sent the brig *Curieux* to warn the Admiralty of the enemy's movements. She not only made a fast passage but sighted Villeneuve's squadron and was able to report that they were steering for Ferrol. With this information the Admiralty was in time to order a reinforcement to Sir Robert Calder, who was cruising off that port. On 22 July, in fog, Calder's fourteen ships of the line intercepted Villeneuve's Franco-Spanish fleet, now of twenty. There followed a confused action in which the Spaniards did most of the fighting, and lost two ships. The next two days were clearer, and Calder could have renewed the action, but he chose to regard the preservation of his squadron as a priority. For this he was subsequently disgraced, since in the strategic situation the crippling or even loss of his ships would have been a price well worth paying to knock out the Combined Fleet. Nelson saw this, as other admirals did, and an officer of Calder's experience should have done the same.

Nevertheless Calder's action did have a major strategic effect: it further demoralised Villeneuve and led him to abandon his orders to push for Brest. On 20 August he entered Cadiz, while Collingwood's little squadron skilfully drew off to a safe distance. Nelson meanwhile had landed at Gibraltar on 20 July, the first time in almost two years that he had been ashore. There he concerned himself with redisposing the ships in the Mediterranean, until on the 25th he had news that Villeneuve had been seen steering for the Bay of Biscay. At once Nelson headed north to rejoin the Channel Fleet, where he left the bulk of his squadron and himself proceeded to Portsmouth to go on leave. Disappointed at his failure to catch the enemy, and ill as he so often was when frustrated, Nelson was astonished to find that his unsuccessful pursuit across the Atlantic and back had fired the public imagination almost as much as a victory. He was now beyond common popularity, and he could not appear in public without being instantly mobbed and cheered. In August Lord Minto (the former Sir Gilbert Elliot)

> met Nelson to-day in a mob in Piccadilly and got hold of his arm, so I was mobbed too. It is really quite affecting to see the wonder and admiration, and love and respect, of the whole world; and the genuine expression of all these sentiments at once, from gentle and simple, the moment he is seen. It is beyond anything represented in a play or a poem of fame.[12]

Nelson landed at Portsmouth on 19 August, the day before Villeneuve reached Cadiz, but the enemy's whereabouts were not known in England until 2 September, when Nelson was re-appointed to the Mediterranean command, including Collingwood's squadron off Cadiz. Napoleon had now abandoned his invasion scheme, and issued orders for Villeneuve to take the Combined Fleet into the Mediterranean to support the intended French invasion of the Two Sicilies. On the 28th Nelson joined Collingwood off Cadiz and took command. Almost as soon as he arrived signs of imminent movement were reported from Cadiz, and early on 19 October the enemy began to get under way. Nelson made no attempt to close until they were well at sea, but his frigates continued to give him very full information of Villeneuve's movements. During the night of the 20th the two fleets closed, and at dawn on the 21st they were in sight south of Cape Trafalgar.

The morning was fine, with a very light westerly wind. The Combined Fleet was heading south, with a view to opening the Straits, in what was meant to be a single line, with a flying squadron under the Spanish admiral Don Federico Gravina ahead and to windward. Nelson's fleet was in its cruising formation of two columns, running before the wind towards the enemy. His tactics at the Battle of Trafalgar have given rise to a great deal of controversy, since it is not clear exactly how he intended to fight, nor how closely he followed his own intentions. For thirty years naval tactics and signalling had been developing rapidly, and Nelson, like his opponents, was familiar with many methods of concentrating on some part of an enemy's fleet. His own ideas were always flexible and eclectic, and their object was not so much to follow any theoretical scheme as to throw the enemy into confusion by swift and unexpected movements. 'The spur of the moment must call forth the clearest decision and the most active conduct', he wrote. 'On occasions we must sometimes have a regular confusion, and that apparent confusion must be the most regular method which could be pursued on the occasion.'[13] 'A Sea-Officer cannot, like a Land Officer, form plans,' he claimed; 'his object is to embrace the happy moment which now and then offers.'[14] His naval contemporaries admired him as a tactician for his unequalled quickness in embracing the happy moment. 'Without much previous preparation or plan', Collingwood wrote, 'he has the faculty of discovering advantages as they arise, and the good judgement to turn them to his use. An enemy that commits a false step in his view is ruined, and it comes on him with an impetuosity that allows him no time to recover.'[15]

Before the battle he circulated a plan of attack in three divisions, the third to be kept to windward under a trusted officer with discretion to throw it into action at the decisive point: 'I think it will surprise and confuse the enemy. They won't know what I am about. It will bring forward a pell-mell battle, and that is what I want.'[16] In the event five ships were away watering on the Moroccan coast, and with only twenty-seven against the enemies' thirty-three, Nelson went into action in two columns. Contrary to all precedent, both he and Collingwood in their powerful flagships were at the head of their respective columns instead of in the middle, and the British went into action under full sail including studding-sails, so that they closed much faster than the enemy can have expected. Even so their progress was slow in the light airs, and there was ample time to prepare for battle, for last-minute letters to be written, and for Nelson to 'amuse' the fleet with the newly introduced 'telegraph' system, which for the first time allowed an officer to compose signals in his own words: 'England expects that every man will do his duty.'

Seeing the enemy bearing down towards his rear, Villeneuve ordered his fleet to wear together, thus reversing its formation and direction. This further disorganised an already loose formation, and introduced a pronounced curve in the Combined Fleet's line. Possibly against Villeneuve's wishes, Gravina's Squadron of Observation bore up and prolonged the rear (as it now was) of the line, instead of keeping its station to windward. The Combined Fleet was now steering northwards, back towards Cadiz, and Nelson probably interpreted the move as a last-minute scramble for safety. Perhaps this caused him to modify his tactics, for instead of turning parallel to the enemy at the last minute, and then bearing up together to cut through the enemy line at many points (the plan he had circulated beforehand) Nelson's column held on, initially towards the enemy van, then altering course to starboard to cut nearly vertically through the middle of the Combined Fleet. Collingwood's column had already cut into the rear. This unconventional head-on approach was dangerous, but besides gaining time, it concealed Nelson's intentions from the enemy until the last moment. Initially fighting at a great advantage against the isolated leaders of the British columns, the centre and rear of the allied line were now subjected to a growing onslaught as ship after ship came into action. Gravina's Squadron of Observation, now absorbed into the rear and engaged by Collingwood's ships, was not in a position to take any initiative, and the unengaged van under Rear-Admiral Pierre Etienne Dumanoir le Pelley, which was, did nothing until the battle was already lost. Firing began about noon, and the battle was virtually over by about five o'clock, with seventeen prizes in British hands, and another burnt.

At about 1.15pm, as he walked the quarterdeck with his flag-captain, Thomas Masterman Hardy, Nelson was hit by a musket-ball fired from the mizzen-top of the French *Redoutable* alongside. The ball entered his left shoulder, passed through a lung and lodged in his spine. It seems unlikely that it was aimed specifically at him; the quarterdeck was crowded and he cannot have been clearly visible through the dense smoke of battle even at twenty yards, nor was a musket accurate at such a range, especially fired from aloft in a rolling ship. Contrary to myth, he was wearing an old uniform coat with inconspicuous cloth replicas of his decorations. There is no evidence that he deliberately sought or recklessly courted death, though he was certainly well enough aware of the risks of action. He was carried below to the cockpit, where he lay, in great pain but conscious until just before he died at 4.30pm. Thus was victory swallowed up in death. 'All the praise and acclamations of joy for our Victory only bring to my mind what it has cost', wrote Collingwood, and the nation grieved with him.[17] Having lain in state in Greenwich Hospital and been borne in procession up the river to Whitehall and through the streets to St Paul's, Nelson received a state funeral of a scale and splendour unprecedented for a commoner. Royal princes squabbled for the right to lead the mourning.

After the battle it was claimed that 'His Lordship's superior arrangement left nothing to be done by signals. The frequent communications he had with his Admirals and captains put them in possession of all his plans, so that his mode of attack was well known to every officer of the fleet'[18] – but this must be an expression of the confidence he aroused rather than a complete description of his methods. So far from being familiar with his plans before the battle, his captains were by no means agreed about them even afterwards, and historians have been debating them ever since. Just as at the Nile and at Copenhagen, Nelson had had very little opportunity to impress his ideas on his officers. Only five of his twenty-seven ships of the line had formed part of the Mediterranean Fleet under his command during the previous two years, and only eight of the captains had ever served with him before. Most of them knew him only by reputation, but he knew how to reach out to officers who knew him little or not at all. 'He was perhaps more generally beloved by all ranks of people under him than any Officer in the Service', in the judgement of Captain William Hotham, 'for he had in a great degree that valuable but rare quality of conciliating the most opposite tempers and forwarding the Public Service with unanimity among men not themselves disposed to accord.'[19] 'He added to genius, valour, and energy, the singular power of electrifying all within his atmosphere, and making them only minor constellations to this most luminous planet ... it was his art to make all under him love him, and own his superiority without a ray of jealousy',[20] wrote Lord Malmesbury after his death.

His unaffected warmth and human sympathy, his generosity (especially his generous table), his concern that every possible comfort should alleviate the boredom and danger of prolonged cruising were known and valued throughout the Navy. 'Is Lord Nelson coming out to us again?' wrote Captain Edward Codrington to his wife in September 1805. 'I anxiously hope he may be; that I may once in my life see a commander-in-chief endeavouring to make a hard and disagreeable service as palatable to those serving under him as circumstances will admit of, and keeping up by his example that animation so necessary for such an occasion.'[21] In less than three weeks he deeply endeared himself to the captains of this squadron. 'He is so good and pleasant a man, that we all wish to do what he likes, without any kind of orders', wrote Captain George Duff, explaining why he was repainting his ship in Nelson's preferred style.[22] 'No man was ever afraid of displeasing him,' wrote Codrington, 'but everybody was afraid of not pleasing him.'[23]

IV

No one-dimensional explanation can account for Nelson's extraordinary popular status in his own lifetime and ever since. As a sea officer he excelled in most, but not all areas of his profession. His judgement of diplomacy and strategy, though improving with experience, suffered from his lack of education, his ignorance of languages and his uncertain feel for politics. As a tactician, however, he deployed a unique combination of very thorough training, delegation to trusted subordinates, and an uncompromising determination to achieve total victory. 'He possessed the zeal of an enthusiast,' Collingwood wrote, 'directed by talents which Nature had very bountifully bestowed upon him, and everything seemed as, if by enchantment, to prosper under his direction. But it was the effect of system, and nice combination, not of chance.'[24] He achieved at sea the same practical and psychological revolution as the French revolutionary generals achieved on land, ushering in an age when victory meant not a modest advantage, but the total destruction of the vanquished. In Minto's words, 'there was a sort of heroic cast about Nelson that I never saw in any other man, and which seems wanting to the achievement of *impossible things* which became easy to him'.[25] Instead of the centralised control which was the ambition of most admirals, because it seemed the essential prerequisite for success, Nelson practised initiative and flexibility. In this he built upon the methods of several of his predecessors, including Anson, Hawke and St Vincent, but he applied them with a unique openness and generosity of spirit. Warm and friendly amongst his brother officers, Nelson was equally direct and approachable to his men. Though other officers might be more advanced in their social views or more relaxed as disciplinarians, Nelson alone gained his people's hearts. In part they were inspired by his matchless gallantry. Though he never wantonly risked his life, no flag officer ever exposed himself with such heroism, or bore so many wounds to show it. No other British officer had such a record of victory, in the long years of endurance against France when victories were so scarce.

The key to Nelson's remarkable personal appeal lay in the amalgam of ardour and naivety. He threw himself into all his undertakings with 'ardent, animated patriotism panting for glory'.[26] He was a stranger to half-measures, to reservations, to fears. Uninterested in appearances, he burnt with direct, uncompromising and entirely unfeigned zeal. Nervous, irritable, sometimes anguished and often ill with the strain of unsupported responsibility, he never tried to conceal his feelings. His vanity was as artless as the rest of his personality, and went with an inimitable magnanimity which rejoiced at the successes of his friends and lamented the misfortunes even of rivals like Hyde Parker and Calder who had treated him badly. His naked thirst for glory was part of his vulnerability and insecurity. He needed emotional support; from the many close friends he found amongst the officers he worked with, from the world at large, and from women. At times vulnerable and weak as a man, Nelson was also the leader of unequalled readiness, courage, generosity and professional genius: 'in many points a really great man', as Minto put it, 'in others a baby'.[27] In that extraordinary combination lies something of his appeal to successive generations.

Notes

1. I make no attempt to provide references for every event of Nelson's very well-known career, which can be followed in dozens of biographies. The general naval background may be found in N.A.M. Rodger, *The Command of the Ocean: A Naval History of Britain, 1649–1815* (London: Allen Lane, 2004).

2. *Nelson's Letters to his Wife and other Documents, 1785–1831*, ed. G.P.B. Naish (Navy Records Society vol. 100, 1958), p. 204.

3. Carola Oman, *Nelson* (London: Hodder and Stoughton, 1947), p. 171.

4. *The Nagle Journal: A Diary of the Life of Jacob Nagle, Sailor, from the Year 1775 to 1841*, ed. John C. Dann (New York: Weidenfeld and Nicolson, 1988), pp. 192, 207–9.

5. Sir N.H. Nicolas, *The Dispatches and Letters of Vice Admiral Lord Viscount Nelson* (London, 1844–45, 7 vols), II,333.
6. Ibid., 343.
7. Naish, *Nelson's Letters to his Wife*, p. 326.
8. Ibid., p. 399.
9. Nicolas, *Dispatches*, III,230.
10. Ibid., 49.
11. Brian Lavery, *Nelson and the Nile: The Naval War against Bonaparte 1798* (London: Chatham, 1998), pp. 155–6.
12. Nina [Kynynmound] Countess of Minto, *Life and Letters of Sir Gilbert Elliot, First Earl of Minto* (London, 1874, 3 vols), III,363.
13. 'Miscellaneous Letters', in *The Naval Miscellany Vol. I*, ed. J.K. Laughton (Navy Records Society vol. 20, 1902), pp. 387–444, at p. 424.
14. Nicolas, *Dispatches*, VII Add.lxi.
15. *The Private Correspondence of Admiral Lord Collingwood*, ed. Edward Hughes (Navy Records Society vol. 98, 1957), p. 130.
16. Nicolas, *Dispatches*, VII,241.
17. Ibid., 239.
18. *Logs of the Great Sea Fights, 1794–1805*, ed. T. Sturges Jackson (Navy Records Society vols 16 & 18, 1899–1900), II,196, quoting Lt. George Brown of the *Victory*.
19. A.M.W. Stirling, *Pages & Portraits from the Past, being the Private Papers of Admiral Sir William Hotham, G.C.B. Admiral of the Red* (London, 1919, 2 vols), I,240.
20. *Diaries and Correspondence of James Harris, First Earl of Malmesbury*, ed. [James Harris] 3rd Earl of Malmesbury (London, 1844, 4 vols), IV,311.
21. [Jane] Lady Bourchier, *Memoir of the Late Admiral Sir Edward Codrington* (London, 1873, 2 vols), I,47.
22. Nicolas, *Dispatches*, VII,71.
23. Bourchier, *Codrington*, I,125.
24. Hughes, *Collingwood Correspondence*, p. 167.
25. Minto, *Life and Letters*, III,374.
26. James Stanier Clarke and John M'Arthur, *The Life of Admiral Lord Nelson, K.B., from his Lordship's Manuscripts* (London, 1809, 2 vols), II,267, quoting the surgeon of Nelson's flagship at Copenhagen.
27. Minto, *Life and Letters*, III,370.

2
Nelson and His 'Band of Brothers': Friendship, Freemasonry, Fraternity

Martyn Downer

'A friend in need is a friend indeed': writing to his agent Alexander Davison in February 1803, Nelson described these words 'an old adage, but not the less true'.[1] Davison and his family were marooned in lodgings at Calais, a tour of France during the Peace of Amiens truncated by the sudden illness of one of their children. Yet even *in extremis* Davison did not neglect the material needs of his 'dear friend' who was seeking funds to improve Merton Place, the house the admiral shared in Surrey with his mistress, Emma Hamilton. 'Command the purse of your ever unalterably affectionate friend', Davison had written without hesitation and with no certainty of being repaid.[2] Although Nelson only needed a few thousand pounds – small beer to a man like Davison who estimated his fortune at £300,000[3] – his agent's casual offer of financial assistance was material proof of the deep well of affection that existed between the two men in the last years of the admiral's life. They had met in Quebec twenty years before, during the American War of Independence. Nelson, then captain of *Albemarle,* was on North Atlantic convoy duty while Davison was running a successful business in the town supplying goods to the British troops arriving in Canada to fight the war as well as to the loyalist émigrés refugees who were pouring across the border from the colonies. Through his carefully nurtured contacts within government, Davison had also secured the lucrative agency to supply presents to the Native American tribes whose allegiance to the crown – so critical to the success of the Canadian fur and fish trades – was being severely tested by the blandishments of the American rebels. The idea of using sweeteners to secure loyalty was a lesson Davison learnt early in his career.

I

At first glance it might appear that the young officer and the merchant had little in common. Nelson, who was twenty-four, had already spent half his life at sea while Davison, the elder of the two men by eight years, had been immersed in trade since his youth. But the nature of international trade in the eighteenth century – which rested so heavily on the sea – caused their worlds to be in constant contact, even before the exigencies of war obliged Davison to rely on the Royal Navy for the safe transport of his goods across the Atlantic. Each, for instance, had passed their childhoods in remote rural areas close to the sea – Nelson in Norfolk, Davison in Northumberland. Nelson's connections with the Navy are well recorded yet Davison, too, was in close proximity to several naval families from a young age. His elder sister Katy married captain, later admiral, Roddam Home and at least two of his contemporaries and near neighbours in Northumberland – Cuthbert Collingwood and John Orde – rose to prominence alongside Nelson in the Navy.[4]

As sons, respectively, of a clergyman and a farmer, Nelson and Davison were products of the 'middle gentry', that mildly impoverished yet ambitious and upwardly mobile breed which was spreading rapidly across the country. In many material respects the interior life of the Davisons' stone farmhouse in the Cheviot Hills would have closely resembled that of the Nelsons' parsonage in Burnham Thorpe. Beyond the physical landscape that cast the young men was empathy in their upbringing, for each was the fourth son to his parents and as such was denied the attention afforded to their elder brothers. For example, neither of them received the benefits of an extended education nor was there enough money to buy either of them a commission in the army or an apprenticeship with one of the large, 'monied' firms in the City of London such as the East India Company. Growing up at opposite ends of the country, both boys must have realised that to a great degree they would have to make their own way in the world. Nelson chose the sea; Davison chose trade.

There were, however, two striking differences in the backdrops to the boys' emotional lives. Perhaps the most significant was the early loss of Nelson's mother when he was just nine years old. By contrast, from surviving family correspondence it is clear that Davison enjoyed a warm and supportive rapport with his mother until her death in his early middle age. Subsequently Nelson's relationships with women, were often awkward, even destructive. 'I know your determination about women', Davison warily told his friend in 1801, whereas he himself was at ease in female company, enjoying a long and happy marriage to Harriett Gosling whilst forging an affectionate friendship with Nelson's wife Fanny.[5] Another notable distinction between the boys was their religious upbringing. Nelson grew up under the watchful eye of his father Edmund, the local parson and a stern advocate of religious orthodoxy. Yet although the Davisons were baptised, married and buried in their local Anglican church, their faith was informed by the prevailing dissenting beliefs of many of their neighbours in the borders. It is known, for example, that they patronised the Presbyterian chapel in Morpeth. Religious nonconformity gave Davison an independence of thought denied to Nelson whose strict spiritual upbringing often left him struggling painfully at moments of personal crisis.

Despite the limitations of their backgrounds, the ambitions of both boys stretched far beyond the bleak view from a draughty Norfolk rectory or an isolated Northumbrian farmhouse. But desire alone was not enough to succeed. To reach their goals – distinction, respectively, in business and in the Navy – Davison and Nelson needed to develop a network of well placed social and professional patrons. For aristocratic endorsement the Nelsons looked to the Walpoles at Houghton Hall, with whom they could claim a distant kinship, while in Northumberland the Davisons fostered a relationship with the powerful Percy family at Alnwick Castle. Meanwhile within their chosen careers Nelson could rely on the support of his uncle Maurice Suckling while Davison's early life in the City of London prospered under the careful supervision of the eminent trans-Atlantic fur trader Robert Hunter. Nelson and Davison viewed their patrons as 'friends' but not in the modern sense of mutually supportive friends chosen voluntarily. Davison later described Hugh Percy, the second Duke of Northumberland, as his 'best' friend, but the duke would never have returned the compliment.[6] The professional lives of the patron and patronised might overlap but their social spheres rarely did. Indeed, despite eventually achieving prominence in their respective fields, both Davison and Nelson were humiliated when they tried to meet their socially superior patrons on an equal footing. Hubris allied with the jealousy of his business rivals would lead Davison to Newgate prison, while Nelson was snubbed at court following the disclosure of his affair with Emma Hamilton.

For social relationships based on disinterested sentiment outside their families, Nelson and Davison looked within their own circles for like-minded acquaintances of similar status. Those circles touched when HMS *Albemarle* moored in the St Lawrence River off Quebec in September 1782. It is not known for certain where Davison and Nelson were first introduced, perhaps at the chateau of the governor or in one of the coffee houses or taverns in the lower town. With Quebec overflowing with troops and refugees it seems likely that Davison offered to put up the young officer at his house on St Peter Street. The only other option for Nelson was to remain in the cramped conditions in his ship. During Nelson's short stay in the town he forged a friendship with Davison based not simply on their similar backgrounds but on their broad emotional and intellectual affinity. Nor was it the first occasion on which the thrusting young naval officer had befriended a like-minded merchant. Until his death Nelson would remain in friendly contact with Hercules Ross, another agent of provisions of northern British descent who he had met in Jamaica in the late 1770s.[7] The personal characteristics Nelson recognised in Davison included a rigorous independence of spirit verging on arrogance; nonconformity in the face of authority and a propensity to impulsiveness which was typified by events involving both men on 14 and 15 October 1782.

Early on the morning of the 14 October, just hours after *Albemarle* unmoored to move downriver to rendezvous with a convoy of troop transports bound for New York, Nelson unexpectedly returned ashore determined to precipitously propose marriage to Mary Simpson, a local beauty he had met in the town during his stay. Fortunately for his career, Nelson was intercepted on the quay by Davison who was able to dissuade his new young friend from taking such a calamitous step. The incident left such an impression on Davison – who had suffered youthful rejection by a sweetheart himself – that he specifically recalled it after Nelson's death. And although Nelson never mentioned it himself, the memory of Davison's timely intervention in such a sensitive matter may have informed his later decision to employ his friend in the unpleasant business of separating from his wife Fanny. Within twenty-four hours, Davison himself was embroiled in a potentially far more serious affair. As *Albemarle* sailed downriver, he fought a duel on the Heights of Abraham, outside the town gates, the result of a hot-headed clash with a business rival. No harm was done to either man, yet the incident leaves the impression of a man sensitive to criticism, and one not afraid to act to protect his reputation.

Beyond the record of a brief meeting in London the following year, there is no record of any further contact between Nelson and Davison until May 1797. Yet they must have occasionally written to each other in the interim, for that month their surviving correspondence bursts suddenly into life with a letter from Nelson addressed to 'My dear friend'[8] – terms he generally reserved for his closest male acquaintances, men like Cuthbert

Collingwood and William Locker. This intimacy; the nature of the letter's businesslike content and the subsequent exhortation of Sir Nicholas Harris Nicolas, the Victorian editor of Nelson's letters, for Davison's son to 'let me have the letters *before 1798'* suggests that some early material has been lost.[9] Perhaps it was not until Nelson's eye-catching exploits at the Battle of St Vincent in February 1797 that Davison thought it worth preserving his friend's correspondence. (Nelson's habit of burning many of his incoming letters probably accounted for Davison's.)

Even so there is scant evidence that the friendship formed in Canada was well maintained before 1797. For instance, Davison's congratulations to Nelson for the daring part he played in the Battle of St Vincent were forwarded to the Mediterranean by Nelson's elder brother Maurice, a clerk at the Navy Office with whom Davison was familiar through his constant business dealings with the Navy Board. In fact Davison's friendship with Maurice can be seen as bridging the lost years of his relationship with Nelson. For a time the two men even worked alongside each other. In 1793, following his appointment as commissary-general to Lord Moira's expeditionary army, Davison invited Maurice to be his assistant. Maurice, who had chafed at the lowliness of his position in the Navy Office, leapt at the chance to double his wages (the commissariat paid him £1 5s a day). He was also undoubtedly flattered by the patronage of his younger brother's influential Canadian friend. After joining Davison at commissariat headquarters on the Isle of Wight, Maurice commented proudly to his wife that: 'I live with Mr D but not lodge, if I may be allowed to judge his friendship increases.'[10] Indeed the friendship between Maurice and Davison grew to become one of genuine affection; greater perhaps in sentimental terms than Davison's relationship with Maurice's illustrious, but generally absent, brother. 'I have lost my Bosom and sincere friend!' Davison cried, following Maurice's early death in April 1801.[11] Terms that can be compared to his regret, after Trafalgar, at the death of 'my late valuable friend Nelson'.[12]

Although sceptical of the wisdom of abandoning the Navy Office for the commissariat Nelson, like the rest of his family, was grateful to Davison for helping his hapless brother. When the commissariat was wound up in 1796 and Maurice safely restored to his former position at Somerset House; Nelson thanked Davison for the 'kind method you have taken for effectually serving my dear brother'.[13] Nor, it seems, was the help Davison extended towards Nelson's family limited to Maurice. As early as 1791 Davison – whose contacts with the government were well known – had been approached by Nelson's brother-in-law George Matcham for help in securing land in the newly settled colony of New South Wales.

Presumably the introduction was made either through Maurice or Nelson himself (who was living in Norfolk at the time) for Matcham, a successful businessman, was clearly acting on a known family interest. So even if direct contact with Nelson himself was limited before 1797, Davison was already widely recognised by Nelson's extended family as a source of valuable patronage. Fanny Nelson later praised his 'very disinterested friendship to all [the family] ...'.[14] The debt of gratitude that Nelson felt towards Davison undoubtedly informed his otherwise surprising decision to award his friend the prize agency for the Battle of the Nile in August 1798. Nevertheless (and even though he had more reason than most to thank Davison for his help in the past) the appointment shocked Maurice who felt that his kinship to the Victor of the Nile should have secured him a role that was seen as a valuable perk by his colleagues at the Navy Office. 'I am free to confess to you,' Maurice wrote to his brother,

> that I feel myself not a little hurt at my not having been named with Mr D as one of the agents to your squadron. It might have put something in my pocket, at least it would have stopped people's mouths who repeatedly say there must have been some misunderstanding between me and you ... I have no doubt you have sufficient reason and content myself in present degrading situation, degrading I call it because I cannot reach the top of my profession.[15]

There were other, more personal reasons why Nelson risked incurring the wrath of his brother in making the appointment. Not only was he sensitive to charges of nepotism – an accusation that could harm his growing reputation – but he was also alert to the shift in official attitude towards Navy Office employees moonlighting as prize agents. Yet there was one further compelling reason why Nelson chose Davison for this prestigious and lucrative job, the roots to which can be traced to their meeting in Quebec fifteen years earlier. This was a reason, moreover, which had remained hidden to biographers of Nelson until the recent discovery of Davison's collection of papers and artefacts. Its emergence confirms the importance of looking beyond the documentary record to reveal the entirety of a person's life.

Among Davison's treasures was a pair of wine coolers commissioned by him from the Derby porcelain factory following the Battle of the Nile. (The Derby showroom in London was next door to Davison's army clothing factory in Covent Garden.) The prominent use of Nelson's coat of arms on the coolers, however, which had been newly augmented by a baron's coronet and the Sultan of Turkey's *chelengk*, make it unfeasible that anyone else except for the admiral himself could have displayed the coolers without causing offence. In all probability the coolers were a gift from Davison to Nelson by way of thanks for his appointment as prize agent. On 21 February 1799 – while Nelson still lingered in the Mediterranean after the battle – Fanny Nelson thanked Davison: 'for some of the most beautiful china I have ever seen'.[16] Unfortunately Fanny does not describe the exact nature of her gift beyond describing 'the devices' decorating it as 'elegant'. In the letter Fanny also reveals how, after she received Davison's lavish present, she passed a happy day with her father-in-law Edmund Nelson: 'in admiring them and disposing of them in various parts of the room' – terms which accord with an attempt to find the best position to display the coolers. And she cheerfully complained that Davison's generosity had unintended consequences for 'one expense brings on others for I shall exert my judgement in forming a plan for something quite out of the ordinary for them to stand on'. For Davison, however, who had long experience of the terms under which gifts were given and received, Fanny's most satisfying comment came towards the end of her letter: 'Your china has been shown and name told,' she wrote, 'so that the Bath talkers will soon be undeceived.'[17] If, as seems likely, the Derby wine coolers were the 'beautiful china' which Fanny received on her husband's behalf in February 1799, they were probably returned to Davison after Trafalgar as Emma Hamilton began haphazardly selling the contents of Merton Place in her struggle to keep her creditors at bay.

Yet the full significance of Davison's gift is only revealed by examining the complicated iconography decorating the tableaux on the reverse of the coolers. These were painted with images symbolic of Nelson's victory off the coast of Egypt, such as a flag draped cannon, a pyramid, palm trees and a sphinx. Yet on close inspection several discrepancies become apparent in the iconography, notably the prominent display of a Roman Corinthian column at the heart of the ostensibly Egyptian landscape. The key to this mystery is, however, literally staring the viewer in the face. Alongside the Corinthian column is a mason wearing an apron.

II

Their shared interest in freemasonry did not forge the friendship between Nelson and Davison but it did invisibly bind them together. It may also account for the otherwise often enigmatic character of a relationship that survived the acrimonious break-up of Nelson's marriage in 1801 and Davison's imprisonment for electoral corruption in 1804. Nelson's contact with masonic culture also informed the loyalty he felt towards other male friends and colleagues in his circle regardless of their often-manifold faults. By comparison this hidden sense of duty was often lacking in his uneasy dealings with women, who were excluded from freemasonry, most notoriously in his treatment of his wife Fanny. By contrast Emma Hamilton may have had at least some knowledge of freemasonry from her marriage to the antiquarian Sir William Hamilton. Emma had accompanied her husband and Nelson on a tour of the famous masonic gardens at Wörlitzpark during their journey through Germany on the way back to England from Naples in 1800. A few months later all three passed Christmas as guests of the exotic aesthete and prominent freemason William Beckford. Intriguingly, in one of the letters he wrote to Emma during Nelson's lifetime, Davison even overtly referred to the 'All Ruling Power', indicating that he knew she would recognise this masonic allusion to God.[18]

There are no surviving records of Nelson's formal membership of a masonic lodge beyond his acceptance – in 1801 – of the regalia for the so-called Ancient Gregorians in Norwich, one of the many fashionable pseudo-masonic friendly societies that were springing up around the country at the time. Davison was initiated as a master mason – the third and highest degree of freemasonry – during a ceremony in Quebec on 22 October 1785. His attainment of this degree indicates that he had been a freemason for some years and almost certainly before Nelson's arrival in the town in 1782. Davison's membership of Merchant Lodge No. 1 in Quebec was not surprising, for freemasonry was the principal social and intellectual activity among the small British merchant community in the province, as it was in other British colonies. By participating in it Davison would have enjoyed the mutual support and encouragement of his peers.

In typical fashion the first lodges had arrived in Canada embedded in the regiments that secured the country after the conquest in 1759. Freemasonry – with its emphasis on equality and fraternity – not only offered the officers a forum for philosophical debate free from the handicaps of status but gave them an opportunity to wine and dine in congenial company thus contributing to *esprit de corps*. Freemasonry struggled, however, to take hold in the less familial atmosphere of the Navy compared to the tight knit culture of the Army. Its rituals may also have been hampered by space restrictions on board a warship.[19] Indeed compared to the dozens – even hundreds – of lodges recognised in the Army, only three ships in the Royal Navy were granted warrants to hold freemason meetings by the Grand Lodge in London: *Vanguard*, *Prince* and *Canceaux*.[20] Nelson, of course, became very familiar with *Vanguard* during the Nile campaign while, by coincidence, *Canceaux* was moored in the River St Lawrence when he arrived at Quebec in September 1782.[21]

In Quebec Nelson would have recognised the colonial masonic milieu that he had experienced earlier in his career in the West Indies. Indeed on at least two occasions he had lodged in Jamaica at the house of Admiral Sir Peter Parker, the provincial grand master of the freemasons in the West Indies who later became his mentor. By the time of Nelson's state funeral at St Paul's Cathedral twenty-five years later – where he controversially led the official mourning in place of the First Lord, Earl St Vincent – the ageing Parker had risen to become the deputy grand master of the freemasons in England, a position second only in executive importance within the masonic hierarchy to the acting grand master, and another conspicuous guest at the ceremony, the Earl of Moira. (In the Cathedral Moira stood alongside the grand master, the Prince of Wales, who was prevented by protocol from leading the official mourning himself.)

Moira, subsequently the Marquis of Hastings, played a major role in Davison's life and a greatly underestimated one in Nelson's. At Davison's trial for fraud in 1809, Moira claimed that they had met on the outbreak of war in 1793 when Davison had been recommended to him as the commissary-general for the army he was preparing to take over the Channel to invade France. Davison's name may have been proposed by the Duke of Northumberland who had fought alongside Moira in the American war, and who shared the earl's aristocratic, Whiggish outlook. When Moira became embroiled in a plot to oust the prime minister William Pitt from office in 1797, he instinctively turned to the duke for help, using Davison as a secret go-between, a role Davison would reprise for Nelson and Emma. In a similar manner, Moira used Davison's influence with Nelson to harness the Victor of the Nile's political appeal. In 1802 Davison told Nelson that Moira was on the verge of being appointed to Henry Addington's new cabinet. Persuaded by the hope that Moira's influence might secure a longed-for government pension for Emma Hamilton, Nelson gave the earl his proxy in the House of Lords believing him 'a distinguished officer, an enlightened statesman and a man of too much honour to abuse so sacred a trust'.[22] Nelson's disappointment was profound, therefore, when not only was Moira not invited to join the cabinet but he began to wield his vote against his interest. On his last leave in England in September 1805 Nelson felt compelled to ask the earl for the return of his proxy, an embarrassing and unpleasant task which he bitterly resented having to do, believing it was Davison's responsibility, but his agent was out of town.

Nelson saw his lavish Derby wine coolers for the first time on his return to England in November 1800. An educated eye would have recognised the obvious Egyptian motifs: obelisks, pyramids and palm trees as well as the conventional symbols for a naval victory: a flag draped gun, trident and anchor. An initiated observer, however, could decipher the hidden masonic code, for each of the images was loaded with rich allegorical meaning. The most striking of these was the Roman Corinthian column which a freemason would recognise as emblematic of strength and wisdom. The column stood alongside an obelisk, another striking masonic image. In due course both would become physical realities. For, with its empty pedestal, the column on the coolers eerily foreshadowed the vast stone monument erected in Trafalgar Square forty years after Trafalgar, whereas Davison himself raised an obelisk in Nelson's memory on his estate in Northumberland.

The coolers offer vivid proof of Davison's guiding philosophy and of his enthusiasm for the voguish masonic conviction that freemasonry could be traced to the ancient world of the Egyptians. Yet the physical manifestation of this previously hidden aspect to Davison's friendship with Nelson did not end there. In November 1798 Davison embarked on an ambitious, and expensive, scheme to give a medal to every man who fought the Battle of the Nile – all six thousand of them. Davison's grand project – which eventually cost him £1,200 – was authorised by his political friend the secretary for war Henry Dundas. Dundas insisted that the medal should not glorify Nelson, rather that it should celebrate the victory as a stepping stone to peace. However, as a prominent freemason himself, the minister turned a blind eye to the encoding of the Nile medal with masonic symbols. In accordance with the government's instructions Davison – who painstakingly designed the medal himself – placed a figure of Hope on the obverse of his medal, to represent the official desire for peace. In contrast the image of Nelson was relegated to a small shield, in blatant contravention of the precedent set by earlier medals for naval victories – such as Earl Howe's victory on the Glorious First of June – when a bust of the commander-in-chief was given prominence. The figure of Hope served a dual function. Alongside her traditional representation as a source of comfort was her providential role as one of the three principal theological virtues of freemasonry (the others being Faith and Charity). To emphasise this point still further, in his design Davison depicted Hope with her right breast bared, in imitation of the masonic initiation ritual. He also insisted that the anchor supporting the figure of Hope – her traditional and, in the context of a naval victory, highly appropriate emblem – should appear exactly as he had sketched it, intending that its partially obscured stock should appear like a coffin, another discreet masonic reference. Matthew Boulton, the famous steam engineer and industrialist who was entrusted with the manufacture of the medal, was unimpressed by the use of so much symbolism believing it to be confusing and in very bad taste. Boulton's objections were ignored and it is only by understanding the deliberate ambiguities within Davison's Nile medal that a solution can be found to its most abiding mystery.

This is the appearance of the sun on the reverse of the medal which depicted the scene within Aboukir bay shortly before the battle commenced. As the action took place at night, the orientation of the Egyptian coastline on the medal suggests that the sun is setting in the *east*. This impossibility had always been assumed to be the unintended error of Matthew Boulton's master die-cutter, a German émigré called Conrad Küchler. Yet from the extensive – almost obsessive – correspondence between Davison, Boulton and Henry Dundas' office in Downing Street over the manufacture of the Nile medal, it seems inconceivable that such an obvious mistake would have been tolerated. Indeed in the final design of the medal – which Davison arranged to be published in the *Anti-Jacobin Review and Magazine* – the sky above the bay was left entirely blank. Why then was the sun added to the design, apparently at the last moment? The answer to this riddle is found in other masonic jewels of the period notably those of the Ancient Gregorians, the obscure pseudo-masonic friendly society which later counted Nelson among its members. In these jewels a *rising* sun often appears as symbolic of the influence of the masonic 'All ruling Power'. The use of the sun to represent Divine providence is analogous within masonic iconography to the more familiar 'Eye of Providence'. The 'Eye of Providence' is seen in 'The Thanksgiving Medal', another medal struck after the battle to celebrate the victory. 'The Thanksgiving Medal' was available to the public in a variety of metals from a leading jeweller in the Strand and it seems impossible that Davison was not aware of it. Placing 'The Thanksgiving Medal' with its pyramid, palm tree, and masonic bi-morph figure, alongside Davison's Nile medal and the Derby wine coolers it is impossible to ignore the extraordinary amalgamation of masonic influences. It seems that Davison was not alone in expropriating Nelson's victory as a triumph of masonic virtues over the threat of tyranny.

There was also a political dimension to Davison's very public act of generosity. Prevented by their constitution from publicly defending themselves, the freemasons, led by Lord Moira, had recently embarked on a discreet campaign to secure exemption from emergency legislation which, although designed to outlaw the secret meetings of Jacobins and

Irish revolutionaries, would have severely restricted their own activities. Within this highly charged political context, Davison's medal can be seen as a mute demonstration of masonic loyalty to crown and country. Accordingly, in addition to the medals struck for the men who fought the battle, Davison ordered a further quantity for his own, carefully targeted, distribution. Two of the first medals were sent to Earl St Vincent and Admiral Sir Peter Parker, neither of whom had been at the battle, while Davison presented one to the king in person, reporting happily to Nelson that they were received 'most graciously and with much joy and pleasure'.[23] St Vincent subsequently returned the favour presenting Davison with one of the gold medals he commissioned from Boulton after he struck his flag for the final time in 1800. Like Nelson, no record survives of St Vincent's membership of the freemasons yet his medal is elegant proof that he, too, was steeped in the masonic culture which informed the very highest levels of the government and military. The medal depicts a marine and a naval officer making a masonic handshake against the backdrop, following the recent union with Ireland, of the newly instituted Union Jack. Above them is the motto 'Loyal and True' – sentiments which resonated through the military and political elite.

The government took the opportunity of Davison's largesse for some strategic gift-giving of its own. Lord Grenville, the foreign secretary, asked Davison to send medals to the emperors of Russia and Germany, the sultan of Turkey and the king of Naples. Davison happily obliged, waving aside offers of payment satisfied as he was with the political capital he was reaping. Nelson – who understood the currency of gift giving – doled out Nile medals liberally until his death. His own medal, which he wore on a ribbon around his neck, was returned to Davison after the Battle of Trafalgar.[24]

III

The material expression of the friends' interest in the culture of fraternity was matched by the language they employed, famously in Nelson's description of his Nile captains as his 'band of brothers'. This striking term is taken, of course, from the king's speech in Shakespeare's *Henry V* yet it seems the idea of employing it in the aftermath of the battle was given to Nelson by his wife. In a letter to her husband written in March 1797, Fanny Nelson casually mentions Lady Spencer, the wife of the First Lord, speaking 'of the admirals and captains as a chosen band, they all can do the same great actions'.[25] 'The band of brothers' was certainly a propitious term in the context of the fraternalism of the freemasons and by expropriating it (then modifying it to the 'brethren of the Nile'), Nelson defined the intellectual environment in which the battle was fought.

So compelling was the prevailing instinct to ritualise fraternal bonds forged in war that barely twenty-four hours after the battle the 'band of brothers' instituted the elite 'Egyptian Club'. With its rules and designated meeting place (though it seems to have only met once), the Egyptian Club mimicked the freemasons and other friendly societies with which the captains were familiar. Back in London, Davison was given the task of organising a deluxe gold and bejewelled presentation sword with its hilt designed as a crocodile for the members of the club to present to Nelson. Replica swords were made for the captains and an elite group of invited members, including the prince of Wales. Davison himself owned at least two Egyptian Club crocodile swords. One was bequeathed by his son to the Royal Naval Hospital at Greenwich in 1873 while another was found among his collection of artefacts.

The Nile medal and the Derby wine coolers indicate the high importance that the friends placed in gift giving. Yet Nelson faced a dilemma. With only limited resources, what could he give a man who quite literally had everything? The answer is found in the will he made out shortly before joining HMS *Victory* in May 1803. In the will, he bequeathed to Davison 'my Turkish Gun, Scimitar and Canteen'.[26] Although of uncertain provenance – Davison subsequently claimed they had been presented to Nelson after the Battle of the Nile by the Sultan of Turkey – these three items of otherwise modest value were carefully selected by Nelson as emblematic trophies of war. As such they held a resonance for Davison far beyond anything Nelson could have purchased and were of inestimable value to him. At the earliest opportunity after receiving his bequest in 1806, Davison was painted by Arthur William Devis – the artist who had just completed his famous work *The Death of Nelson* – ostentatiously carrying Nelson's 'scimitar' (in reality, a captured French cavalry sabre.) At a stroke the painting identified Davison to posterity as an intimate of the nation's hero. The sabre was gifted to the Royal Naval Hospital although in the event only its gilt scabbard was received with the sabre believed lost until it resurfaced among Davison's lost treasures.[27]

Alongside his bequest to Davison, Nelson gave another indication in his will of the significance he attached to those objects he felt were invested with emotional significance. This was his mention of a diamond star which he left to Emma Hamilton 'as a token of my friendship and regard'. Nelson had previously described the star – which was incontrovertibly a gift from the Sultan of Turkey – in a letter to Emma as a 'memento of friendship, affection, and esteem' presumably because it had witnessed the onset of their affair.[28] After Nelson's death, Emma asked Davison to take the diamond star to John Salter, her jeweller on the Strand, 'as he is to do something to it'.[29] Thereafter the star disappears, to be replaced in Emma's collection by a 'brilliant anchor'; probably the same jewel – decorated with Nelson's initials – which was found two hundred years later with Davison's descendants and which was the key to the discovery of his lost treasures. As with the Derby wine coolers, Emma presumably sold the diamond anchor to Davison as her fortunes dramatically declined after Nelson's death.

Davison's role in altering the diamond star is one practical demonstration of his integration into Nelson's closest inner circle, placing him at the heart of a dense web of relationships. Following his appointment as Nelson's prize agent in 1798, Davison used his experience in business to quickly extend his interests until they encompassed virtually the entire management of Nelson's civilian life including the admiral's legal and financial affairs, his domestic household, his tax returns, even the management of his post. When called upon, Davison was also expected to lend his friend money without charging interest, something which he happily, and frequently, did – although the scale of his debt came to trouble Nelson. This mixing of private and professional duties between friends was characteristic of a period where there were few other outside resources to rely on. In this way Davison's mansion in St James's Square became the hub of Nelson's world, a place to which all those in the admiral's inner circle looked for advice, or influence; and none more so than Nelson's wife Fanny. Davison's papers reveal that during her husband's long absence in the Mediterranean after the Battle of the Nile – as his affair with Emma Hamilton gathered momentum – Fanny was effectively adopted by the Davison family. Her letters mention shared suppers, walks, evenings of whist and her warm affection for Davison's children and for his young wife Harriett. In June 1799 Fanny stood as a sponsor to the Davisons' sixth child, Alexander Horatio Nelson Davison, though she excused herself from the baby's christening pleading the lack of a suitable gown.

It was against this intimate background that Davison received Nelson's deplorable instruction in April 1801 to 'signify to Lady N. that I expect, and for which I have made such a very liberal allowance to her, to be left to myself'.[30] Davison dutifully replied that 'I shall implicitly obey and execute your wishes at the proper time ... I will break the subject in the most delicate manner I possibly can and in a way to give least offence to Lady N.'[31] And yet, handicapped by his close friendship Davison did nothing. Indeed to the contrary, despite all he knew, he continued to give Fanny hope that rapprochement with her husband was still possible. Davison may even have believed this himself, anticipating that widespread social and professional opprobrium at Nelson's behaviour, combined with the admiral's jealous regard for his own reputation, would crush the affair. Also found among Davison's papers was a revealing letter from Captain Edward Parker, one of Nelson's young protégés, written in August 1801. In his letter Parker referred to Emma Hamilton as a 'B[itch]' who would 'play the deuce with him [Nelson]'.[32] That Parker felt able to describe Emma in such withering terms to Nelson's closest male friend indicates not only that he believed he had a sympathetic ear but also that he was expressing a widely held sentiment.

So Davison did nothing, his duty to Nelson outweighed by compassion for Fanny. In this perilous state he received a startling letter from Fanny which reveals her as every bit as passionate as her glamorous rival. 'You or no one can tell my feelings', she wrote:

> I love him I would do anything in the world to convince him of my affection – I was truly sensible of My good fortune in having such a husband – surely I have angered him – it was done *unconsciously* and without the least *intention* – I can truly say, my wish, my desire was to please him – and if he wil have the goodness to send for me – I will make it my study to obey him in every wish or desire of his – and with cheerfulness – I still hope – He is affectionate and possesses the best of hearts – He will not make me miserable – I hope I have not deserved so severe a punishment from him.[33]

Davison took a month to reply. 'I have long wished to write to you', he began, his words betraying his obvious discomfort:

> Which nothing but the want of something to say to you prevented. I have nothing to relate in particular, yet it is with unspeakable pleasure I can assure you, that Lord Nelson is in better health that I had ever reason to expect … I hardly need to repeat how happy I should have been to have seen him with you, the happiest. His heart is so pure and so extremely good that I flatter myself he never can be divested from his affection. I have the same opinion I ever had of his sincere regard for you. I have no right to doubt it.[34]

Davison's letter is further evidence of an emerging consensus that Nelson had been led astray by his mistress. Fanny described her husband as 'deluded'[35] while the Reverend Edmund Nelson lamented that his son 'is gone a little out of the straight road – He will see his error – and be as good as ever'.[36] This attitude brought with it some comfort, and a little hope, but made the inevitable denouement still more devastating. This arrived in December 1801 when Fanny sent a letter to her husband under cover to Davison's house in St James's Square, the one place where she believed her husband might read it away from the gaze of Emma Hamilton. 'My dear husband', she wrote:

> The silence you have imposed is more than my affections will allow me … Do, my dear husband, let us live together. I can never be happy till such an event takes place. I assure you again I have but one wish in the world, to please you. Let everything be buried in oblivion, it will pass away like a dream. I can now only entreat you to believe I am most sincerely and affectionately your wife, Frances H. Nelson[37]

Davison was now forced to choose between his friends. His decision was inevitable, given the value to him of his role in Nelson's life and the strength of the hidden loyalties that existed between them. But it was none the less painful. The same evening Fanny received her letter back. On the address leaf was written – like a short stab to her heart: 'Opened by mistake by Lord Nelson, but not read. A. Davison'.[38] Davison's loyalty to his friend, which he pursued at great personal cost (the thoughts of Harriett Davison on her husband's role in the separation of the Nelsons may be imagined), was not entirely reciprocated. From Nelson's surviving correspondence to Emma Hamilton it seems that in the last months of his life the admiral was cooling in his regard for his old friend, a situation exacerbated by his anger and embarrassment at the abuse of his proxy vote by Davison's patron Lord Moira. The news in 1804 that Davison had been imprisoned in the King's Bench for electoral corruption was greeted with a distinct smug satisfaction. 'I am quite hurt about his getting into such a scrape,' Nelson commented, 'he always told me: "Oh! I know my ground – leave me alone – I cannot be deceived". It often turns out that these very clever men are oftener deceived than other people.'[39]

Emma, who had clashed with Davison over the cost of her improvements to Merton Place, undoubtedly stirred things up. Matters deteriorated to such an extent that in one of the last letters Nelson wrote to Emma, he confided that: 'I don't think Davison a good hand to keep such a secret as you told him. I fear I cannot even write him a line.' The nature of the 'secret' which Emma divulged to Davison is not known. Perhaps she revealed to him the true parentage of her four-year-old 'ward' Horatia.

Nelson was also eager to escape from Davison's financial grasp, confiding to Emma in May 1805 that: 'I know I am most deeply in debt to Davison, and I want his account that I may close it, for it must not run on in the way it has, but I cannot get it, nor do I know how I stand with their banking house, I get no account.'[40] Yet despite his inner thoughts, the last letter Nelson wrote to his friend, from *Victory* on 13 October 1805 showed no sign of any lessening of affection. In the letter – which Davison carefully preserved – Nelson expressed his hope that 'some happy day I hope to get at their fleet and nothing shall be wanting on my part to give a good account of them'.[41]

IV

Davison stayed loyal beyond Nelson's death. He erected an obelisk on his estate dedicated to their 'Private Friendship' and, to his credit, did his best to support Emma Hamilton as she struggled with her rising debts. Learning that Davison had raised a consortium of investors to bale her out of her debts, Emma wrote that: 'to my last breathe I shall feel a glory in having had Alexander Davison as my friend; as did Nelson, to his death, die loving & respecting you more than he did any man living. Relations not excepted.'[42] In the event, Davison's unhappy fate was scarcely less humiliating than Emma's. In 1809 he was found guilty of defrauding the public purse in his capacity as a government contractor and was again sent to prison, this time for two years. On his release Davison embarked on an ill-advised and costly attempt to clear his name. Although eventually vindicated, his campaign, combined with the failure of his bank, cost him much of his vast fortune. In 1817 his mansion in St James's Square was sold and the contents auctioned in a spectacular fourteen-day sale. Alongside his magnificent collection of works of art and paintings were numerous souvenirs of his relationship with Nelson although Davison preserved those of particular sentiment, including the diamond anchor, Nelson's Nile medal, the Derby wine coolers and the bloodstained purse which his friend had carried to his death at Trafalgar.

Lot 972 on the last day of the auction was a copy of Jeremy Taylor's *Doctor Dubitantium or The Rule of Conscience*. Taylor, an influential seventeenth-century theologian, believed that a good friend should be 'wise and virtuous, rich and at hand, close and merciful, free of his money and tenacious of a secret, open and ingenuous, true and honest' for 'a fool cannot be relied upon for counsel; nor a vicious person for the advantages of virtue, nor a begger for relief, nor a stranger for conduct, nor a tattler to keep a secret, nor a pitiless person trusted with any complaint, nor a covetous person with my childes fortune ... nor a suspicious person with a private design'.[43] In subsequent biographies of Nelson and even – as a contemporary caricature reveals – during his lifetime, Davison has been vilified for exploiting his friendship with the hero. Yet it seems that he largely fulfilled Taylor's dictum and that, on balance, it was Davison who was ill-advised in his choice of friend.

Notes

1. Nelson to Davison, 8 February 1803. N.H. Nicolas, *The Dispatches and Letters of Vice-Admiral Lord Viscount Nelson* (London, 1846), vol. V, p. 42.
2. Davison to Nelson, 3 February 1803. T.J. Pettigrew, *Memoirs of the Life of Vice-Admiral Lord Viscount Nelson, K.B.* (London, 1849), vol. II, p. 282.
3. In 'State of my affairs according to my books to the 31st December 1803', Davison estimated his net personal worth at £307,940. (Private collection.)
4. Davison introduced his nephew William Home, then serving in *Blanche*, to Nelson during a visit to Yarmouth in February 1801 shortly before the fleet sailed on the Baltic campaign.
5. Quoted by Nelson in a letter to Emma Lady Hamilton, 7 March 1801. Pettigrew, *Memoirs*, I, p. 438.
6. Davison to his son William Davison, 8 December 1810. (Private collection.)
7. Davison and Ross must have known each other, if only by repute. In a letter dated 11 June 1801 Nelson asked Davison for assistance in a matter involving Ross' nephew. Nicolas, *Dispatches*, IV, p. 408.
8. Nelson to Davison, 27 May 1797. Nicolas, *Dispatches*, VII, p. cxxxviii.
9. Sir Nicholas Harris Nicolas to Percy Davison, 17 December 1844. BL EG MSS 2241.
10. Maurice Nelson to Sukey Ford, 27 March 1794. NMM HAM/81.
11. Davison to Nelson, 24 April 1801. NMM CRK/3.
12. Davison to Admiral Cuthbert Collingwood. NMM DAV/52 fo. 44.
13. Nelson to Davison, 27 May 1797. Nicolas, *Dispatches*, VII, p. cxxxviii.
14. Frances Nelson to Davison, 3 May 1801. NMM DAV/2/43.
15. Maurice Nelson to Nelson, 25 November 1798. BL ADD MSS 34988.
16. Frances Nelson to Alexander Davison, 21 February 1799. NMM DAV/2 fo. 6.
17. Ibid.
18. Davison to Emma Hamilton, undated, probably November 1804. A. Morrison, *The Hamilton and Nelson Papers* (1893), vol. II, p. 247.
19. J. Harland-Jacobs, '*The Essential Link': Freemasonry and British Imperialism, 1751–1918*, unpublished D. Phil. dissertation (Duke University, 2000), p. 46n.
20. F. Smyth, 'The Master-Mason-at-Arms: A Short Study of Freemasonry in the Armed Forces', *Ars Coronatorum*, 104 (1991).
21. In *Horatio Lord Nelson Was he a Freemason* (1998) John Webb points out that during Nelson's tenure the Great Cabin of *Vanguard* was carpeted by a piece of sailcloth marked out in black and white squares as if for a masonic ritual. Webb states that this checkerboard sailcloth was subsequently transferred to *Victory*.

22. Nelson to William Haslewood, quoted in T. Pocock, *Horatio Nelson* (London: Bodley Head, 1987), p. 310.
23. Davison to Nelson, 6 April 1799. BL ADD 34910.
24. In 1866 the medal was recorded in a family inventory by Davison's son, Sir William Davison, as 'the gold nile medal worn by the immortal Nelson when he fell 21st October 1805 at Trafalgar'. It was Lot 8 in *The Alexander Davison Collection*, Sotheby's London, 21 October 2002 selling for £26,290.
25. Frances Nelson to Nelson, 11 March 1797, in G.P.B. Naish, *Nelson's Letters to his Wife and other documents 1785–1831* (Navy Records Society, 1958), p. 350.
26. The will is printed in full in Nicolas, *Dispatches*, VII, pp. ccxxi–ccxl.
27. The sabre was Lot 84 in *The Alexander Davison Collection*, Sotheby's London, 21 October 2002, selling for £336,650.
28. Nelson to Emma Hamilton, undated but probably February 1801. Pettigrew, *Memoirs*, I, p. 428.
29. Emma Hamilton to Davison, 7 June 1806. NMM LBK/7.
30. Nelson to Davison, 23 April 1801. Nicolas, *Dispatches*, VII, p. ccix.
31. Davison to Nelson, 4 May 1801, in Lot 70 *The Alexander Davison Collection*, Sotheby's London, 21 October 2002.
32. Edward Parker to Davison, 9 August 1801, in Lot 53 *The Alexander Davison Collection*, Sotheby's London, 21 October 2002.
33. Frances Nelson to Davison, 26 June 1801. NMM DAV/2 fo. 50.
34. Davison to Frances Nelson, 12 July 1801. Naish, *Nelson's Letters to His Wife*, p. 588.
35. Frances Nelson to Davison, 15 March 1801. NMM DAV/2 fo. 32.
36. Quoted in Frances Nelson to Davison, 27 July 1801. NMM DAV/2 fo. 51.
37. Frances Nelson to Nelson, 18 December 1801. Naish, *Nelson's Letters to His Wife*, p. 596.
38. Ibid.
39. Nelson to Emma Hamilton, 22 May 1804. Pettigrew, *Memoirs*, II, p. 392.
40. Nelson to Emma Hamilton, 13 May 1805. Pettigrew, *Memoirs*, II, p. 474.
41. Nelson to Davison, 13 October 1805. *The Alexander Davison Collection*, Sotheby's London, 21 October 2002, Lot 76.
42. Emma Hamilton to Davison, 21 December 1808. NMM MSS 9640.
43. Jeremy Taylor, *A Discourse of the Nature, Offices and Measure of Friendship* (London, 1671), pp. 27–8.

3
Nelson and the People: Manliness, Patriotism and Body Politics

Kathleen Wilson

'The fittest man in the world for the command' of the Mediterranean, Lord Minto declared of Horatio Nelson on 24 April 1798, following Nelson's inventive assault on Spanish ships off Cape St Vincent. 'Admiral Nelson's victory [at Aboukir, the mouth of the Nile] ... [is] one of the most glorious and comprehensive victories ever achieved even by British valour', the *London Chronicle* exulted later that year. Nelson's breath-taking exploits on the high seas, his courage and aggression in combat, and his quixotic generosity to his men, had quickly catapulted him to fame, enmeshing his reputation with the best of the English national character. '[W]ith the brilliant qualities of a hero, Lord Nelson unites a feeling and generous heart, a quick discernment of occasion, and popularity of manners' affirmed the *Gentleman's Magazine* in 1801, surveying the acclaim of the people on Nelson's tour to Fonthill.[1]

We are so familiar with Nelson the legend that the historical mechanics and the cultural significance of his extraordinary reputation as England's greatest admiral are rarely examined. Yet the making of Nelson's almost instantaneous apotheosis in his own day has much to reveal to us in our effort to re-discover the man and the myth. First, it demonstrates new departures in the popular politics, forged through a century of British war, which continued even in the age of Pitt's Terror. Secondly, Nelson's fame and the iconic significance of his dismembered body marked a larger shift in the politics and practices of representation, away from the transparent and universal forms of an eighteenth-century public sphere, towards the fragmented body and body politic of nineteenth-century modernity. Finally, the figure of Nelson mobilised and concentrated a version of stoic, affective, masculinist patriotism in the service of the nation-state, the main characteristics of which have yet to be entirely effaced. These three themes in popular, body and gender politics provide the focus of this chapter.

I

From the long eighteenth-century perspective, Nelson's celebrity was in itself nothing new. Since Marlborough's victory at Blenheim, triumphal military and naval figures had increasingly seized the British imagination in ways that rivalled and even exceeded kings and queens. The Royal Navy in particular produced heroes that personified the kind of wars that many people felt Britain should be fighting – expansionist blue-water conflicts that extended British trade abroad and protected constitutional liberties at home. Hence in 1739, at the start of the War of Jenkins's Ear, Vice-Admiral Edward Vernon wrenched a victory over Spain at the Panamanian fort of Porto Bello and was wildly celebrated as a hero in towns and villages across England, Ireland and North America. An opposition Whig, hostile to the corruption of the Walpolean state and to its pacific foreign policy, and resentful of the profiteering that riddled the Royal Navy, Vernon was identified with a host of libertarian issues in the domestic polity as well as British expansion abroad. Vernon's image and the plan of attack on Port Bello were accordingly festooned on tavern signs, mugs, prints and plates (see Plate 1).

Most importantly for our purposes, Vernon was fêted by his admirers for many of the same qualities for which Nelson would become known. Vernon was intrepid and aggressive – prior to the war, he had declared in parliament, in the face of ministerial stalling, that he could take Porto Bello with six ships and three hundred men, and so it would prove. He was disdainful of rank, declining the offer of a knighthood in 1742, and he was a just and fair commander, willing to implement reforms to improve morale and health and to press sailors' rights in parliament. Hence he appealed to a wide range of British people, who saw in British expansion overseas and a reformist domestic agenda at home a recipe for national greatness. Above all, Vernon and the popular politics he mobilised helped crystallise an idealised notion of the national character as comprised of the 'manly' qualities necessary for military triumph and successful colonisation: independence, fortitude, courage, daring, resourcefulness and paternalistic duty.[2]

Of course Vernon was only the first of a series of naval and military figures who would attain celebrity as well as opprobrium among the people in the public sphere of eighteenth-century politics.[3] The Duke of Cumberland, fondly known as 'Billy the Butcher' for his bloody dispatch of Highlanders, Frenchmen and other Jacobite rebels in 1745–46, was wildly celebrated by the same social groups who had rioted on Vernon's behalf a few years earlier. Alternatively, the unlucky Admiral John Byng was burnt in effigy by crowds across Britain and then executed by the government for failing to launch a futile but aggressive counter-attack on the French as they conquered the island of Minorca in 1756. With the humiliation of Minorca still fresh in the public mind, General James Wolfe led a dangerous and reckless assault on French forces in Quebec in 1759, and died in the effort on the plains of Abraham; but the resulting victory and death exuded the requisite dose of testosterone-fuelled predatory aggression. Indeed, the victory at Quebec was pivotal to British success in capturing this part of North America, and Wolfe's heroic fall in the effort provided empirical and symbolic assurance of British ability to triumph on land as well as sea.[4]

The painting by Benjamin West, on which the print included here is based (see Plate 2), commemorates this patriotic death by depicting a Highlander, a native American, and several other men known not to be there, all sharing in the contemplation of the greatness of the fallen hero of empire. The filial nature of Britain's next war – with the American colonies – made the national celebration of bloodthirsty admirals a touchier affair; but Admiral Keppel and Howe's victories over French forces in the Channel and the West Indies were celebrated by people of all political persuasions, eager to see evidence of British fighting mettle. And so it went, all the way up to Horatio Nelson's triumphs, the aftermath of which is, as they say, history.

Each of these high-profile men's fate and reputation were exploited in political struggles at home; and each was celebrated or faulted for demonstrating or failing to display the high levels of initiative, will and courage that had come to define public conceptions of patriotic virtue. Rooted in classical ideals about citizenship and embellished by early modern civic humanism and neo-classical stoicism, Georgian patriotism demanded that these forms of manliness be put at the service of the nation-state. Addison's play *Cato*, whose namesake forswore sexual passion to give his life for the cause of liberty against the tyrannical Caesar, epitomised its central features. Whether inflected with radical or loyalist political associations or, after 1760, modulated with the empathy directed by the cult of sensibility, the true patriot was the austere, forceful and independent masculine subject who would resist, often at considerable personal cost, the illegitimate powers that threatened to overtake the polity: men who distinguished themselves by resolve and self-control, whose 'inner authenticity had allowed them to achieve self-sovereignty'.[5] Though modelled on Roman precedents, this was, arguably, a bourgeois ideal: in the age when ideas about natural rights and social contract were challenging old regime corporatism, this version of patriotism required each person to represent his own political body, in conscious opposition to old public values of aristocratic display, conspicuous consumption and self-glorification. Manly patriotism was disdainful of 'womanly' qualities in men, such as tenderness or pity, which were considered signs of a failed masculinity or effeminacy, but it still gave women a job to do: promoting the stoicism and love of country within the home that produced a manly and intrepid fighting service at the front. Hence in the aftermath of the infamous Battle of Falkirk (1746), when panicked British troops fled from Jacobite Highlanders without firing a single shot, the famous actress Peg Woffington appeared at Drury Lane in the dress of a redcoat, admonishing the 'Patriot-Fair' to 'vindicate the glory of our Isle' by refusing their favours to cowards and deserters.[6]

Certainly, as this example indicates, the national celebration of aggressive conquering masculinity had its dark side. For much of the century, it was lauded in no small measure as the antidote to recurring fears of national impotency and failure. First, military debacles such as Falkirk, the loss of Minorca, and the poor performance of British troops in the early years of the Seven Years War had conjured up images of an effeminised and enervated British nation becoming a province of – curiously – an allegedly feminised and foppish France. Further, conquests of both territorial and sexual varieties were believed to be ambiguous in their results, the first allowing luxury, and effeminacy to contaminate the body politic, as civic humanists warned, and the second blurring the boundaries between domination and submission (as when the male climax becomes the female triumph, leaving him 'spent' and her invigorated). But partly because of these complexities, the conquering masculine version could readily seize the individual and national psyche, and generate the propensity for identifying oneself with a Brutus, a Cato, or a Wolfe. Given this context, it is perhaps unsurprising that the young Horatio Nelson, convalescing from malaria in 1776 after an East Indian tour, realised through 'a sudden glow of patriotism' that the defence of king and country would be the animating goal of his life. 'Well then,' he exclaimed, 'I will be a hero, and confiding in Providence I will brave every danger.'[7]

II

The earliest years of Nelson's career contained events that would later be represented as intimating his future greatness. As a midshipman, he had accompanied Captain Phipps' polar expedition to try to find a north-east passage to the Pacific (a voyage also attended by another current celebrity of eighteenth-century studies, Olaudah Equiano). Here Nelson purportedly engaged a polar bear in hand to paw combat, after his musket misfired (see Plate 3). He infuriated his captain for taking this unnecessary risk – Nelson had wanted to kill the bear to bring the skin home to his father, and escaped with his life only because the ice floe broke in two. But the incident became part of his legend, so the painting was commissioned for Clark and McArthur's biography of 1802. A greater and more significant portion of his early career was spent in the Americas, serving as post-captain during the years of the American war. Here he protected the islands from French and Spanish attack, and married Fanny Nesbit, daughter of a senior judge on the island of Nevis. He also led a daring raid on the Spanish fort one hundred miles up the St John River in present day Nicaragua, scaling the wall with a hundred men and fighting the Spaniards with their own guns. This incident probably inspired Richard Brinsley Sheridan and Phillipe de Loutherbourg's theatrical spectacular staged for British audiences in the midst of the American war called *The Storming of Fort Omoa*, which featured the astonishing spectacle of a brave British officer climbing the wall of the fort while he furnished an unarmed Spaniard with a cutlass, conquered him and then spared his life.[8]

But the true take-off of Nelson's fame began in 1794–95, when France's best general, Napoleon Bonaparte, was in charge of the Italian campaign, and the revolutionary armies had struck across Europe. The British people were bitterly divided over the course of the war, as they had been over the Revolution itself. Corresponding societies and Jacobin clubs were remarkably effective not only in articulating middling and plebeian discontent with the government, but in drawing it to the attention of a wider public. In response, local elites and ministerial supporters in many places presided over celebrations of naval victories meant to bolster Church and King.[9] Yet even naval victories over the revolutionary forces could not tamp down radical dissidence. In Harwich in 1794, the town refused to illuminate for the victory of Howe over the French off Brest in 1794, and refused again, significantly, after the victory at Cape St Vincent. At the latter date, the national thanksgiving for the victory was marred by anti-Pitt sentiments and the demands for peace, for its elaborate ritual seemed to mock the increasing taxes, poor harvests and spiralling prices borne by ordinary people. City Foxites declared the procession to St Paul's but a 'Court Thanksgiving', with nothing to offer ordinary citizens; the night before, journeymen coachmakers staged a mock execution of Pitt for tripling assessed taxes on horses and carriages; and the prime minister was burnt in effigy in 'twenty different parts' of the metropolis.[10]

The Royal Navy itself had felt the burn of disaffection and desire for radical change; the great fleet mutinies at Spithead, Yarmouth and Nore included among the mutineers some respectable tradesmen (probably entering the service under the Quota Act of 1795, by which each county and seaport had to raise recruits), who used Painite language to demand justice and their 'natural rights'.[11] The ferocity of Pitt's Gagging Acts, or 'Pitt's Terror' as radicals liked to call it, did much to force radicalism and peace sentiment underground, but it was Napoleon himself who did the most damage to radical agitation. As his ambitions and Grand Design became clear, his standing as a revolutionary general in radical circles declined, and naval victories began to be celebrated as anti-French festivals by conservatives and radicals alike. Napoleon's targeting of the British empire had thus done what his previous campaigns had not, and the war effort united most people behind the massive effort to save the country, the empire and the world from French perfidy and tyranny.

This political context and the shifting politics of the war help us appreciate the nuance and novelty of Nelson's celebrity. In the years between 1794 and 1797, his daring insubordination and relentless determination made his countrymen take notice. Nelson frequently chafed at what he saw as the indecision of his commanding officers: in the days before the siege of Bastia, he complained to Sir William Hamilton, 'when before was the time that 2000 British troops ... were not thought equal to attack 800 French Troops, allowing them to be in strong works? What would the immortal Wolfe have done?'[12] At the siege of Calvi, later that summer, he impetuously led a battery of seamen on shore before receiving the wound to his right eye that cost him his sight. The next year, under the command of Vice-Admiral Hotham, Nelson's first fleet action in March 1795 off Genoa was to launch a murderous assault from his frigate the *Agamemnon* on the French ship *Ça Ira*, a double-shotted broadside which raked her from stem to stern and left the sail and mast in tatters. Swift response from other French ships to save her led Hotham to order Nelson away, and the battle was indecisive. But it confirmed in Nelson his desire to command: 'In short I wish to be an admiral and in the command of the English fleet,' he wrote to his wife Fanny; 'I should very soon either do much or be ruined. My disposition can't bear tame and slow measures.'[13]

This was soon borne out at the Battle of Cape St Vincent in 1797. Commodore Nelson's commander-in-chief, Sir John Jervis, had fought with Wolfe at Quebec, and had just assisted in the capture of the French sugar islands of Guadeloupe and Martinique. But it was Nelson's attack on the Spanish fleet on his own initiative – falling out of line to throw his ship across the path of the escaping enemy squadron, engaging and boarding the 80-gun *San Nicolas*, and then crossing it and boarding the 112-gun *San Josef*, and capturing it as well – that won the day (see Plates 4 and 5). Jervis's dispatch to the Admiralty the day after the battle did not mention Nelson or his capture of two ships. But fortunately for us, Nelson did, and most of what we know about the victory came from Nelson himself. In letters to the Duke of Clarence and to Fanny, his wife, Nelson outlined his actions and their importance in the overall victory; hence his description of 'Nelson's Patent Bridge for boarding First Rates' appeared in *The Times* and *The Sun*. Coming at a time when Bonaparte was advancing to Vienna and rumblings of mutiny could be heard among the fleet at Spithead, the victory was greeted with widespread rejoicings all over the country. Significantly, at the Theatre Royal, Bristol, 'Cape St Vincent, or British Valeur Triumphant' replaced 'The Siege of Quebec' as the favoured afterpiece to boost nationalist and patriotic sentiment, closing with rousing audience choruses of *Rule Britannia*.[14] Jervis was made Earl St Vincent, and Nelson Knight of the Bath; in April he hoisted his own flag as Rear-Admiral of the Blue.[15]

Nelson's Patent Bridge had made him famous; the attack on Tenerife, where he lost his right arm after engaging in hand to hand combat with the enemy, began to turn him into a legend. But of course the crowning jewel of Nelson's glory in this period was the Battle of the Nile. In early 1797, invasion fears and news of a French mobilisation had emptied many coastal towns and galvanised militia organisation. As Nelson trolled the Mediterranean for an elusive French squadron, he became convinced Bonaparte was after India. On 28 July he learned the French were in Egypt; he set sail for Alexandria on the afternoon of 1 August, and found the French fleet of thirteen ships of the line and four frigates in Aboukir bay, a few miles north-east of Alexandria. Nelson having neither eaten nor slept for many preceding days, now chose the moment to order dinner to be served. Presiding over table he remarked, 'Before this time tomorrow, I shall have gained a Peerage, or Westminster Abbey.'[16] Daring shallow shoals to surround the unprepared French ships on both sides, he began the battle at 6.00pm; at 10.00pm *l'Orient*, the flagship of French admiral Bruey, blew up, with bodies, masts, yards, cannons and wreckage blazing down upon all the ships (see Plate 6). Both sides were so shocked at the disaster that for some minutes, firing ceased. Bruey was mortally wounded; Nelson struck on the forehead by flying iron shrapnel; and of the thirteen French ships of line, nine had been taken. It was obliteration new to naval warfare, and Nelson remarked, 'Victory is not a strong enough name for such a scene as I have passed.'[17]

Contemporary historians and biographers have seen in the spectacle of Aboukir Nelson's will to annihilate: he was a 'natural born predator', as Terry Coleman said, a manic-depressive who had a thirst for blood.[18] But what such assessments overlook is that the British nation participated in this desire. Like Wolfe, who has similarly been reassessed in current histories as a ruthless killer, Nelson exhibited the complete devotion to victory, whatever the cost, that many people in Britain felt was the only recourse when faced with French ambition.[19] As such, the nation was quick to respond. In press and parliament, on medals, tavern signs pottery and prints, and in civic fêtes, street festivals, and thanksgivings, the victory at the Nile was hailed as something the likes of which the nation and the national history had never before beheld – 'pre-eminent even in the Naval History of this country, for its daring gallantry and most happy success', as the *True Briton* declared. His new arms, as Baron Nelson of the Nile and Burnham Thorpe, engravings of his left and right hand autographs, and battle plans were displayed on prints, broadsheets and in newspapers; verses and songs celebrated his daring, gallantry and courage; and the papers also carried accounts of processions, illuminations and bonfires from towns all over England, Scotland and Ireland and the empire, from Antigua to Calcutta.[20] In Norfolk Street, a transparency of the gallant admiral depicted him 'standing on the deck of his own Ship, with his Sword drawn, and L'Orient near him in flames, as the figure of fame sounded her Trumpet and the words "Rule Britannia" came out'.[21] All this in addition to the foreign and international acclaim festooned upon him: a dukedom from the king of Naples, a *chelengk*, or Plume of Triumph, and a star and crescent set with diamonds, from the Grand Signior or sultan of the Ottoman empire; and the adoration of the ladies in Naples and Britain on his return from the coast of Egypt.[22]

Nelson, as usual, did his part to enlarge his celebrity; he was always his own best publicist. His dispatch to Earl St Vincent, commander-in-chief, after the battle, which subsequently appeared in all the newspapers in England, began 'Almighty God had blessed his Majesty's arms in the late battle by a great victory over the fleet of the enemy', and went on in the next sentence to commend the men of his squadron: 'their high state of discipline is well known to you, and with the judgment of the Captains, together with their valour, and that of the Officers and Men of every description, it was absolutely irresistible'.[23] This show of humility, faith and loyalty to his men, contrasting with French atheism and arrogance, was described in editorials as 'properly adapted to the state and feelings of the public mind rendered in a high degree gloomy and desponding, by the hasty progress of the Republican arms and principles, subversive of all order, religion, property and every social compact ....' In the House of Lords, Lord Minto spoke about the 'fervent and sincere piety of our Christian Conqueror' and the scale of his achievements, 'those prodigies of valour and conduct never equaled, before in the History of War'. And coming as it did in the wake of mutinies and radicalism at home, loyalist writers could use the Nile victory to remind British seamen and soldiers that their best chances lay in following their officers: as one writer pointedly asserted, Lord Nelson's actions must convince 'every British seaman, in whatever quarter of the globe he may be extending the glory and interests of his country ... [that] courage alone will not lead him to conquest, without the aid of direction, exact discipline and order ... submissive obedience, and willing subordination' to the 'courage, judgment and skill of their superior officers'.[24]

Alas, the meaning of Nelson's acclaim and the lessons to be drawn from his successes were not so clear-cut, and were fought out on a public stage in the tussles between Whigs and Tories, King and People. Members of the London Corresponding Society had been clear that although France seemed 'widely remote from the enjoyment of liberty' their hostility to invasion should not be construed as support for Pitt's government, especially not in the face of the 'savage system of coercion now pursuing in Ireland'. The opposition newspaper *The Sun* asked archly if in fact Nelson 'had not been sent out to the Mediterranean to *prevent* the French fleet from reaching Egypt?'[25] The Foxites still hoped that Nelson's victory at the Nile would lead to a 'speedy and honorable peace' with France.[26] Their measured response was satirised by the caricaturist James Gillray, whose cartoon, *Nelson's Victory, or Good News Operating upon Loyal Feelings* (1798) shows the various Whig leaders mortified by the destruction of the French fleet. But Fox and his supporters continued to be quite astute observers of the war effort, and were among the most vocal of the critics of Nelson following the Naples 'betrayal' of 1799, when Nelson went back on a treaty to deliver republican rebels to the vengeful sovereign.[27] Clearly, conventional opposition and radical dissidence were far from dead. Nevertheless, and simultaneously, English people of all persuasions were becoming sceptical of 'French liberty'. Gillray's *The British Hero*

Cleansing the Nile (1798) captured this shift, depicting Nelson, fictionally, with a hook on his right stump, lassoing the 'revolutionary crocodiles' as Alexandria looms in the background.

III

The celebration of Nelson's heroism would be embellished in the aftermaths of the Battle of Copenhagen in 1801 and of course Trafalgar in 1805. A closer look at the popular – in the sense of socially inclusive – political shows of support for Nelson reveals not only a widened political consciousness, but also a more sophisticated understanding of the ways in which such festivals and rituals and their representation functioned to create theatres of identification within the tenets of an ambiguous patriotism. On his triumphal return to England in November 1800, with Lord and Lady Hamilton in tow, Nelson was pursued by city and provincial elites who desired to host a visit from the hero and his entourage. Freedom of boroughs, swords and silver plates were presented, guns were fired, and local volunteers paraded, all participating in Nelson's reflected glory. Similar events punctuated his Midlands and West country tour, again with the Hamiltons, during the brief peace of 1802. 'It is a singular fact,' declared the *Morning Post*, 'that more éclat attends Lord Nelson ... than attends the King.'[28]

One example can crystallise both Nelson's affective power and the reverberations of its social circulation. En route to Fonthill for a spectacular fête in his honour put on by William Beckford, Nelson and the Hamiltons stopped at Salisbury. In the vast crowd before the Council House Nelson caught sight, remarkably, of two men who had served under him at Tenerife. To both he exchanged greetings, called them forth, and gave them gifts. One, who had been present at the amputation of Nelson's arm, removed 'from his bosom a piece of lace which he had torn from the sleeve of the amputated arm, declaring he would preserve it to his last breath in memory of his late gallant commander, whom he should always deem it the honour of his life to have served'. The exchange was gone over in detail in the press, in order, as one writer asserted, 'to observe the minutest action, listen to the slightest word, and dwell upon every tint or shade of character, which may furnish opportunity of tracing, in the favourite object, either resemblance or dissimilitude ... to ordinary men'.[29] Such minute description, like the performances of identification and subjection, humility and obeisance by Nelson and his men, twinned Nelson's achievements and fate with that of every common seaman and soldier and beyond, to every spectator or witness, uniting them all in the 'qualities of a hero': 'a feeling and generous heart, a quick discernment of occasion, and popularity of manners'.

Certainly, as the deliverer of his country from a foreign menace, Nelson could serve as a figurehead for mobilising the 'nationalist patriotism' that the government was attempting to implant, with its voluntary contribution schemes and associations for defence.[30] But if the Nile victory could consolidate this kind of state-promoted patriotism, its longest lasting effect would be a more critical identification of ordinary people with the body politic. Nelson's own self-conscious empathy with his subordinates aided this process, and amplified the meanings of his celebrity to include a rather pointed critique of the establishment. First, his audaciousness was only exceeded by his insubordination: at St Vincent, he had intercepted the Spanish on his own initiative; at Copenhagen, he famously put the telescope to his blind eye in order to ignore Sir Hyde Parker's orders to disengage the Danish fleet. In a war seen increasingly in terms of sacrifice, Nelson's manly stoicism, initiative and disregard for his own safety were incredibly important to his reputation. At the same time, he showed care and respect for his seamen, attending to health and victualling, but being particularly vigilant in attempting to ensure that they received their due recognition. He caused a stir when he billed the Admiralty for £60,000 in prize money for French ships fired after the Nile, writing to Earl Spencer, 'An Admiral may be amply rewarded by his feelings and the approbation of his superiors, but what reward have the inferior Officers and men but the value of the Prize?'[31] The famed 'Nelson touch', his ability to electrify his seamen with his own desire for victory and the will to achieve it, demonstrated this very personal power. Not surprisingly, he never had a problem manning his ships.

To the bravery and daring of conventional heroes, then, Nelson added compassion and empathy. He frequently expressed doubt about the wisdom of his superior officers many times in his letters, but never failed to laud the bravery and discipline of those who laboured below him. This is in contrast with most other commanders in the service, who at best maintained a polite but chilly distance between themselves and their subordinates, or at worst, like Wellington, called them 'the scum of the earth'.[32] Nelson's strong sense of camaraderie was displayed by his agreeing to give testimony on behalf of Colonel Edward Despard in 1803, on trial for treason. Despard, a United Irishman and member of the Society of United Britons, was accused of having plotted to assassinate George III and seize the Tower of London, but he had been with Nelson during the Nicaraguan expedition of 1780 and helped him scale the wall of the fort. Despite Nelson's plea for leniency, Despard was hanged, along with six of his co-conspirators in the Grenadier Guardsmen, but Nelson then attempted to obtain a pension for his widow.

Nelson's own background may have also contributed to his easy identification with his junior colleagues. Distantly related to Robert Walpole, 1st Earl of Orford, through his maternal grandmother, and having a maternal uncle who was comptroller of the Navy, he was still by the standards of the day fairly limited by birth and connection. In the aftermath of the Nile, his supporters, such as Admiral Hood, objected to the comparatively trifling peerage offered him, saying it was unworthy of his great achievements. But Earl St Vincent and Pitt insisted that Nelson's elevation was the most that could ever be given to an admiral who had not been commander-in-chief, an excuse which Hood described to Nelson as 'flimsy beyond reason'.[33] In the event, Nelson's importuning of the Admiralty and government for favours for his family and friends were usually unsuccessful. And his eccentricities, his unconventional love life, his childish vanity in wearing his many decorations, and his physical presence had all worked to make him and his mistress, Lady Hamilton, herself of low birth, outcasts in conventional high society. In Gillray's *The Hero of the Nile* (Plate 7), Nelson is caricatured as a haggard-looking dwarf, sagging beneath the weight of his medals and stars, a look which contrasts markedly with Gillray's representation of a 'typical' British tar (Plate 8), whose apparent lack of mental alertness is compensated for by his physical robustness.

Yet these very characteristics for which he became the butt of elite jokes endeared him to the people. His scarred and dismembered body made him an instantly recognisable figure; but it was also made to bear the weight of larger cultural and political change. The nature of the change can be seen in two portraits, Rigaud's *Captain Horatio Nelson* (Plate 9), painted when Nelson was a young captain and Guzzardi's *Rear-Admiral Horatio Nelson* (Plate 10), and painted after his death. These portraits are more than a commentary on youth and age. Rather, they show a shift in the representation of Nelson's body that should be seen in relation to changing notions of the body politic. The promising young captain depicted against the Nicaraguan coast gives way, in the later piece, to a figure in the full dress uniform of a rear-admiral; his right arm pinned to his coat, he wears the ribbon and star of a Knight of the Bath, the St Vincent naval medal, and the Turkish *chelengk* on his hat. The hat is pushed back on his head, to prevent discomfort to the wound scar on his forehead; and his left eye appears slightly out of focus. Nelson is emaciated-looking, pale and rather wan as he points limply to the battle scene of the Nile.

His deteriorating body became something of an obsession with some of his contemporaries. 'His weight cannot be more than 70 pounds; A more miserable collection of bones and wizened frame I have never yet come across', a Lutheran pastor asserted after seeing Nelson and the Hamiltons on their grand progress across Europe. Aristocratic observers seemed even more repulsed. Lord Elgin, passing through Palermo on the way to Constantinople in 1799, was appalled: 'He looks very old, has lost his upper teeth, sees ill of one eye, and has a film coming over both of them. He has pains pretty constantly from his late wound in the head. His figure is mean, and in general, his countenance is without animation.'[34] Elgin clearly found the figure of the man to be unworthy of his deeds; indeed, whether it was class or disability, Nelson was in his eyes a grotesque, a physically deformed specimen unworthy to represent the British nation. The contest over body politics at work here was that between the sacralised, classical forms of monarchical and patrician culture, and the particularised and peculiarly individual forms of an industrialising society, in which the far from uniform body was a force of production and a generator of individual rather than political sovereignty.

This was made very clear, conversely, by people who looked at Nelson and saw the icon. Charles Macready, then a schoolboy son of the Birmingham theatre manager, remembered seeing Nelson at the theatre during his Midlands tour. He recalled:

Nothing of course passed unnoticed ... the right-arm empty sleeve attached to his breast, the orders upon it, ... but the melancholy expression of his countenance and the extremely mild and gentle tones of his voice impressed me most sensibly. When with Lady Hamilton and Dr. Nelson (his brother) he entered the box, the uproar of the house was deafening, and seemed as if it would know no end ... the crowded house was frantic in its applause ... Lady Hamilton, laughing loud and without stint, claped with uplifted hands and all her heart, and kicked with her heels against the footboard of the seat, while Nelson placidly and with his mournful look ... bowed repeatedly to the oft-repeated cheers.[35]

Such spontaneous acclaim – Nelson could not walk in any streets in Britain without attracting enormous crowds – contrasted markedly with the more studied royal spectacle during the wars. In this way, he acted as cynosure for national sentiment and sensibility in ways that George III's managers could only dream about.

Nelson's own preference for a portrait was one by an unknown artist (Plate 11) and which he personally owned. It shows him in bloodstained shirt and bandage, watching *l'Orient* blow up at the Battle of the Nile, his St Vincent medal on a ribbon round his neck. The stump that remained of his right arm hangs starkly, graphically, with no effort at disguise; his posture is somewhat theatrical, echoing, perhaps, one of the 'attitudes' of his lover Emma, Lady Hamilton. This portrait probably was painted as a love token for her. It revealingly represents Nelson as a dismembered and romantic figure, who looks rather stunned at what he has accomplished and what he has yet to do. He is stoic in the neo-classical sense, having self-sovereignty at a critical moment, and thereby embodying the spirit of self-sacrifice and fortitude that must characterise the British nation as a whole. Nelson, in other words, had carried out the injunction of modernity to represent the body politic with his own, and enjoined his lover, by this image, to provide a similar bulwark of feminine resolve.

Emma, of course, provided another cause of mirth at Nelson's expense and further soured his relations with the establishment. Nelson and the Hamiltons' ménage à trois was a delicious scandal in Europe, but less pleasing to onlookers in England, especially after the two of them went to live with Nelson at Paradise Merton beginning in November 1800. Gillray led the assault of cruel caricatures, among them *Dido in Despair*, which shows a hugely fat Emma sobbing over her departing lover, with the accoutrements of her husband's antiquarian pursuits all about her. Among his well-born supporters, Nelson's attachment to Emma was clearly seen as compromising his virility rather than enhancing it, effeminising and rendering ridiculous the Hero of the Nile. Lord St Vincent called her an 'infernal bitch' who 'could have made him poison his wife or stab me, his best friend … [their affair] will reflect eternal disgrace upon [his] character which will be stripped of everything but animal courage.'[36] But her origins and brash character only increased his standing with the people, who seemed to appreciate her ability to let the wind out of the sails of elite snobbery and self-regard.

I have been arguing that Nelson and his status as an icon marked a new departure in popular politics, in terms of the reflexivity and sophistication of their organisation and in the valencies of their representation of the individual and the body politic. Certainly he was the people's conquering hero, in some respects like Vernon and Wolfe had been; but that people's relationship to the great and to the state had changed since mid-century. Seventy years of war had promulgated more expansive definitions of the rights and liberties of the people, and new views of the just relationship between the individual and the state. Pitt's Terror and an increase in royal ceremonial could not stamp out these legacies, and the wars against France, while temporarily amplifying nationalistic patriotism, also made clear how dependent the patrician state was on the mass military endeavour. Lord Liverpool estimated in 1805, that out of a British population of 15 million, 3,750,000 were capable of bearing arms, and of these 386,621 were in the army and navy, 385,000 in volunteers, and 30,000 more were sea fencibles, for a total of 803,621.[37] In other words, more than one in five were directly involved in the war. Nelson and his representation may have helped give a face to this mass mobilisation, and re-imagine common soldiers and sailors as potential heroes and patriots; his battered and torn body also made clear the costs and physical sacrifices that such an effort required. As a writer for the *Edinburgh Review* argued in 1804, 'modern warfare consists in reducing men to a state of mechanical activity, and combining them as parts of a great machine'.[38] Nelson, who engineered a recognisably modern system of command, based on consultation and coordination rather than strict hierarchy, in many ways inaugurated the age of the body as a machine, a war machine that changed the way in which society, state and the body politic would be looked at thereafter. Nelson was its fulcrum, appropriately annihilating himself in its service, as he knew he would and should. As he wrote in a briefing for Prime Minister Pitt, hours before the Battle of Trafalgar, 'it is annihilation that the country wants, and not merely a splendid Victory ... numbers only can annihilate'.[39]

The vulnerability of the human body in such a matrix is eloquently expressed in Arthur William Devis's painting, *Death of Nelson* (Plate 12). Here Nelson lies dying in the cockpit of the *Victory* after Trafalgar; Hardy stands over Nelson, his hand on the ship's knee against which Nelson reclines, his surgeon and his steward look on in distress, while a sailor grieves in the shadows to the right. Nelson is here divested of his uniform, his sole arm extended in comfort to his friends, as he looks Christ-like, eyes upward, bathed in light. To quote Walter Benjamin, writing about another, later world war and the modernity it both inaugurated and traduced, 'beneath those clouds, in a field of force of destructive torrents and explosions, was the tiny, fragile human body'.[40] Nelson was thus the screen upon which all those who had fought in the war machine, who had lost their limbs or senses or a loved one to its cruelties, could project their own experience, identifications and desires for recognition; a national body equally dismembered by battles, taxes and gagging orders, yet still fighting for vindication and redemption. At Nelson's funeral in St Paul's in January 1806, the king refused to attend, and women were excluded. But thousands of men, women and children filled the streets to pay respects to the fallen hero; and once again the spontaneity of the people and their respect took centre stage. As Lady Bessborough remarked to Lord Granville, of the procession to St Paul's,

> Amongst other things the silence of that immense mob was not the least striking ... the moment the car appeared which bore the body, you might have heard a pin fall, and without any order to do so, they all took off their hats. I cannot tell you the effect this simple action produced; it seem'd one general impulse of respect beyond anything that could have been said or contriv'd.[41]

IV

Two images of Nelson's death thus provide an appropriate conclusion to this exploration of Nelson and the People. The first – the most conventional – is Scott Pierre Nicolas Legrand's *Apotheosis of Nelson* (Plate 13). It adapts a classical reading of an apotheosis, depicting a deified Nelson being received into immortality among the gods on Olympus. Men grieve below, while the Battle at Trafalgar rages on. Neptune supports his ascent while Fame holds a crown of stars, and Britannia kneels on the right, as Mars, the god of war, waits to receive Nelson. Hercules and other gods are here, but what is most notable is the figure of Nelson – he is made whole. His left arm is concealed, but his right arm broadly gestures.

The second – Benjamin West's *The Immortality of Nelson* (Plate 14) – envisions a radically different apotheosis, despite its rendering in neo-classical style. This painting emphasises Nelson's heroism but also his sacrifice. Nelson's dead body is offered to Britannia by Neptune, Britannia is in shadow, to show the grief of the Nation; and Winged Victory supports him from behind. Winged putti surround him to represent the continuity of life, as one holds a scroll inscribed with his famous signal at the Battle of Trafalgar: ENGLAND EXPECTS EVERY MAN WILL DO HIS DUTY. But here Nelson ascends to the gods without his right arm, forever dismembered and scarred, even in the heavens, the first modern, profane hero to enter the pantheon: for his victory had come at the highest price, one which the classical vision of the body politic could neither recognise, nor represent.

Notes

1. Gilbert Eliot to Lord St Vincent, quoted in Edgar Vincent, *Nelson: Love and Fame* (New Haven and London: Yale University Press, 2003), p. 219; *London Chronicle*, 2–4 October, 1798; *Gentleman's Magazine*, 71 (1801), 207–8.

2. Kathleen Wilson, *The Sense of the People: Politics, Culture and Imperialism in England 1715–1785* (Cambridge: Cambridge University Press, 1995), chap. 3.
3. The following three paragraphs are based on Wilson, *Sense of the People*, and Kathleen Wilson, *The Island Race: Englishness, Empire and Gender in the Eighteenth Century* (London: Routledge, 2003).
4. For a recent assessment of Wolfe as hero, see Nicholas Rogers, 'Brave Wolfe: The Making of the Hero', in Kathleen Wilson (ed.), *A New Imperial History: Culture, Identity and Modernity in Britain and the Empire, 1660–1840* (Cambridge: Cambridge University Press, 2004), pp. 239–59.
5. Dorinda Outram, *The Body and the French Revolution* (New Haven: Yale University Press, 1989), p. 72.
6. Ibid., p. 74; Wilson, *Island Race*, p. 109.
7. J.S. Clark and J. McArthur, *The Life of Admiral Lord Nelson, KB from His Lordships's manuscripts*, 2 vols (London, 1802), vol. I, p. 9.
8. *Aris's Birmingham Gazette*, 30 August 1780.
9. See Gerald Jordan and Nicholas Rogers, 'Admirals as Heroes', *Journal of British Studies*, 28 (1989), 215–24.
10. *The Sun*, 19 June 1794; *London Chronicle*, 2–4 March 1797; *Morning Chronicle*, 19, 21 December 1797; Jordan and Rogers, 'Admirals as Heroes', pp. 212–13.
11. Gerald Jordan, 'Admiral Nelson as Popular Hero: The Nation and the Navy, 1795–1805', in *New Aspects of Naval History* (Baltimore: United States Naval Academy, 1985), pp. 109–10.
12. Sir Nicholas Harris Nicolas, *The Dispatches and Letters of Vice Admiral Lord Viscount Nelson* (8 vols, London: 1845–46), vol. I, pp. 377–8.
13. George P.B. Naish, *Nelson's Letters to his Wife, and other documents 1785–1831* (London: Navy Record Society, 1958), pp. 203–4.
14. Nicolas, *Dispatches and Letters*, II: 344–7; *The Times*, 21 March 1797; *The Sun*, 22 March 1797; University of Bristol Theatre Collection, Kathleen Barker papers, KB/4/3, 11 July 1796; 11 November 1797.
15. Terry Coleman, *Nelson* (London: Bloomsbury, 2001), pp. 124–8. *The Times*, 13 March 1797; *The Sun*, 15 March 1797.
16. Nicolas, *Dispatches and Letters*, III: 55.
17. Naish, *Nelson's Letters*, p. 399.
18. Coleman, *Nelson*, p. 1 and passim; Vincent, *Nelson*.
19. E.g. Frank McLynn, *1759: The Year Britain Became Master of the World* (London: Jonathan Cape, 2004).
20. *True Briton*, 4 October 1798; *London Chronicle*, 2–4 October 1798; *Manchester Mercury*, 9 October 1798; *Gentleman's Magazine*, 68 (1798), 68i, 891–912, 1096. In London, a grateful East India Company voted him a donation of 10,000l; in White Town, Calcutta, residents followed the metropolis in contributing to the Subscription fund for the benefit of the wounded seamen and marines, and the families of those killed, raising over £1,000. *Calcutta Gazette*, 18 June 1801, 14 May 1801; for the initiation of the fund, see *London Chronicle*, 11–13 October 1798.
21. *The Sun*, 4 October 1798.
22. See Lady Spencer to Nelson and the accounts of his reception in Naples in Nicolas, *Dispatches and Letters*, III: 74, 135–6; and his sister, Catherine Matcham's report that the young ladies in Bath would 'eat him up alive': British Library, Add MS 34,988, quoted in Coleman, *Nelson*, p. 167.

23. Nicolas, *Dispatches and Letters*, III: 55–7; *London Chronicle*, 2–4 October 1798.
24. *Gentleman's Magazine* (1805), 1069–70; Nicolas, *Dispatches and Letters*, III: 77–8; *Gentleman's Magazine*, 69 (1799), 67–70.
25. Mary Thale (ed.), *Selections from the Papers of the London Corresponding Society 1792–99* (Cambridge: Cambridge University Press, 1983), pp. 429–32, 434.
26. *The Sun*, 3 October 1798; *London Chronicle*, 9–11 October 1798.
27. *Morning Chronicle*, 4 February 1800; *Whitehall Evening Post*, 5 February 1800. For Fox's speech, see William Cobbett, *Parliamentary History of England* (London, 1803), vol. XXIV, pp. 1391–6.
28. Jordon, 'Admiral Nelson', p. 114.
29. *Gentleman's Magazine*, 71 (1801), 207.
30. J.E. Cookson, *The British Armed Nation, 1793–1815* (Oxford: Clarendon Press, 1997), pp. 214–15.
31. Jordan, 'Admiral Nelson', p. 113.
32. Linda Colley, *Britons* (New Haven and London: Yale University Press, 1992), p. 284.
33. Nicolas, *Dispatches and Letters*, III: 85.
34. Vincent, *Nelson*, p. 341; Thomas Kosegarten, *Meine Freuden in Sachsen* (Leipzig, 1801), quoted in Coleman, *Nelson*, p. 393.
35. Sir Frederick Pollock (ed.), *Macready's Reminiscences and Selections from his Diaries* (London, 1875), vol. II, p. 78. For a more detailed treatment of the all-important tour of 1802, see David Howarth and Stephen Howarth, *Nelson: The Immortal Memory* (London: Conway Maritime Museum, 1988).
36. Evelyn Berckman, *Nelson's Dear Lord* (London: Macmillan, 1962), pp. 180, 240, quoted in Jordan, 'Admiral Nelson', p. 116.
37. Colley, *Britons*, pp. 284–5; Cookson, *British Armed Nation*, Appendix 1.
38. *Edinburgh Review*, 5 (1803), 10–11.
39. Nicolas, *Dispatches and Letters*, VII: 80.
40. Walter Benjamin, *Illuminations* (London: Fontana, 1968), p. 84.
41. *Lord Granville Leveson Gower: Private Correspondence*, 2 vols (London, 1916), vol. II, p. 154.

4

Nelson and Women: Marketing, Representations and the Female Consumer

Kate Williams

During the Napoleonic Wars, Nelson was presented in a manner that appealed to a female audience. His image was pervasively sentimentalised in consumer goods marketed to a female purse, and women writers presented him in various ways that correspond to the domestic, amorous, and political desires of their audience. Such extravagantly sexualised and romanticised representations of Nelson were ubiquitous at the time but have since been overlooked by modern scholarship. This chapter proposes that such neglect is undeserved. Women's portrayals of Nelson are not inconsequential, nor the unmediated results of pro-war government propaganda, but vital interventions into the public representation of the hero and important revelations about their opinions towards the Napoleonic Wars. Largely deprived of official representation and a political voice, women wrote novels that exploited patriotic sentiment and sexual feeling about Nelson, expressed dissent and appreciation, offered fantasies about how sailors should behave, and tested new theories about Nelson, heroism, and the role of sailors in the wider culture.

Scholarship on Nelson tends to focus on how men commemorate and represent him. In the years following the Battle of Trafalgar, many monuments, street names, and squares were dedicated to Nelson.[1] As John MacKenzie shows in this volume, Nelson was constructed to fit the political needs of male groups. But, as Linda Colley has argued, the Napoleonic Wars attracted unprecedented female interest, primarily because women believed themselves at personal risk from an invasion.[2]

As Margarette Lincoln's pioneering recent study revealed, women's representation of the Navy questions notions that men and women inhabited 'separate spheres' in the eighteenth century.[3] This chapter endeavours to show how women expressed their interest in contemporary events by representing Nelson and I am indebted to the work of Colley, Kathleen Wilson, and Lincoln, who have demonstrated how women understood and portrayed military conflict.[4] The first part of this chapter interprets contemporary Nelson souvenirs, the second section reclaims forgotten bestsellers and reads familiar texts anew for representations of him, and the final part considers how Nelson was represented to women in the nineteenth and twentieth centuries.

Unlike dashing and aristocratic Wellington, Nelson was not an obvious sex object. Spare, nervous, emaciated, and of middling height, his hair was white (and had previously been red) and he was not conventionally handsome. As a foreign newspaper observed, he was 'small and lean, the skin pale, the cheeks hollow [...] and his hair was combed into his face'.[5] He had a large nose, slightly droopy eyelids, his face was scarred, and his complexion was uneven from the ravages of tropical disease. He was missing his right arm from the shoulder and he had also lost the sight of his right eye. Recurrent hernias may have caused him to limp. His background was undistinguished and he was comparatively uneducated and inarticulate, as well as being insecure and quick to take offence. He lacked sexual charisma: his love life before he became famous was characterised by repeated rebuffs. Only Frances Nisbet, a widow with a young son, encouraged him and she was desperate for a home of her own. Lady Elizabeth Foster wrote that he 'is covered with wounds, has lost the sight of one eye and his right arm, is of a slight, rather delicate make, but his countenance is full of fire and animation, and it was delightful for us to see and converse with the Hero of the Nile'.[6] As her account indicates, success at Aboukir rendered an unprepossessing man an object of desire. By 1805, Lady Foster related the following tale:

Lady Hamilton told him [Nelson] to embrace me. I consented with great pleasure and hurried away. Lady H. told him also to embrace Lady Percival. When we were in the carriage my son, who had not seen Nelson embrace me, said, 'Are you not jealous?' 'No', I said, 'for he embraced me also.' 'Do you think,' said Lady Percival with some humour, 'that I should otherwise have ventured to have got into the same carriage?'[7]

The Ladies Foster and Percival were not alone in joking about women cat-fighting over the Nile hero. Thousands of British women fell in love with Nelson and the manufacturers of ornamental goods and the writers of popular fiction reflected, encouraged, and exploited their sexual preoccupation with him.

I

The Battle of the Nile produced, in Carola Oman's words, a 'shower of souvenirs' for Nelson's eager public.[8] Manufacturers targeted female consumers with Nelson fans, ribbons, rings, charms for charm bracelets, earrings, brooches, enamelled boxes for storing beauty 'patches', jewellery boxes, muslins, bags, and shawls. Women wore gold anchors commemorating Nelson, who 'relieves the World at the Mouth of the Nile' (see Plate 15).[9] Milliners produced a Nelsonian marmeluke hat and a 'Nelson cap' in coquelicot velvet.[10] Every possible item of clothing was adorned with his insignia. Before Nelson arrived in Naples in 1798, Lady Hamilton (who was only acquainted with him at this point) wrote that: 'My dress from head to foot is alla Nelson. [...] Even my shawl is in Blue with gold anchors all over.'[11] Lady Hamilton's showy devotion to Nelson, her fashions 'alla Nelson' and her general personal style, in addition to her demands that her guests wear Nelson fashions, set the tone for English shoppers (see Plate 18). A piece of Nelson jewellery or a Nelson fan became an important badge of loyalty and status at social gatherings across England. One of such fans commemorated Nelson, listed the English and French fleets and then detailed eighteen new dances, including 'Sprigs of Laurel for Lord Nelson'.[12] Nelson's romance was commemorated too: a colourful ribbon survives printed with laurel, an anchor and the words 'Baron Nelson of the Nile' and the words that Nelson and Emma used to excuse their affair in Naples: 'Tria Iuncta in Uno'.

The 'alla Nelson' range extended to home decoration. Stoneware jugs were shaped after his head or bust.[13] Whole dinner services appeared decorated in Nelson symbols, as well as expensive porcelain vases, and tea and chocolate sets. Cheap Pratt ware jugs and mugs bore a relief-moulded Nelson.[14] Nelson ordered a porcelain beaker decorated with a picture of himself embraced by a Fame who resembles Lady Hamilton.[15] According to Lord Minto in 1802, Lady Hamilton decked Merton, the home she shared with Nelson with 'representations of his naval actions, coats of arms, pieces of plate in his honour, the flagstaff of *L'Orient*, etc', and she even named the garden stream the 'Nile'.[16] Her taste in decoration was repeated on smaller scale throughout Britain. There was a fashion for draping curtains to recall Nelson: red curtains gathered with gold anchors at the side and blue and white overdrapes topped with a plaque of the hero.[17] Curtains were also printed with scenes from the life of the hero.[18] Even the most private detail could manifest devotion: Bilston enamel manufacturers produced enamel drawer handles painted with portraits of Nelson.[19]

Nelson's death at the Battle of Trafalgar produced an unparalleled (and never equalled) outpouring of commemorative goods. William Tassie, one of the foremost cameo makers of the day, worked feverishly to satisfy the demand for cameo heads of Nelson for jewellers to set in rings and brooches (see Plate 16).[20] Commemorative ivory lockets issued for the Nile were decorated with sailors crying 'Nelson for ever'; those after Trafalgar showed weeping ladies, who resembled Lady Hamilton, dressed in white (see Plate 17).[21] Large linen tablecloths and matching napkins bore the plan of the Battle of Trafalgar, and clocks, boxes, and trunks also appeared.[22] One furniture maker claimed to be selling the exact table and sideboard that Nelson ordered before his death.[23] As Amanda Vickery has shown, women tended to purchase such household objects, perceive them as an expression of their social identity, and invest them with emotional significance, a process she calls 'sentimental materialism'.[24] Since eighteenth-century families reinforced relationships with clients, colleagues and relatives by dining at home, a woman's choice of Nelson candlesticks or tableware was not a private matter of taste but a semi-public declaration of opinion and loyalty.

Such high-fashion goods would have been costly. Manufacturers seized the opportunity to represent purchasing images of Nelson as an expression of patriotic devotion. If the shopper bought Nelsonia, her act was not, as contemporary critics of consumer culture suggested, frivolous or enervating. Buying Nelson-themed commodities was an expression of patriotic fervour and of a more general support for the very economy that the war aimed to defend (the Navy was particularly concerned to protect British trade routes).[25] Women who decked themselves and their houses in Nelson insignia presented themselves as loyally supportive of England's belligerent foreign policy. The conflict brought prosperity to middle-class Britons at comparatively minimal personal cost (there was no income tax and the poor were most vulnerable to impressments and death in service).[26] The mercantile classes glossed their pursuit of their own interests by indicating that the war was fought in the cause of virtue and established this idea of virtue by reproducing Nelson as a domestic object. Genteel women's passion for Nelson reflected a class interest: their devotion to him elided and sentimentalised the reality that the war that he fought brought them personal gain.

The flood of Nelson commodities directed at female consumers reflected their new financial and social independence: many wives were newly in charge of the household budget and others gained a sense of purpose from fundraising and organising supplies.[27] In 1798, the same year as women were buying Nelson goods, so many women contributed to the state-sponsored Voluntary Contribution to the war that *The Times* raised the possibility of a ladies-only subscription list.[28] By purchasing Nelsonia, a sailor's wife was able to support her husband's actions. Furthermore, women's excessive devotion to the hero constituted a derisory comment towards men who had refused the opportunity to fight.[29] A scene from Alexander Korda's *That Hamilton Woman* (1941) suggests the ambiguous sexual significance of their practices. Throughout a scene where Emma (Vivien Leigh) resists Sir William's demands that she renounce Nelson, Korda concentrates the light on a giant diamante 'N' that Leigh wears on a chain about her neck. The glittering 'N' signifies Lady Hamilton's loyalty to Nelson and thus the futility of Sir William's efforts. Women's efforts to drape themselves 'alla Nelson' hinted to their spouses and male relatives that they were emotionally independent and that their sentiments were invested in the grander nationalistic and patriotic cause.

Women also created their own versions of Nelson. The Maritime Museum holds a framed embroidery, sewn by Lady Hamilton, which represents Nelson and herself as Yorick and Maria from Laurence Sterne's novel, *A Sentimental Journey* (1768). Yorick has one of his most erotic experiences with a lady from Amiens. Lady Hamilton's representation of her lover as the excitable parson suggests a subtle joke on how the Peace of Amiens (March 1802–May 1803) gave the couple a honeymoon period of passion in Merton. Excluding Sir William from the picture, as well as Horatia, and the members of Nelson's family, Emma fashions Nelson into a sentimental hero and herself as Maria, the innocent erotic object of Yorick's effusive sentimental feelings. Never a skilled needlewoman, Lady Hamilton must have worked from a pattern, a background canvas printed with the design. Nelson's death featured on many such patterns, which were then turned into pictures, cushions, and fire screens. Younger women practised their skills on Nelson samplers.[30] Trafalgar even became the name of an embroidery stitch. The Trafalgar Stitch, which presumably resembled Nelson's favoured formations, appears to have been tricky: Jane Austen's sister-in-law, Mary, joked about her difficulty with it.[31] Ladies less handy with the needle could amuse themselves instead with a Nelson jigsaw.[32]

Whilst the men of a town clubbed together to make a Nelson monument, a town's female population expressed a more individualised interest in Nelson by turning him into a treasured object or an intimate item of clothing. They wore Nelson-themed clothes, accessories, and keepsakes, and they embroidered him as a sentimental hero or recalled him when sewing the stitch named after his final battle. They also enjoyed representations of Nelson in literature that were as sentimentalised and intimate as those on necklaces or fans. The hero's most persistent and enduring representations came, as the next section shows, in novels that exploited his figure to gain readers.

II

Novelists in the late 1790s and early 1800s were as quick as cameo manufacturers to capitalise on interest in Nelson. His very public affair was for ordinary Britons both a source of fascination and a welcome respite from otherwise worrying and sometimes dreary news. Although they have been forgotten and are now excluded from surveys of naval literature in reference books and on internet sites, many novels by women were published in which characters resemble Nelson and members of his circle (an elementary library search for books published in the period of Nelson's success yields many possible texts).[33] The references are not subtle: Horatio is a recurrent name, and there is a Horace Nevare (Nelson preferred to be called Horace), a Lord Nelvil, and, curiously, a Henry Thompson. Other characters are called Frances, Fanny, Lady Hamilton, Sir William, and versions on Emma or Amy such as Amelia. This chapter considers one novel published after Nelson and Emma arrived home from Naples and a select group of novels published after the Battle of Trafalgar. After Nelson's death, writers represented his adulterous affair as the ultimate sentimental romance.

The conversion of a distant and complex battle into a form able to produce a familiarly affecting emotional response was achieved in these works through symbolic substitution: the victory, the sailors, the tactics, and the political machinations that produced the battle and won it are condensed and converted into the figure of Nelson, who becomes the virtuous hero in a domestic drama. Such texts typically showed a sensitive but melancholic hero restored to spirits by his passion for the expressive heroine. Both characters are young, although Lady Hamilton turned forty in 1805 and Nelson was seven years her senior. Horatio, the protagonist of Lady Morgan's *The Wild Irish Girl* (1806), travels and falls in love with Glorvina, whose dress and dance moves recall those of Lady

Hamilton. Writers exploit Nelson's adultery at the same time as excusing it by presenting him and the heroine as experiencing a deep sentimental friendship and by intimating that the domestic Englishwoman is an inadequate partner for him. The hero's disposition is so exceptionally passionate that he can only be matched by a theatrical and excitable woman, preferably one, like Lady Hamilton, brought up by an old man in a foreign country (see Plate 19).

The daughter of an army surgeon and sister of a navy surgeon, Anna Maria Porter wrote over fifteen novels and many of these dramatise military and naval themes. The hero of *A Sailor's Friendship and a Soldier's Love* (1805) is Captain Byron, a naval commander who has many common features with Nelson. As Lady Frances informs Lady Mary:

> You and all the rest of the world know Captain Byron by reputation; his splendid services even in the beginning of the war, when but a youth, have justly rendered him the idol of the public.

Few other naval men could be said to be 'the idol of the public' in 1805. Lady Frances continues that 'in private life, he is as amiable as he is great, his countenance is strongly charactered by the fire and intelligence of his mind; and his temper is of the very sweetest imaginable'. Her words resemble the description of Lady Foster, cited above. Both Porter and Foster were probably repeating a description of Nelson that had been already disseminated in the newspapers. Like Nelson, Captain Byron is dynamic and reviles appeasement. The novel opens with Byron's complaint that he has returned from a 'very stupid cruise, which has neither brought me money nor fame (for not an enemy's ship did we fall in with)'. Ambitious to fight, he feels a 'phrenzy' of anger when he is passed over because 'the spirit of party' prevails at the naval board. But when he finds battle, he is successful and writes:

> I have executed the business assigned me by my country, (vide the newspapers): success has smiled upon my enterprise; – and so, damaged only by a wounded shoulder, I sit down [...] to give you some serious counsel.

Like Nelson, the captain is wounded in the arm after defeating the enemy fleet. But soon after his victory, Byron weeps with anger when he hears about the Peace of Amiens. As the people around him shout with joy and seem 'transported out of themselves', he writes that:

I saw all the brave companions with whom I have served, and whom I have seen fall, dropping again by my side. To think they had sacrificed themselves for nothing! – After the most dreadful slaughters, the severest sufferings, the most brilliant victories, we were just in the very place from which we had set out ten years before: it seemed to me then, as if we had fought only to make widows and orphans.[34]

Nelson did not believe, as Colin White comments, that the treaty would last.[35] Porter uses her Nelson figure to make a political point: the Peace of Amiens was a mistake.

Captain Byron is the ultimate romantic hero. He even tears off his neckcloth to treat a wounded man and trembles from sensibility. Lady Frances extols:

Is he not firm in principle, noble in sentiment – in sensibility tender as a woman – in understanding, equal to any of that sex, of whom intellect is the boast? Are not his habits of purity and self-restraint, proofs that his principles are not mere speculations, but the very life of his character? [...] His reputation I do not dwell on, because that is an ornament, not a part of his beautiful character.

To render Nelson a perfect hero, however, an author must address the problem of Lady Hamilton. Porter excuses his attachment to her by vindicating her as Castara, a sensitive and virtuous girl whose passionate nature makes her the ideal partner for the emotional Nelsonian hero. An English girl who, like Lady Hamilton, lives overseas with her low-class mother, Castara is a talented singer and dancer but her lack of education dissuades potential suitors. She is rescued when she is discovered to be the illegitimate daughter of an aristocrat, Sir James. His sister, Lady Frances, as genteel, restrained, and lonely as Lady Frances Nelson, decides to adopt Castara after she realises that she is forty and entirely a 'lone unloved creature' (Lady Nelson was forty-four in 1805). Lady Frances recruits the 'philosophic' gentleman and intellectual, Sir William Hereford to educate Castara. In real life, Lady Frances Nelson and Sir William Hamilton were unhappy witnesses to the affair between their spouses. Porter revises the miserable love triangle and renders them parent figures who instil Castara with the education and etiquette necessary to be a fit partner to the naval captain.

Nelson spent most of the period of the Peace of Amiens romancing Lady Hamilton. Amiens allows Byron to court Castara, 'intoxicated with new and delightful feelings'. Castara falls in love with him when he becomes ill, just as Nelson began his affair with Lady Hamilton after he collapsed with a fever at Naples. At this point, however, the story splits: Castara marries another man and broken-hearted Byron sails to the West Indies. A dairy maid, Ruth, follows him (Emma's old protector, Sir Harry Featherstonehaugh married his dairy maid), having adopted the 'wild romantic resolution of assuming the dress of a man'. She nurses him when he falls ill with yellow fever and he surrenders to the 'enchantment' of her 'beauty and tenderness' and excellent virtue and marries her. Lady Hamilton recurs in Castara and Ruth. Porter's book reflects a confusion over whether high birth automatically endowed a person with virtue and whether those from labouring classes could be honourable and virtuous (such prejudices characterised the real-life responses to Lady Hamilton). In the novel, the first heroine becomes a fit wife for the Nelson hero because she is discovered to have an aristocratic background, and the second is justified as a partner because she is virtuous and affectionate.[36]

In the second volume, another Emma-figure appears, the engaging and graceful Amelia (Lady Hamilton was christened Amy) who falls in love with Lieutenant Camelford. Camelford is dependent on the whims of his uncle, Sir William, who wishes him to marry a court beauty, Lady Lucy Hamilton. After refusing Lady Hamilton, the despairing Lieutenant travels to the 'French West India Islands', where he befriends the rich widow of a planter and her son. She dies, leaves her money to him, and, newly rich, he defies Sir William and marries Amelia.[37] Porter's tale is an intriguing revision of Nelson's marriage to Frances Nisbet: a widow living in the West Indies provides the money that allows the Nelson and Emma characters to marry. *A Sailor's Friendship and a Soldier's Love* contains three versions of the Nelson–Lady Hamilton story. Sir William is at first a kindly tutor, then a cruel uncle, and Lady Nelson is first a childless woman who adopts the heroine and encourages the match and then a rich widow whose bequest enables the pair to marry.

A Sailor's Friendship and a Soldier's Love blends political comment and sentimental romance about naval heroes. Porter, like the other writers surveyed in this chapter, shapes and produces response to national events by converting them into a form – the sentimental courtship – that held emotional meaning for the reader. Her premise is consolatory: true love prevails over class or social divisions and poor girls can marry rich men. Porter attempts to valorise an adulterous affair into an acceptable romance by revising Hamilton and Lady Nelson into sponsors to the affair and by representing Nelson as a sensitive man with complex emotional needs. She also builds on her efforts to romanticise Nelson by intimating that service at sea encourages a man's ability to love, and his appreciation of domestic sentiment. The hero who cannot separate love and duty becomes both a better sailor and a better lover. Nelson, as Byron, becomes a fantasy romantic hero: ambitious and determined but sensitive and capable of deep affection. Porter adopts Nelson to make a more general point: the truly virtuous leader allows sentiment and private feeling to define public duty.

In *The Convict; or, The Navy Lieutenant* (1806), Eliza Parsons blatantly exploits the story of Nelson and Lady Hamilton. Although little is known about Parsons' life, we know that her father victualled the Navy in Plymouth. *The Navy Lieutenant* invokes a readership interested in naval matters: Parsons digresses to complain that a lieutenant's pay is insufficient, particularly in 'expensive stations' overseas. But the point of the novel is not factual: Parsons casts Nelson as Henry Thompson, the sentimental hero who proves that 'sailors fight like lions for their king and country, but they have hearts like lambs to relieve distress and misery'. Most crucially, Parsons revises and excuses the most controversial aspect of Nelson's life: his illegitimate daughter by Emma, Horatia.[38] The name 'Henry' may have been a common substitution for 'Horatio'. As Colin White observes, Horatio was difficult to scan and the name Henry sometimes replaced it in songs and poems about Nelson.[39] Nelson was so fond of citing Shakespeare's *Henry V* that he may have even occasionally dubbed himself Henry. Most intriguingly of all, Nelson and Lady Hamilton corresponded about Horatia under the names Mr and Mrs Thomson or Thompson whilst Nelson was at sea in 1801. Parsons would have been familiar with Plymouth gossip and her choice of Thompson as a surname indicates that Nelson's activities might have been more widely known than he believed. It was certainly a fortuitous choice in a novel that addressed the problem of Nelson's child.

The hero's background and career resembles Nelson's. The novel begins: 'Mr. Henry Thompson was the third son of a country curate, and had been placed in the navy at eleven years of age, to make his way progressively in his profession without the smallest hope of assistance from interest or fortune.' Although Nelson was the fifth son of his Norfolk rector father, two of his brothers died, so he was, in a manner of speaking, the third son. Henry's elder brother, like Nelson's, becomes a parson. Like Nelson, Thompson goes to sea early and he is promoted to the rank of lieutenant and joins the *Vengeance*, a name that echoes Nelson's *Victory*. Thompson speaks in 'plain, adulterated language' and his are the 'effusions of an honest heart'. Like Nelson, he gains the respect of the men under his command, but his inability to appreciate the importance of internal politics leads to him being retired from the service on half pay.

Thompson is travelling through London, on his way to join a ship to the East Indies, when he encounters Ellen, the convict of the title, a fallen woman and a prostitute. He is unable to suppress the 'sympathetic drop that fell on his manly cheek' and volunteers when she begs someone to adopt her infant daughter:

> [The] lieutenant, who had stood the brunt of many a well-fought engagement without shrinking, was now overcome, and whilst with trembling arms he regained the fallen child, large drops fell on its face as he hugged it to his breast.

He claims that charity makes it his 'duty to be father to the child', who is innocent of her mother's crimes. Thompson names the child Frances and delights in his new 'Fanny Thompson'. He employs his agent (a 'just and benevolent man') to pay a woman to care for her. Parsons celebrates Nelson by denigrating Lady Hamilton. Ellen's tale of ruin resembles Lady Hamilton's teenaged experiences with Sir Harry Featherstonehaugh and Charles Greville. We later find that her name was Ellen Thompson and so the story tells of Henry Thompson and Ellen Thompson (when Nelson and Lady Hamilton were, in their secret correspondence, Horatio Thomson and Emma Thomson). At seventeen, Ellen was taken as a mistress by a twenty-six-year-old aristocrat, and she became close to one of his friends, the thirty-year-old Sir Gilbert, but her first seducer ruined her, prostituted her and imprisoned her in an 'infamous house'.[40]

In *The Navy Lieutenant*, Nelson's child is not the product of an adulterous affair but the result of his self-sacrificing and virtuous act of charity. Kindly Thompson, untainted by lust or cynicism, adopts the daughter of a prostitute to give her a better life. Nelson's affair and Horatia's birth might have seemed to some an example of the new class of powerful middle-class men behaving like aristocrats: without compunction and believing themselves above morality. But in Parsons' novel, the daughter of a fallen woman, adopted by a naval hero, exemplifies the new moral order of sentimental and virtuous charity. Nelson becomes a virtuous hero whose efforts rebut the exploitative actions of aristocrats, such as Ellen's first seducer, and introduce a reformatory order.

Mary Charlton's *The Wife and the Mistress* (1802) offered another version of the love triangle. Charlton, writing when the scandal was at its height, is more eager to excuse the participants. Nothing is known about her background, but she appears to have been familiar with naval affairs.

An earlier novel, *The Pirate of Naples* (1801), made sly points about the Neapolitan rebellion. In *The Wife and the Mistress*, Horatio Nelson becomes Horace Nevare, an individualistic and romantic hero who is superior to trivial amusements and courts virtuous Laura, without caring that her parentage is obscure. Charlton also adds characters named Mrs Hamilton, a Fanny and a Sir William. Mrs Hamilton is the epitome of virtue, whom the heroine wishes she could question on issues of etiquette. Horace Nevare eschews superficial codes of behaviour and follows the truth of his heart. Charlton, like Parsons and Porter, suggests that the virtue of her hero, and thus Nelson, inheres in his feeling personality: the truly great man is the emotional man for whom every act is an expression of feeling. Such a virtuous portrayal of England's most sensational love story proved appealing to Lady Hamilton herself. Although she fled with the minimum of personal belongings to France, *The Wife and the Mistress* was found in her effects after her death. Perhaps, in her dying and graceless final days, she cherished the representation of herself in Charlton's novel as the virtuous Mrs Hamilton or as innocent Laura, courted by handsome Horace Nevare. It would appear as if even Lady Hamilton cherished the idealised and fictionalised versions of Nelson.

A similarly independent hero recurs in *Corinne* (1807), by a Frenchwoman, Madame Germaine de Staël. Madame de Staël's novels were immediately translated and, in Europe, along with Sir Walter Scott, Byron, and Goethe, she was the most read living author of the time.[41] Unlike the other writers surveyed so far, she was comfortably off and her writing was more concerned to make a political point. *Corinne* is a pro-British and pro-Nelson novel. Staël hated Napoleon and she detested how he had conquered Italy and she calls for Europe to rise up against him. The Nelson-type hero was ideally suited to such a project.

In *Corinne*, the Nelsonian figure is a sensitive and thoughtful hero, Lord Nelvil. Whilst touring Italy in 1794, he falls in love with Corinne, a handsome Englishwoman who fled to Italy and became a famous actress and poetess. Like Lady Hamilton, Corinne is tall, her 'shape [was] majestic; but rather inclining to fullness – the general air that of a Grecian statue', dances the Tarantella, and specialises in Attitudes. Because she is independent and artistic, stiff Englishmen such as Mr Edgermond mistake her for a kept mistress whose favours can be bought. Nelvil meets Corinne in a way similar to the very public meeting between Nelson and Emma in Naples when she is conducting a dramatic performance to the wild acclamation of the Italian crowd. As in the case of the real Nelson and Lady Hamilton, Nelvil later collapses (but from an excess of feeling), Corinne nurses him, and he falls in love with her. But his family wish him to marry a dutiful and insipid English girl, Lucile, a Lady Nelson figure, a perfect domestic woman. Torn between the two women, even the sublime sight of Vesuvius tortures Nelvil's 'peturbed imagination'. As the author exclaims, susceptible minds suffer great 'struggles between passion and conscience'. Staël's allegory of England's most famous love triangle identifies Nelvil's inability to choose between Corinne and Lucile with his 'feeling heart and ardent mind', his emotional and acutely sensitive temperament. Nelvil is not only sensitive, he is also a natural leader. When a passenger on a boat in a storm:

> Lord Nelvil assisted the sailors by his advice, and sustained the passengers; and [...] when he for a moment supplied the pilot's place, he displayed a degree of dexterity and strength which were evidently not the effect of corporal ability only, but shewed that his whole soul was engaged in every action.[42]

Lord Nelvil, and, by implication, Nelson is the ideal sentimental hero: his heart and his whole soul is engaged in every action. Once more, his capacity for feeling is the basis of his courage. The true hero does not separate private emotion and public endeavour.

Staël turns the adulterous affair into a chaste mingling of minds. Corinne is no mistress and her acting is an indication of her devotion to art rather than immorality. Although they travel together alone, Corinne and Nelvil are not physically intimate; their love is purely platonic and spiritual. As in *The Navy Lieutenant*, where the reality of Horatia's illegitimate birth was turned into a virtuous adoption, *Corinne* elides the tricky issue of extra-marital sexual activity (which no respectable novelist could portray) by revising the relationship into an expression of generous and chaste sentimental feeling. *Corinne*, like the other imaginative literature I survey in this chapter, is amenable to diverse readings and the figure of Nelvil is open to many interpretations. My point is that Nelson became a crucial figure to contemporary women and the issues about love, loyalty, and sexual morality, which he came to signify, were similarly compelling. Staël, like the other writers considered here, exploited public fascination with Nelson and glossed the aspects of the affair that were an affront to public morals by sentimentalising him as a man of feeling engaged in a lofty romance with an equally idealised (and virginal) Lady Hamilton.

The potential readership of these novels was large. As Margarette Lincoln notes, naval matters affected the 'domestic lives of thousands of women'.[43] N.A.M. Rodger has estimated that out of the 140,000 sailors working at the height of the Napoleonic Wars, around 25 per cent were married, and most of these married men were officers, petty officers, and older seamen.[44] There was thus about 35,000 wives of officers at home in Britain and such women would have been literate and likely to read for pleasure. Single sailors had mothers, sisters, and sweethearts at home. Girls who lived in port towns, such as Plymouth, where Parsons grew up, eagerly anticipated the arrival of ships and their cargo of handsome young officers who attended their social gatherings.[45] All these women – and those generally interested in the Navy – would have been attracted to naval novels. Many women writers had naval links, perhaps because officers and female writers tended to be of a similar middle-class origin. Porter's brother was a naval surgeon, Parsons' father had been a victualler to the Navy, and two of Austen's brothers were naval officers.

Naval novels by men were judged according to the perceived verisimilitude of their representation of life at sea.[46] Women's desires were less pragmatic. Benedict Anderson has argued that the growth of 'print capitalism' in the period enabled the development of 'imagined communities' of readers for whose benefit and in whose interest national and international news was condensed and refracted.[47] The 'imagined communities' invoked by the Nelsonian novel were groups who wished to read a sexual and sentimental fantasy of the hero. Nelson was, in reality, a practical, efficient, and at times ruthless naval commander but women writers represented him as guided by sentiment and emotion. They romanticised the figure of Nelson and appropriated his figure to express how they wished their heroes – and men in general – would behave. Nelson's obsession with Lady Hamilton and his seeming inability to separate his private desires and public ambitions made him the ideal for representation as a man who never forgot his womenfolk, a consolatory figure to a lonely and anxious sailor's wife.

The heroes of these tales are prone to exhaustion and Captain Byron is wounded in the arm. Nursing proves a romantic occupation for Castara, Ruth, and Corinne. These writers move towards creating a man as physically damaged as Nelson a hero, without being so blatant or daring. For Nelson's wound was axiomatic to his appeal to women: it was a direct mark of his valour and proved him a fighter who led from the front. It was also emblematic of the wounds suffered by countless sailors and soldiers during the Napoleonic Wars. Nelson's missing arm came to signify all the missing limbs and scared bodies of Britain's wounded fighters as he became the representative victim, and hero, of the long and bloody war, a signification magnified by the fact that he died in battle. Thanks to his final words about Lady Hamilton, his death fused military glory and public sacrifice with his fame as a lover. Nelson's wound made him vulnerable: the great warrior was also disabled. He simultaneously projected a sense of strength and weakness, appealing to the nurturing feelings of English women even while he fulfilled the role of a powerful protector. Nelson allowed women to feel both protected and needed. His figure came to stand for a conflation of public and private realms of service, emotion, and sacrifice.

III

When Jane Austen was writing, ten years after Parsons, Porter, Charlton, and Madame de Staël, it was harder to be romantic about Nelson's affair with Lady Hamilton. A book of Nelson's letters was published in 1814. Emma claimed that they had been stolen from her, but the public was shocked by her treachery and by the revelation of Nelson's intimate thoughts. Austen would have followed the developments for she had been exposed to first-hand news about Nelson. Her beloved brother, Frank, was one of Nelson's favoured captains. His ship, *Peterel*, carried a dispatch to Lord Nelson at Palermo in 1799 and Frank sent his lieutenant to deliver the letter to Nelson, possibly to the Palazzo Palagoni where Nelson, Emma, and William Hamilton lived together.[48] Austen also met one of those capitalising from the country's obsession with him. In 1815, at the invitation of the Prince of Wales, she met James Stanier Clarke, the Prince's librarian, ex-chaplain of Captain Jack Willet Payne, who claimed to have been an early lover of Lady Hamilton. Clarke was the author with John McArthur of the decorous two-volume *Life of Nelson* (1809), which glossed over Nelson's private life. Austen's representation of Nelson has not been carefully considered. But she would have read novels by Porter, Parsons, Charlton, and particularly Staël. Our awareness of the content of these novels allows us to read her work anew as engaged in the debate about Nelson and the representation of heroes that they began.[49]

On the publication of Robert Southey's *Life of Nelson* (1813), Austen described herself as 'tired of Lives of Nelson' even without reading any.[50] Her objection was not to writing about Nelson, but to the outpouring of masculine tribute to Nelson and the Navy after Trafalgar.[51] One of Austen's heroines decried such conventional or 'top down' and male-centred versions of world events as 'very tiresome': the 'quarrels of popes and kings, with wars or pestilences in every page [...] hardly any women at all'.[52] Endeavours to applaud victory by focusing on acts in battle alone negated the trials of women. Austen situated the Navy and its hero in a domestic setting and reminded readers about the pain suffered by wives and female relations waiting for news. Challenging Clarke's and

McArthur's effort to minimise the importance of Nelson's private life, she follows precursors such as Porter by establishing the issue of the love triangle as central to portrayals of Nelson. But her work rebuts their valorisations of expressive and unconventional women. Her heroes prove their excellence by choosing the restrained Fanny Nelson figure over the vivid Lady Hamilton character.

Like her predecessors, Austen represented naval men as sensitive individuals who are preoccupied with private sentiment. In *Persuasion* (1818), Captain Bentick is 'deeply afflicted' (he suffers what we would call a nervous breakdown) by the death of his wife, Fanny. Like heroes such as Captain Byron and Lord Nelvil, Bentick has a disposition 'of the sort which must suffer heavily, uniting very strong feelings with quiet, serious, and retiring manners'.[53] But the ideal partner for feeling men such as Bentick and Captain Wentworth is not the Emma Hamilton figure, but Anne Elliot, the domestic woman who shares their 'retiring manners'. Austen reworks the love triangle of texts such as *Corinne* in which the hero's choice of the retiring woman dooms him to misery. *Emma* (1816), which was dedicated to the Prince of Wales, establishes a rivalry between Emma Woodhouse, as flirtatious and extravagantly headstrong as Emma Hamilton, and Jane Fairfax, who is as controlled and self-sacrificing as Frances Nelson. Emma teases Jane as ruthlessly as Lady Hamilton slandered Lady Nelson and we might also see a little of Sir William in Mr Woodhouse, cosseted by Emma and blind to her faults. Despite of Emma's energy, however, she only marries after she has been taught that she must behave more like Jane.

Austen sets up a similar rivalry in *Mansfield Park* (1814) between proper Fanny Price and daring Mary Crawford. Whilst living with her uncle, an admiral, Mary tells Edmund she met many naval men and a 'circle of admirals'. She could 'say a great deal' about 'the gradations of their pay, and their bickerings and jealousies'. But, she claims, they think themselves 'all passed over, and all very ill used'. As she concludes, 'Of *Rears*, and *Vices*, I saw enough. Now, do not be suspecting me of a pun, I entreat.'[54] The speech is pure Lady Hamilton, whose critics accused her of being boastful, prone to exaggeration, wont to ignore the women to flirt with men, and fond of coarse sexual innuendo. But in *Mansfield Park*, the Lady Hamilton figure loses the battle to the domestic Fanny. Flamboyant, showy women, Austen suggests, make poor wives. In Austen's novels, if not in real life, Fanny wins against Emma.

Austen's *Sanditon* (1817) reflected how the world was changing. Mr Parker tells the heroine about his guest house, Trafalgar House, but continues, 'I almost wish I had not named [it] Trafalgar – for Waterloo is more the thing now'.[55] The name Waterloo 'will give us the command of visitors': he hopes to build an extension and call that Waterloo instead. By 1817, the cultural commodity that was Nelson: stitches, necklaces, shawls, tablecloths, and *Lives of Nelson*, was falling out of favour. Wellington had become the ultimate hero: in 1814, the Countess of Spencer opened a subscription list to erect a statue of Wellington in Hyde Park, which became Britain's first nude statue of a public figure.[56]

The Victorians found Nelson's unabashed adultery difficult to tolerate and art forms aimed at women no longer represented him as the ideal hero. William Makepeace Thackeray's *Vanity Fair* (1847–48) promotes Wellington as the ideal because his controlled behaviour inspires the nation's 'resolute faith' and identifies Nelson with a bygone age. In one episode, Thackeray's female protagonist, Becky Sharp, is in conversation with Lady Crawley, endeavouring to win her affection. It is the summer of 1813 (so Emma Hamilton would still be alive). Lady Crawley waxes about recent scandals about men who elope with women of ill repute.

> 'That was the most beautiful part of dear Lord Nelson's character,' Miss Crawley said. 'He went to the deuce for a woman. There *must* be good in a man who will do that. I adore all imprudent matches. [...] I wish some great man would run away with *you*, my dear; I'm sure you're pretty enough'.

Women, Thackeray suggests, found Nelson attractive because he seemed willing to risk reputation and status for Lady Hamilton. But in *Vanity Fair*, society no longer celebrates those who hazard everything for a woman. Heroic Captain Dobbin always remembers his duty.

Becky Sharp is the Lady Hamilton figure. A dancer and artist's model, Becky infiltrates an aristocratic family, receives a marriage proposal from the elderly patriarch, Sir Pitt, flirts with the Prince of Wales, exploits her connections to aristocratic men, and makes Rawdon Crawley 'go to the deuce' for her. Becky even performs Attitudes at parties:

> The band plays the awful music of 'Don Juan', before the statue enters. [...] Clytemnestra glides swiftly into the room like an apparition – her arms are bare and white – her tawny hair floats down her shoulder – her face is deadly pale – and her eyes are lighted up with a smile so ghastly, that people quake as they look at her.
>
> A tremor ran through the room. 'Good God!' somebody said. 'It's Mrs Rawdon Crawley.'

Scornfully she snatches the dagger out of Ægisthus's hand, and advantances to the bed. You see it shining over head in the glimmer of the lamp, and – and the lamp goes out with a groan, and all is dark.

In the novels of Porter and Staël, the charisma of the Lady Hamilton figure inhered in the fact that she had been a model, actress and dancer. But Becky's earlier occupations identify her as a disgraceful woman who should be reviled. In a contemporary illustrated version of the text, a section that raises the possibility that Becky murdered Jos Sedley for his life insurance is flanked by a picture of her as Clytemnestra: her ability to act such postures reveals that she shares similarly destructive sentiments. As Lady Jane Crawley cries, such a woman is not fit to dine with a Christian family, and, it seemed, neither was Nelson.[57]

Nelson was less fashionable, although he was evoked when a writer sought a hero who learnt humility from his experience of weakness. Linda Colley argued that Charlotte Brontë recalled her early devotion to Wellington to figure Mr Rochester in *Jane Eyre* (1847).[58] But if Wellington recurred in Rochester, Brontë turned the Iron Duke into a Nelsonian figure: the pair cannot truly love until he is wounded, blind, and dependent on Jane's nursing. Charlotte's father surely recalled Nelson's title, Baron of Brontë, when he changed the family's surname from Brunty. In Wilkie Collins's *No Name* (1864), the machinations of the false Horatio, Captain Horatio Wragge, are beaten by kindly sailors, one of whom, old Mazey, keeps a room full of model ships and portraits of captains, including 'Lord Nelson on one wall, in flaming watercolours'.[59] Like the sentimental heroes of earlier novels, Mazey is easily weakened into mercy by the sight of a young pretty woman in distress. Nelson was never quite forgotten and then, in the twentieth century, when women's support for military activity was solicited, he became fashionable once more.

Alexander Korda's film, *That Hamilton Woman* was intended to raise patriotic sentiments in the Second World War. Lawrence Olivier plays Nelson and Vivien Leigh is Emma. Winston Churchill loved it and claimed to have written some of the more stirring lines about tyranny, Europe and democracy.[60] A romantic film aimed at women, the scene where Emma sends Nelson to fight urges female viewers to push their men to the front. But the film also manipulates its audience more subtly by encouraging them to eroticise the figure of the wounded man. Korda achieves this by fictionalising the beginning of their affair. The film shows – as was the case – that Lady Hamilton was unimpressed by Nelson at their first meeting in 1793. Then, as we know, in 1798, she fell in love with Nelson's reputation as the hero of the Nile before he arrived in Naples and she staged an extravagantly dramatic welcome to win his heart. But in the film, she falls in love with him when she realises he is wounded.

Lady Hamilton/Leigh visits Nelson/Olivier in his cabin to discuss supplies, before the Battle of the Nile. When Nelson steps forth from the shadows, she struggles to contain her feelings for him when she realises that he has lost an arm and an eye. She says, in a romantic close up, 'They told us of your victories but not of the price you paid.' The long gaze between the pair marks the beginning of their affair. In 1941, it was important that women believed in the sexualised appeal of the wounded man. Thousands came home injured. Korda's film renders wounds desirable and erotic: it intimated that the sacrifice represented by a man's wound would inspire women's adoration.

In the latter part of the twentieth century, Nelson was absent from romantic fiction. Georgette Heyer wrote courtship novels set in the eighteenth century and although Wellington appears, notably in *An Infamous Army* (1937), Nelson is missing. He is similarly absent from the novels of Barbara Cartland. In Barbara Taylor Bradford's *A Woman of Substance* (1979), the heroine, Emma Harte, is a twentieth-century reworking of Lady Hamilton. Harte is a young girl from a Yorkshire mill village, when Lady Hamilton was born in a Lancashire mining village, her brother, Winston, joins the navy as a boy, against the wishes of his family (there were rumours that Lady Hamilton met Jack Willett Payne when attempting to save her young male relative from going to sea), and, after she has been seduced by the weak son of the local landowner, Edwin Fairley, Harte flees to the nearest big city and pretends she is a sailor's wife. She is determined to revenge herself on the aristocrats who have mistreated her, just as Lady Hamilton refused to be rebuffed by the snobbery of those she encountered. In one episode, Harte, now a successful businesswoman, is trying to name a range of fashions she has designed. Her friend, David Kallinski, tells her that they should name them after 'the first Emma Hart. That's Hart without the "e"'. Harte decides that the name 'Lady Hamilton Clothes' had 'a catchy ring to it and it was rather classy. She remembered that Nelson was Winston's great naval hero'. Lady Hamilton Clothes becomes highly profitable and crucial to the development of Harte's Department Store empire.[61]

But, for apparently the first time in a novel about Lady Hamilton, there is no Nelson. Men are a pitiful species in *A Woman of Substance*: the heroine's father dies, and her brothers, lovers, husbands, and sons are all weak. None deserve a woman as resilient and resourceful as Emma Harte. We might argue that the advent of feminism had made women less disposed to hero-worship, or that Cold War had made conventional heroes redundant. Nelson, it seems, was a hero for a previous time.

IV

This chapter has offered a brief survey of how women and art forms aimed at women represented Nelson. Women adopted Nelson as a sex symbol in an attempt to accredit themselves with some control in a world where their choices were made for them. They accustomed themselves to their dependence on the successes of one man, who existed for them only as an image, by domesticating him into a household object or sexualising him into an aspect of their self-adornment. Women readers demanded a similarly personalised and romanticised version of him and novelists endeavoured to satisfy their desire by representing him as a fantasy hero, a man of deep feeling. By celebrating his emotional needs, writers excused his adultery. They also made the wider point that feminine modes of behaviour should intersect with the public sphere: a great leader should not subordinate his private desires to duty but allow sentiment to define those public responsibilities.

Powerful men are habitually sexualised. Women manage their position of political weakness and legal subjection by eroticising their relationship with those who control their lives. Nelson was nearly fifty in 1805 and thus old enough to be the father of most of the women buying representations of him, writing about him, and reading about him. By turning him into a youthful sex object and thus eroticising their link to him, they confer themselves with a measure of power that they would not possess if they represented the hero as their father. Fanny Nelson and Emma Hamilton, who epitomised different strategies of attracting and maintaining male attention became, along with Nelson, sites upon which women projected complex worries, fantasies, and ambitions about their changing notions of their roles and responsibilities as lovers and wives in a period of war. Women's anxieties about themselves, their ability to love wounded men, and the political situation were channelled through representations of Nelson and the women who rivalled for his affections. No hero was more intensely sexualised than Nelson and the attention he attracted was due to the aspects of him that appealed to women: he was wounded and he seemed to risk his reputation for love. Nelson was represented differently over the years but each time he was evoked, his figure was explicitly marketed to the female consumer.

Notes

1. See Colin White, *The Nelson Encyclopaedia* (London: Chatham, 2002), pp. 176–8; Flora Fraser, 'If You Seek His Monument', in *The Nelson Companion*, ed. Colin White (Stroud: Sutton, 1995), pp. 129–51.

2. Linda Colley, *Britons: Forging the Nation 1707–1837* (1992; repr. London: Vintage, 1996), p. 268.

3. Margarette Lincoln, *Representing the Royal Navy: British Sea Power, 1750–1815* (Aldershot: Ashgate, 2002), pp. 137–60.

4. Colley, *Britons*, particularly pp. 251–96; Kathleen Wilson, 'Empire of Virtue: The Imperial Project and Hanoverian Culture c. 1720–1785', in *An Imperial State at War: Britain from 1689 to 1815*, ed. Lawrence Stone (London: Routledge, 1994), pp. 128–64, and Wilson, *The Island Race: Englishness, Empire and Gender in the Eighteenth Century* (London: Routledge, 2003), p. 105.

5. *Grazer Zeitung*, 18 August 1800. Cited in Thomas Blümel, *Nelson's Overland Return in 1800* (Slinfold: The Nelson Society, 2000), pp. 8–9.

6. Lady Elizabeth Foster, journal entry, 12 November 1800, cited in Dorothy Stuart, *Dearest Bess* (London: Metheun, 1955), p. 88.

7. Foster, 7 September 1805, cited in Stuart, *Dearest Bess*, p. 124.

8. Carola Oman, *Nelson* (1947; repr. London: Hodder and Stoughton, 1950), p. 270.

9. Rina Prentice, *A Celebration of the Sea: The Decorative Art Collections of the National Maritime Museum* (London: HMSO, 1994), p. 33.

10. Park Honan, *Jane Austen: Her Life* (1987; repr. London: Phoenix, 1997), p. 162.

11. Cited in Hugh Tours, *The Life and Letters of Emma Hamilton* (London: Gollancz, 1963), p. 121.

12. Lionel Cust (ed.), *Catalogue of the Collections of Fans and Fan-Leaves Presented to the Trustees of the British Museum by the Lady Charlotte Schreiber* (London: Longmans, 1893), p. 4; see Prentice, *Celebration of the Sea*, p. 32.

13. R.K. Henrywood, *Relief-Moulded Jugs, 1820–1900* (Woodbridge: Antique Collectors' Club, 1984), p. 199. For a reproduction of this jug, see Desmond Eyles, *Royal Doulton Character and Toby Jugs* (Kent: Westerham Press, 1979), p. 29.

14. John May, 'Nelson Commemorated', in *The Nelson Companion*, ed. White, pp. 81–101 (p. 83).

15. See *The Nelson Dispatch*, 7, part 11 (2002), 747.

16. Cited in Oman, *Nelson*, p. 434; see Nelson to Lady Hamilton, 14 March 1804, cited in Tours, *Life and Letters*, p. 206.

17. See Lincoln, *Representing the Royal Navy*, colour plate 6.

18. May, 'Commemorating Nelson', in *The Nelson Companion*, ed. White, p. 94.

19. See Prentice, *A Celebration of the Sea*, p. 32.

20. See Shirley Bury, *Jewellery: 1789–1910*, 2 vols (Woodbridge: Antique Collectors' Club, 1991), vol. I, pp. 174–5.

21. See Prentice, *A Celebration of the Sea*, p. 33; Ann Louise Luthi, *Sentimental Jewellery* (Princes Risborough: Shire Publications, 1998), p. 9.

22. See Prentice, *A Celebration of the Sea*, pp. 36–7.

23. See Tom Malcomson, 'Commemoration Meant Commerce for Some, Advertisements from *The Times* after the Death of Nelson', *The Nelson Dispatch*, 6, part 9 (1999), 386–90 (p. 387).

24. Amanda Vickery, *The Gentleman's Daughter: Women's Lives in Georgian England* (New Haven: Yale University Press, 1998), particularly pp. 187–93 (p. 193). On shopping and social identity, see Grant MacCracken, *Culture and Consumption: New Approaches to the Symbolic Character of Consumer Goods and Activities*

(Indianapolis: Indiana University Press, 1988), p. 19; on 'social emulation', see *The Birth of a Consumer Society: The Commercialisation of Eighteenth-Century England*, ed. John McKendrick, John Brewer, and J.H. Plumb (Bloomington: Indiana University Press, 1982), p. 11.

25. On how the period saw two key debates, to define the meaning of consumerism and come to an acceptable ideological construction of the female subject, see Elizabeth Kowaleski-Wallace, *Consuming Subjects: Women, Shopping, and Business in the Eighteenth Century* (New York: Columbia University Press, 1997), p. 5.

26. On the 'discriminatory' policies of the wartime state, see Nicholas Rogers, *Crowds, Culture, and Politics in Georgian Britain* (Oxford: Clarendon Press, 1998), pp. 114–21.

27. On patriotic effort, see Colley, *Britons*, pp. 273–6; Lincoln, *Representing the Royal Navy*, pp. 140–6; Wilson, *Island Race*, pp. 105–7.

28. Colley, *Britons*, p. 274.

29. On how recruiting officers encouraged women to press their men to fight, see Wilson, *Island Race*, p. 105.

30. May, 'Commemorating Nelson', in *The Nelson Companion*, ed. White, p. 94.

31. Honan, *Jane Austen*, p. 222.

32. May, 'Commemorating Nelson', in *The Nelson Companion*, ed. White, p. 96.

33. For example, the website, advertised as a comprehensive list of naval novels, <www.boat-links.com>, cites Samuel Taylor Coleridge's 'The Rime of the Ancient Mariner' (1798), but excludes all novels by women.

34. Anna Maria Porter, *A Sailor's Friendship and a Soldier's Love*, 2 vols (London, 1805), vol. I, pp. 199, 200, 2–3, 89, 144.

35. Colin White, *The Nelson Encyclopaedia* (London: Chatham, 2002), p. 56.

36. Porter, *A Sailor's Friendship*, I, 220, 229–30, 74–5, 151, 197, 238, 307–9.

37. Porter, *A Sailor's Friendship*, II, 22, 116.

38. Eliza Parsons, *The Convict; or, The Navy Lieutenant* (London, 1806), 4 vols, vol. I, pp. 13, 11.

39. Colin White, 'Nelson and Shakespeare', in *The Nelson Dispatch*, 7, part 3 (2000), 145–50 (p. 150).

40. Parsons, *The Navy Lieutenant*, I, 1, 98, 77, 97, 79, 111, 73, 7, 10, 27, 121, 21, 129, 23, 148; II, 19.

41. John Isbell, 'Introduction', to *Corinne; or, Italy*, ed. Sylvia Raphael (Oxford: Oxford University Press, 1998), p. vii.

42. Madame de Staël, *Corinna; or, Italy*, translator unknown, 3 vols (London, 1807), vol. I, pp. 58–9, 320, 54–7, 298, 3, 9.

43. Lincoln, *Representing the Royal Navy*, p. 147.

44. N.A.M. Rodger, *The Wooden World: An Anatomy of the Georgian Navy* (London: Harper Collins, 1986), p. 79.

45. See Wilson, *The Island Race*, p. 107.

46. John Sutherland, *The Longman Companion to Victorian Fiction* (Essex: Longman, 1998), pp. 455–6.

47. Benedict Anderson, *Imagined Communities: Reflections on the Origin and Spread of Nationalism* (London: Verso, 1983), pp. 50–79.

48. See J.H. Hubback and Edith C. Hubback, *Jane Austen's Sailor Brothers* (Stroud: Hodgkins, 1986), pp. 61–7.

49. On Austen's representation of the Navy, see Brian Southam, *Jane Austen and the Navy* (London: Hambledon, 2000).

50. Jane Austen to Cassandra Austen, 11–12 October 1813, in *The Letters of Jane Austen*, ed. Deidre Le Faye (Oxford: Oxford University Press, 1995), p. 235.

51. On this point, I disagree with Park Honan. See Honan, *Jane Austen*, p. 165.

52. Austen, *Northanger Abbey*, ed. Anne Ehrenpreis (1972; repr. Harmondsworth: Penguin, 1985), p. 123.

53. Austen, *Persuasion*, ed. Gillian Beer (Harmondsworth: Penguin, 1998), p. 87.

54. Austen, *Mansfield Park*, ed. Kathryn Sutherland (Harmondsworth: Penguin, 1996), p. 51.

55. Austen, *Sanditon*, ed. Margaret Drabble (Harmondsworth: Penguin, 1974), p. 169.

56. On the statue, see Colley, *Britons*, p. 273.

57. William Makepeace Thackeray, *Vanity Fair*, ed. John Carey (Harmondsworth: Penguin, 2001), pp. 325, 119–20, 598, 183, 642.

58. Colley, *Britons*, pp. 272–3.

59. Wilkie Collins, *No Name*, ed. Mark Ford (Harmondsworth: Penguin, 1994), p. 516.

60. See Andrew Lambert, *Nelson: Britannia's God of War* (London: Faber, 2004), p. 353.

61. Barbara Taylor Bradford, *A Woman of Substance* (London: Granada, 1979), pp. 78, 400–1.

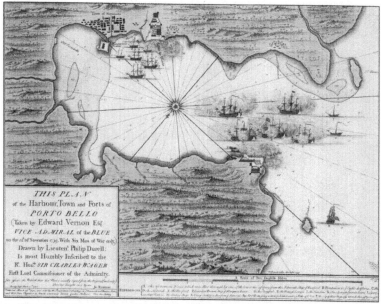

1. *Plan of the Harbour, town and Forts of Porto Bello* (Taken by Edward Vernon Esq., Vice-Admiral of the Blue ...With Six Men of War Only), 1740, National Maritime Museum, Greenwich.

2. *The Death of General Wolfe* After West, 1760, National Maritime Museum, Greenwich.

3. *Nelson and the Bear* Richard Westall, c.1806, National Maritime Museum, Greenwich.

4. *Nelson Receiving the Surrender of the San Nicolas* Richard Westall, date unknown, National Maritime Museum, Greenwich.

5. *Nelson Boarding the San Josef* George Jones, 1829, National Maritime Museum, Greenwich.

6. *The Destruction of l'Orient* at the Battle of the Nile, on 1 August 1798, George Arnald, 1825–27, National Maritime Museum, Greenwich.

7. *The Hero of the Nile*
James Gillray, 1798,
National Maritime
Museum, Greenwich.

8. *A True British* Tar James
Gillray, 1795, National
Maritime Museum,
Greenwich.

A TRUE BRITISH·TAR.

"Damn all Bond-Street-Sailors! say, a parcel of smell-smocks!
they'd sooner creep into a Jordan, than face the French!—damn me!"

9. *Captain Horatio Nelson*
   John Francis Rigaud, date
   unknown, National
   Maritime Museum,
   Greenwich.

10. *Rear-Admiral Horatio Nelson*
    Leonardo Guzzardi, 1799,
    National Maritime Museum,
    Greenwich.

11. *Rear-Admiral Horatio Nelson 1758–1805*
Unknown artist, c. 1800, National Maritime Museum, Greenwich.

12. *Death of Nelson* 21 October 1805, Arthur William Devis, 1807, National Maritime Museum, Greenwich.

13. *Apotheosis of Nelson* Scott Pierre Legrand, c. 1805–18, National Maritime Museum, Greenwich.

14. *Sketch for a Monument to Lord Nelson* Benjamin West, 1807, Yale Center for British Art, New Haven, CT.

15. Some of the thousands of Bilston enamel boxes (used to store patches and other cosmetic items), made to celebrate the Battle of the Nile, and an anchor and chain inscribed to Nelson. National Maritime Museum, Greenwich.

16. Some of the best selling mourning jewellery for Nelson. The three items on which Nelson faces right are based on a design by James Tassie. National Maritime Museum, Greenwich.

17. Pendants and brooches made to commemorate Nelson after the Nile and after Trafalgar. National Maritime Museum, Greenwich.

18. 'Dresses à la Nile respectfully dedicated to the Fashion Mongers of the day'. A print from October 1798 gently pokes fun at the British craze for wearing Nelson fashions.

19. *Emma Lady Hamilton as A Bacchante* Louise Elizabeth Vigée-Le Brun, 1790–91. Beautiful, artistic, glamorous, and compelling, Lady Hamilton recurred again and again in eighteenth-century novels as the desirable, talented, and often virtuous heroine.

20. *Rear-Admiral Lord Nel*
Lemuel Francis Abbott
1800, National Maritir
Museum, Greenwich.

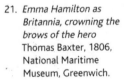

21. *Emma Hamilton as
Britannia, crowning the
brows of the hero*
Thomas Baxter, 1806,
National Maritime
Museum, Greenwich.

22. *Lieutenant Nelson boarding an American prize* Richard Westall, 1806, National Maritime Museum, Greenwich.

23. *Victory at Trafalgar* J. M. W. Turner, 1822–24, National Maritime Museum, Greenwich.

24. *England's Pride and Glory*
Thomas Davidson, *c.*1890
National Maritime
Museum, Greenwich.

25. Nelson's 'Trafalgar' coat,
National Maritime
Museum, Greenwich.

26. *Funeral procession of the late Lord Viscount Nelson, from the Admiralty to St Paul's, London, 9th January 1806* M. Merigot after Augustus Charles Pugin, 1 April 1806, National Maritime Museum, Greenwich.

27. *Interment of the Remains of the late Lord Viscount Nelson, in the Cathedral of St Paul, London on the 9th January 1806* Frederick Christian Lewis after Augustus Charles Pugin, 1 April 1806, National Maritime Museum, Greenwich.

28. *Nelson's Tomb, Crypt of Saint Paul* Anonymous, date unknown, National Maritime Museum, Greenwich.

29. *The Death of Lord Nelson* Benjamin West, 1806, Walker Art Gallery, Liverpool.

30. *The Sailor's Monument to the Memory of Lord Nelson* William Holland, 1806, National Maritime Museum, Greenwich.

31. *Greenwich Pensioners at the Tomb of Nelson* H. Macbeth-Raeburn after Sir John Everett Millais, date unknown, National Maritime Museum, Greenwich.

32. *The United Service* Andrew Morton, 1845, National Maritime Museum, Greenwich.

Part Two
Legacy

5
Nelson Apotheosised:
The Creation of the Nelson Legend

Colin White

On the morning of 21 October 1805, at about 8.00am, Vice-Admiral Lord Nelson went down to his cabin on the upper gun deck of HMS *Victory*. Most of his furniture and belongings had been packed up and stowed in the hold, earlier at daybreak, when the ship's company had cleared for action, but canvas screens had been erected to give him a little privacy and some essential items left behind, such as his portable writing desk. Taking a small pocket notebook, in which he habitually made brief notes of each day's events, he wrote:

> Monday Octr: 21st 1805 at day Light saw the Enemys Combined fleet from East to ESE bore away made the Signal for Order of Sailing and to Prepare for Battle the Enemy with the heads to the Southward. At 7 the Enemy wearing in succession.

He then carried on without a break:

> May the Great God whom I worship Grant to my Country and for the benefit of Europe in General a great and Glorious Victory and may no misconduct in anyone tarnish it, and may humanity after Victory be the predominant feature in the British fleet. For myself individually I commit my life to Him who made me and may his blessing light upon my endeavours for serving My Country faithfully, to Him I resign myself and the Just cause which is entrusted to me to defend. Amen amen amen.

That prayer is a well-known part of the Nelson story. What, however, is not so well known is that there are two versions of it – the one in Nelson's pocket notebook, is now preserved in the National Archive at Kew; another, on loose, unbound pages is in the National Maritime Museum. Both are identical in wording and spelling; even the way the words are arranged on the page is exactly the same. They have been carefully examined by experts to see if one is a facsimile, or even a very clever fake, but there is general agreement that both are genuine. In other words, it would appear that Nelson wrote the prayer out twice.[1] Clearly, this means that he wanted to make sure that the prayer survived. Which means, in turn, that it was not a private prayer at all but one written quite deliberately with posterity in mind.

The pocketbook containing the prayer also contained Nelson's famous 'codicil' to his will in which he left his mistress Emma Hamilton and their daughter Horatia as 'a legacy to my King & Country'. So the book was treated as a legal document and was therefore seen by Nelson's executors who quickly realised the importance of the prayer and decided that it should be published. A special pamphlet was printed and, as a result, the prayer featured early on in accounts of Trafalgar and Nelson's death, and quickly became a central feature of the traditional story. In 1854, it was the inspiration for a famous painting, by Thomas Barker. Barker worked hard to make sure that every detail was correct, even down to the design of the writing slope. But he made one major mistake. Following a number of erroneous contemporary accounts, he showed Nelson dressed in full dress uniform, thus helping to perpetuate a myth, that continues to this day, that he was covered in medals and gold braid on the day of battle. In fact he was wearing his rather threadbare everyday undress uniform coat, with very little decoration and only small sequin and wire facsimiles of his stars, rather than the gaudy jewels themselves.[2]

The prayer has continued to inspire generations of servicemen ever since. Printed versions of it were distributed in Royal Navy ships in both World Wars and it is still read out every Trafalgar Day during the traditional service of remembrance on the quarterdeck of HMS *Victory*. In the story of the prayer, we can see all the essential elements of the development of the Nelson Legend.[3] First, there is Nelson's own role in its creation: in this case, he acts consciously and deliberately to ensure that the prayer survives the battle. Second, there is the active involvement of the British Establishment in publishing the prayer, linked with the fixing of the story by the production of a striking heroic image. And third, the prayer becomes part of the traditional manner in which Nelson and Trafalgar are remembered to this day.

I

Nelson was, above all, 'a performance leader'.[4] For him leadership was a role, which was consciously acted out and, like an actor, he used appropriate dress and also actions and gestures to express his role. Taking dress first: he understood the need for a leader to stand out in a crowd, so that he could be easily recognised. The famous portrait by Lemuel Francis Abbott, painted in 1799 and now in the collection of the National Maritime Museum, shows two key ways in which he did this (see Plate 20). Most obvious are his decorations. His famous refusal to change his coat, or even to cover his decorations, at Trafalgar has been often misinterpreted as an act of mindless vanity – or, most ludicrously, as an indication of suicidal tendencies.[5] That Nelson was vain is undeniable – but his refusal to cover up his stars is much more subtly nuanced. He knew that his men needed to see him; to know that he was there among them, sharing the danger with them; and if, as a result, he was also more easily seen by the enemy, then that was a price he was willing to pay. As he said sharply when his well-meaning officers begged him to change, 'This is no time to be shifting a coat!'[6]

The second distinctive feature in the portrait is so familiar now that it is often forgotten – the missing arm. Nelson made good use of his disability. He gave his stump a nautical nickname referring to it as his 'fin' and he often used it to identify himself. In the Baltic, in 1801, the small boat in which he was travelling was challenged by one of the ships under his command. He stood up, threw back his boat cloak and shouted, 'I am Lord Nelson – see, here is my fin'. He also used the stump to forge bonds with his men. When he visited the hospital in Great Yarmouth following the 1801 Baltic campaign he chatted to a young sailor who had lost his arm and said with a smile, 'Well then Jack, you and I are spoiled for fishermen!'[7] The fact that he could use that phrase 'you and I' with true sympathy, was one of the bedrocks of his success as a leader.

As for his actions and gestures: his battered body showed that his deeds matched his words. Visibly, and obviously, he was a man who led from the front: whether it was charging up the side of the *San Nicolas* to capture the even larger *San Josef* at the Battle of Cape St Vincent (see Plate 5) or jockeying with the *Temeraire* for the lead position in the British line at Trafalgar. Nor were his actions and gestures only warlike. For example, in July 1799, he wrote to the First Lord of the Admiralty, Lord Spencer:

> If under all the circumstances I am not removed from my situation, and the St: Joseph is not otherwise disposed of, it would flatter me

very much to have her for the Ship destined to bear my Flag. I press it no further relying on your goodness.[8]

At a superficial level, that can be read as a particularly blatant example of Nelson's tendency to self-promotion. But it is also subtler – like so much else that he wrote. For it shows he instinctively appreciated the importance of symbolic gestures in leadership: in this case, the victor of the Battle of the Nile, flying his flag in the greatest of his trophies, captured at the Battle of Cape St Vincent. Spencer was shrewd enough to understand the underlying purpose of Nelson's request and personally ordered the *San Josef* to be reserved for him. And indeed he did fly his flag in her for a few weeks in early 1801, before transferring to the more shallow-draughted *St George* for the Baltic campaign.[9]

Nelson also demonstrated a strikingly modern attitude towards the press and used the popular newspapers to promote his own deeds and those of his men. Throughout his later career, he issued what amounted to press releases – usually in the form of letters to friends with specific instructions that they should be published.[10] The most famous example is the account he wrote of his exploits at the Battle of Cape St Vincent, which he sent to his friend, Captain William Locker, with the instruction,

> if you approve of it you are at perfect liberty to insert it in the newspapers … as I do not write for the press there may be parts of it which require the pruning knife which I desire you will use without fear.[11]

Locker duly obliged (although in fact he made very little use of the 'pruning knife') and so Nelson's account appeared in the popular press at almost the same time as the formal report of his commander-in-chief, Admiral Sir John Jervis (which did not mention Nelson's exploits), was printed in the official gazette.[12]

Additionally, new evidence has recently emerged showing that Nelson took a personal interest in the work of the print makers who produced engravings of his portraits and battles. For example, in 1802 he corresponded with James Fittler about a print of the Battle of the Nile, giving him instructions about the right coronet to use.[13] In the same year, he gave the artist Thomas Buttersworth very precise instructions about the details of a print showing all the ships Nelson had been involved in capturing between 1793 and 1801:

> The name of each ship to be wrote between the Main and Foremast. The ships to be put in rotation as captured. L'Orient will then be placed as at present

The Portrait disapproved. To be like the outline formerly sold by Mr Brydon.[14]

The mention of the 'portrait formerly sold by Mr Brydon' is significant. Nelson meant an engraving published by Brydon based on a pencil sketch of his left profile drawn hurriedly at a banquet, sometime in late 1800 by Simon de Koster. Although it is one of the most ordinary, and unheroic likenesses of him, we know that he thought it was 'the most like me' (see Fig. 5.1, p. 102).[15] So we can conclude that, although he was certainly concerned with how his image should be presented, he actually *preferred* to be depicted as an ordinary, approachable person, rather than in a more distant, heroic guise.

Other recently-located correspondence shows that Nelson kept a stock of these prints and distributed them to people whom he wished to impress or whom he thought might benefit from his example. Similarly, he had stocks of the medal awarded for the Battle of the Nile by his friend Alexander Davison, together with off-prints of a biographical article published in the *Naval Chronicle* in 1800, which he also distributed.[16] For example, on 12 April 1801, just ten days after battering the Danes into submission at the Battle of Copenhagen, he wrote to the Commandant of the Danish Naval Academy, Captain Hans Sneedorf:

Lord Nelson's Compliments to Captain Schneider [*sic*] and begs leave to present to the Academy under his able direction two medals, one struck in Commemoration of the Battle of the Nile the other on that of my reconquest of the City of Naples & of the Kingdom ...

I send you also a Short account of my life it cannot do harm to youth & may do good, as it will show that Perseverance and good conduct will raise a person to the very highest honors and rewards, that it may be useful in that way to those entrusted to your care is the fervent wish of Your Most Obt: Servt:

Nelson & Bronte[17]

Another key player in the early development of the Nelson Legend was Emma Hamilton. She was the celebrant of his fame and the rewarder of his exploits – a role he consciously encouraged her to play. Here he is, writing to her from the West Indies at the height of his chase of the Combined Fleet in the summer of 1805:

My dearest Beloved Emma Your own Nelsons pride and delight, I find myself within six days of the Enemy, and I have every reason to hope that the 6th: of June will immortalize your own Nelson your fond Nelson. May God send me Victory and us a happy and speedy meeting. Adl: Cochrane is sending home a Vessel this day. therefore only pay for my success and My laurels I shall with pleasure lay at your feet and a Sweet Kiss will be an ample reward for all your faithful Nelsons hard fag, for Ever and Ever I am your faithful ever faithful and affectionate
Nelson & Bronte[18]

Emma performed the role with characteristic relish and gusto while Nelson lived, and continued to do so after his death. An engraving based on a drawing by Thomas Baxter and published only a month after the news of Trafalgar had arrived in Britain, shows her as Britannia crowning the brows of the hero with laurel (see Plate 21). She also contributed a rich fund of improbable stories to early biographers – especially James Harrison, whose *Life of Nelson*, published in 1806 contains a number of anecdotes that are clearly the product of Emma's inventive gift. There is, for example, her version of her parting from Nelson in September 1805 in which the hero, reluctant to leave his loved ones, is persuaded by a brave Emma/Britannia that his country needs him – a patriotic gesture to which he responds theatrically, 'Brave Emma, good Emma! If there were more Emmas, there would be more Nelsons!'[19] That Nelson was reluctant to leave Emma and Horatia after such a short time with them, is clear from the letters he wrote at the time – but in suggesting that he had to be persuaded into doing his duty, Emma did his memory a lasting disservice.

Emma Hamilton also became the first Nelson Curator, lovingly preserving relics of him, and also carefully recording the provenance of the key items in her care.[20] Both the great Nelson collections, at Greenwich and Portsmouth, include scraps of paper covered in her wandering handwriting relating to these objects. For example, there are her characteristically overblown notes about a silver-gilt christening cup that Nelson purchased for their daughter, Horatia, during his brief leave in England in 1805:

The Victor of Aboukir Copenhagen & Trafalgar etc etc etc the glorious the great & good Nelson, bought this for his daughter Horatia Nelson August 30th 1805. She used it till I thought it proper for her to lay it by as a sacred relic. Emma Hamilton.[21]

II

Nelson was often used as a symbol by the Establishment during his lifetime. As Marianne Czisnik has demonstrated, Nelson's popularity following the Battle of the Nile was skilfully exploited by the government, using various media to promote his public image.[22] Again, in 1801, Nelson was appointed commander-in-chief of the special anti-invasion forces in the Channel, principally because of the power of his name, rather than for any specific operational reason.[23] However by far the most important, and dramatic, expression of the take-over of Nelson by the Establishment was his magnificent State Funeral in January 1806. The splendour and scale of the ceremonies were unprecedented for any commoner. First the body lay in state for three days in the Painted Hall at Greenwich; there was then a river procession from Greenwich to London, then a street procession from Whitehall to St Paul's and finally a three-hour religious service with all the trappings of a full heraldic funeral. It was almost as if a medieval knight was being taken to his rest (see Plates 26 and 27).[24] As if to underline just how much of an Establishment occasion it was, there were the usual disputes over precedence. As Timothy Jenks has shown, the Prince of Wales originally wished to attend in his official capacity but was forbidden to do so by the king. He then decided to attend as a private citizen only to find that the Lord Mayor of London could now claim precedence over him! In the end a place was found for him in the procession just astern of the hearse bearing the body.[25]

The Prince of Wales also played a role in the creation of one of the main foundation stones of the Nelson Legend – the monumental biography (indeed 'hagiography' is not an inappropriate term) published in 1809 by the prince's chaplain, Rev. James Stanier Clarke in collaboration with John M'Arthur.[26] The book was in fact M'Arthur's idea. Formerly a purser in the Royal Navy he knew Nelson well, having served with him in the Mediterranean during the early years of the war against France. He had begun assembling material for a major biography when, in late January 1806, he read an advertisement in the papers announcing that the Nelson family had selected a gentleman 'of high respectability and rank' to write the life and asking all those who had letters from Nelson in their possession not to make their material available to anyone else.[27]

Faced with this potential competition, M'Arthur wrote to Earl Nelson, protesting that Nelson himself had asked him to write his life – a spurious claim, for which there is no evidence in Nelson's letters. He pointed out that he had already incurred a great deal of expense in preparing his book – for example, he had commissioned a set of paintings that would be engraved as illustrations. At the same time the Earl was under pressure from the Prince of Wales who wanted his librarian and chaplain, Rev. James Clarke, to write the book. A protracted negotiation ensued and eventually it was agreed that Clarke and M'Arthur would combine their efforts – but, even then, there was a dispute over whose name would come first on the title page. Eventually, in February 1807 a deal was struck and a prospectus was issued saying that the work 'is sanctioned by Earl Nelson and his family'. The book was eventually published in 1809 in two bulky volumes and with a list of patrons that reads like a roll call of the 'A' List of Regency Britain.

There was little likelihood, therefore, that the book would be detached or dispassionate in its treatment of Nelson's story. From the start, everyone involved was anxious that it should present The Hero in the best possible light and that it should not upset any of its numerous supporters. In M'Arthur's papers in the Rosenbach Library in Philadelphia is a letter from Frances Nelson, dating from December 1806. She had made a number of her husband's letters available to the editors and now she was worried about a passage in one of them that she feared might offend Lord Spencer, the former First Lord of the Admiralty. She wrote:

> I am under personal obligations to Lord & Lady Spencer they were of the very few who had the independence and Virtue enough to Notice a poor deserted wife.[28]

The Nelson family also contributed some tall stories, particularly about Nelson's childhood, that have continued to be repeated in subsequent biographies and it is only recently that they have been effectively challenged and discarded.[29]

Nelson's heroic image was further enhanced by the superb set of illustrations, based on paintings commissioned by M'Arthur from the President of the Royal Academy Benjamin West; leading marine artist Nicholas Pocock and Richard Westall.[30] Most of them are now very well known, having been endlessly reproduced in subsequent biographies, and so they have become an integral part of the Nelson Legend – indeed, it is arguable that they have influenced its development even more than the text of the book. The studies by Richard Westall, of five key moments in Nelson's career,[31] are particularly stylised and romantically heroic. For example, in 'Nelson boarding a captured ship' a young Lieutenant Nelson steps gracefully down into a tossing boat, at the height of a gale, without holding on – for all the world like Christ quelling the storm on Galilee (see Plate 22). It is, in passing, an interesting 'link' of cultural history that Westall went on produce one of the most famous of the romantic portraits of Byron and also the illustrations for the first edition of *Childe Harold*.

However, Clarke and M'Arthur's most profound influence on the Legend was through their editing of Nelson's letters. Having assembled a large amount of his correspondence, they decided to construct their text by using what they called, 'His Lordships own manuscripts'.[32] Sadly, however, they were not content to let Nelson's manuscripts stand as he had written them. Instead, they edited the letters, 'improving' the grammar and style, cutting out some passages altogether and even taking sections from a number of different letters and combining them. It has always been known that they mishandled their material but the full extent of their depredations has only recently begun to emerge as a result of the findings of the Nelson Letters Project.[33]

A good example of their editorial vandalism is the way they dealt with Nelson's correspondence with the Duke of Clarence, later King William IV. Nelson first met Prince William Henry, as he then was, while serving in North American waters in 1782 and they later served together in the West Indies. In the late 1780s they began a correspondence that lasted until Nelson's death. We now know that Nelson wrote over seventy letters to the Duke but, when Clarke and M'Arthur asked permission to publish them, they were allowed access to only half. The remaining letters were suppressed and have remained unknown, and unused by biographers, until they were recently relocated during the course of the Nelson Letters Project. Now that they have been fully transcribed for the first time, some fascinating new material has emerged.[34] For example, on 4 April 1801, two days after the Battle of Copenhagen, Nelson wrote to Clarence:

> I believe I may congratulate Your Royal Highness on the recent success of our Incomparable Navy which I trust has not tarnish'd its ancient splendour. It was my good fortune to Command such a very distinguish'd sett of fine fellows, and to have the arrangement of the attack, the loss of services in the stations assigned to them of three sail by their getting on shore prevented our success being so compleat as I intended, but I thank God under those very untoward circumstances for what has been done.[35]

The suggestion that the British success was not 'so compleat as I intended' is especially significant. In all his public pronouncements, Nelson talked up the victory: here in a private letter to a trusted friend he reveals his true assessment of the battle.

Figure 5.1 Pencil sketch of Nelson by Simon de Koster.

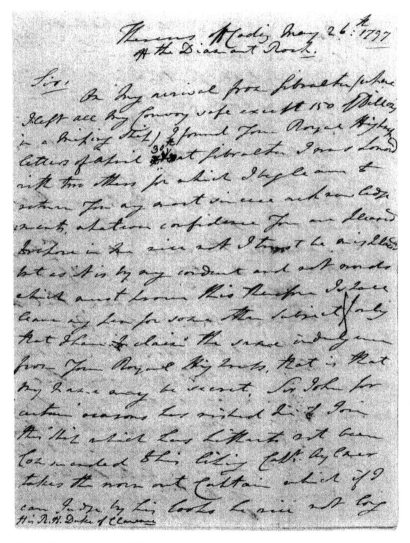

Figure 5.2 Letter from Nelson to the Duke of Clarence, showing crosses where material is to be omitted.

We also now know, that even those letters that were published were often edited to remove confidential, or potentially embarrassing, material. So, for example, in May 1797, when the news of the Spithead Mutiny first reached Cadiz, where Nelson was serving with Lord St Vincent's fleet, his first reaction was to sympathise with the mutineers:

> to us who see the whole at once we must think that for a *Mutiny* (which I fear I must call it having no other Name) that it has been the most Manly that I ever heard of, and does the British Sailor infinite honour. It is extraordinary that there never was a regulation by authority for short Weights and Measures and it reflects on all of us to have suffer'd it so long. But I hope our Seamen, as they say, will hate the French as much as ever.[36]

That passage was considered far too controversial in 1809 and was edited out by Clarke and M'Arthur – indeed close examination of the original reveals large crosses in the text, indicating where the cuts were to be made (see Fig. 5.2).

But Clarke and M'Arthur were not content merely with omitting letters or editing them: at times, they even defaced and altered them. Recent research in the Huntington Library in California in the summer of 2003, revealed an archivists' nightmare: among a batch of original letters from Nelson to Admiral Lord Hood were some that had been literally defaced.[37] Some of the text was heavily scored through; new text had been added in M'Arthur's handwriting in the margins and between the lines. In places, scraps of paper bearing extracts, ripped from the heart of other letters, had been pasted to the top and bottom of the page. Apparently a number of people who lent letters to Clarke and M'Arthur had great difficulty in getting their property returned – now we know why!

In fact the Clarke and M'Arthur biography did not sell well. It cost nine guineas and the two massive volumes weighed over twenty pounds, which made them difficult to read without a bookstand. An abridged edition was produced in 1810 and a second edition, in three small volumes, in 1839/40. But even these attempts at popularising the book did not succeed in making it attractive to a wider market and its influence on the Nelson Legend might well have been insignificant had it not been for the intervention of Robert Southey, the Poet Laureate. In 1810, Southey wrote an article for the *Quarterly Review*, reviewing the existing Nelson biographies, including Clarke and M'Arthur, and, as a result, he was commissioned by John Murray to write a full-length book. The resulting *Life of Nelson*, published in two small volumes in 1813, was an instant success and has never been out of print since. It has therefore been very influential in the development of the Nelson Legend and, because Southey used much of the material he found in Clarke and M'Arthur – including the heavily edited versions of the letters printed by them and the fanciful stories of childhood prowess – these became embedded in the Legend. Southey's book is great literature and still reads superbly – but its facts and its judgements need to be treated with care.[38]

Another important step in the development of the Legend was the establishment of the Naval Gallery in the Painted Hall at the Royal Naval Hospital at Greenwich. Originally the idea of Nelson's former commanding officer the Deputy Lieutenant of the Hospital, Captain William Locker, it was finally brought into being by his son Edward Hawke Locker in 1824. It did not just feature paintings of Nelson and his battles – but they predominated.[39] The paintings were acquired in a number of ways. Some were already in the hospital's possession. Some were donated – for example, in 1829, King George IV presented Turner's magnificent *Victory at Trafalgar* (Plate 23) which quickly became one of the best-known images of the battle. There was even a competition, organised by the British Institution, with a prize of £500 for paintings celebrating British naval achievements and this resulted in the acquisition of some of the most famous images of Nelson's exploits, including a painting of him boarding the *San Josef* by George Jones and one by George Arnald of *l'Orient* blowing up at the Battle of the Nile (Plates 5 and 6). Both are now well-known images of Nelson's battles and have featured in many of the biographies. The Gallery was open to the public and quickly became a popular tourist attraction, inspiring generations of young sailors (Plate 24) until its contents were finally absorbed into the National Maritime Museum in 1937, where they continue to form the core of the museum's unrivalled Nelson collection.

During the same period, monuments to Nelson had been erected throughout the British Isles and overseas, starting with the menhir at Taynuilt erected immediately after Trafalgar by the workers in the local ironworks. By the time that Edward Bailey's massive heroic statue was finally installed atop the column in Trafalgar Square in 1843, there were twelve other publicly funded monuments already in place, as well as a number of privately sponsored ones.[40] The year after the Trafalgar Square column was completed perhaps the most enduring, and certainly the most influential, monument to Nelson was produced – this time a literary one. Sir Nicholas Harris Nicolas's magnificent *Dispatches and Letters of Lord Nelson*, published in seven volumes between 1844 and 1846 is by any yardstick a remarkable work of scholarship. Nicolas assembled and transcribed some three thousand letters and then published them with copious footnotes and additional material relating to Nelson's career. As a result, it reads almost like a biography – the reader can follow Nelson from the proud youngster writing to his brother to announce his promotion to lieutenant in 1777, to the hero writing his incomparable prayer in the great cabin of HMS *Victory* in 1805. It has formed the bedrock on which every subsequent biography has been founded and it has acquired a formidable reputation – in 1947, Carola Oman, arguably the greatest of all Nelson's twentieth-century biographers – called it 'the Bible of the Nelson student'.[41]

Yet it was, just as much as Clarke and M'Arthur, the Painted Hall and the monuments, a creation of the Establishment – as the dedication to the Prince Consort, Prince Albert, makes clear. It was, moreover, not a primary source as has sometimes been mistakenly suggested.[42] Like any other biography, it was an artificial construction and we now know that Nicolas missed a fair amount of important material. Once again, as with Clarke and M'Arthur, the findings of the Nelson Letters Project have thrown fascinating new light on the material that Nicolas missed and it has become clear that he, and his collaborators, made selections from the material at their disposal, discarding letters that did not match the image of Nelson they were seeking to create.[43]

First, there are letters that were withheld from Nicolas. He relied on the owners of Nelson letters to let him see the originals, or to provide him with transcripts. Many of Nelson's former friends and colleagues, or their descendants, made such material available but the new research has shown that some selected letters from those in their possession, rather than simply sending Nicolas everything they had. So, for example, the papers of the politician Henry Addington, Lord Sidmouth, now in the Devon Records Office, include letters from Nelson that have been annotated 'Not to be shown to Sir HN', indicating letters that were not to be published at all; or 'Stop here', indicating where cuts were to be made. Among the former, is a charming letter congratulating Addington – wrongly as it turned out – on the award of the Order of the Garter:

My Dear Sir
Having addressed My letters Public & private to Lord Hobart, I only take up one moment of your time to congratulate you on the Blue Ribbon which the French papers tell us you have got. Without a Compliment I do not believe it could have been more properly bestowed, and may you live in health and happiness many years to enjoy it is the most sincere wish of My Dear Sir Your Attached Friend
Nelson & Bronte[44]

Then, there are letters that Nicolas himself rejected. Sometimes, he did so because of the sheer volume of the material with which he was confronted – for example, in Nelson's official letter books covering the period when he was Commander-in-Chief Mediterranean in 1803–05. But, on occasion, it would appear that Nicolas omitted letters because he felt their content was 'ephemeral'. A notable example is a short letter containing some mock 'operational orders' written by Nelson to his nephew Horatio in late 1800:

> Mr Horatio Nelson
> You are directed to come here and bring with you Mrs Nelson & your Sister. This is a positive order
> Nelson
> Lord Nelson begs Mrs Nelson will allow the party to comply with my directions[45]

We know that Nicolas saw the file containing this letter, since he printed letters on either side of it omitting only this one.

Then, there are letters that Nicolas was not even aware existed. Most important in this category are Nelson's Public Order Books, none of which were seen by Nicolas. Three such books have so far been located – one for the period 1798/99 while he was in command in the Mediterranean;[46] one for the Baltic campaign of 1801,[47] and another for the Channel campaign of the same year.[48] They give illuminating glimpses of Nelson exercising command on a daily basis and, because of their immediacy, conjure up his leadership style vividly. Here he is addressing his widely scattered forces shortly after taking up the Channel command:

> Whenever the Enemy can be discovered they are to be closed with and attacked with all the Vigor which is possible and as they will be followed by our own Ships & Vessels from their own Ports it is hoped that their diabolical design of burning and laying waste our Country will be frustrated & not one of them should be able to land on British soil.

> As much of our success must depend on the cordial unanimity of every person I strongly recommend that no little jealousy of Seniority should be allowed to creep into our Minds but that the directions of the Senior Officer or the judicious plans of the Senior should be adopted with the greatest cheerfulness.

As it is impossible that I can be at all times in every part of my extensive Command I rely with confidence on the Judgement and Support of every Individual under my Command and I can assure them of my readiness to represent their Services in the strongest point of view to the Admiralty.[49]

Other material that Nicolas did not see has been found, thanks to modern electronic cataloguing, in the archives of people not obviously associated with Nelson. So, for example, a letter was found in the British Library to General Sir Robert Wilson in which Nelson succinctly sums up his approach to leadership:

The very handsome manner you are pleased to speak of my Services demands my warmest thanks. Your gallant and ever to be lamented Chief[50] proved in the manner he fell what an old French general said when ask'd what made a good or bad general. He replied two words – *Allons* – *Allez*. Your Chief & myself have taken the first and Victory followed, and the medal which you so deservingly wear proves that you have imbibed the same sentiments.[51]

By far the most significant omission from Nicolas is the material contained in the 'pressed copy' books of Nelson's correspondence during his time in command of the Mediterranean Fleet in 1803–05, now in the British Library.[52] Detailed analysis of the contents of these books, and comparison with Nelson's official letter books, has demonstrated that they include material that Nelson regarded as secret or private and which was therefore not copied into the official books. So, since Nicolas did not use the pressed copy books (presumably believing that they were simply duplicates of the official books), he missed crucial correspondence for a period that is arguably the most important in Nelson's career.[53] Despite these limitations, Nicolas's *Dispatches* is still an invaluable tool for biographers and those who study Nelson. But the work has acquired a legend of its own and, if we are to obtain the maximum benefit from it, we need to strip away that legend and see his great book for what it is – a mid-nineteenth-century construct, giving a consciously mid-nineteenth-century view of Nelson.

III

The third stage in the development of the Nelson Legend was the evolution of traditional ways of celebrating Trafalgar Day. Two main focal points for such celebrations emerged: Trafalgar Square in London and HMS *Victory* in Portsmouth. The story of the development of the ceremonies in the square belong to the latter half of the nineteenth century and so are outside the scope of this chapter.[54] But the involvement of the *Victory* began much earlier.

Finally placed in reserve in 1812, after over fifty years in almost continual active service, the *Victory* remained 'in ordinary' in Portsmouth until the early 1820s, when it seemed likely that she would be broken up. Sentiment prevailed however and, instead, in 1824, a new role was found for her as the flagship of the Port Admiral in Portsmouth. She was moved to moorings off Gosport where she remained for almost a hundred years. Increasingly, she became more of a tourist attraction than a serving warship, although she continued to be manned by naval personnel.[55] By the 1840s, the custom was established of dressing the ship overall on Trafalgar Day, and hoisting laurel wreaths between her masts as a sign of mourning for Nelson. In 1844, Queen Victoria was in Portsmouth *en route* from a stay in her new palace of Osborne, on the Isle of Wight and, noticing the old ship decorated in this way, she asked the reason. On being reminded that it was Trafalgar Day she decided to go on board and was conducted all over the ship, including the quarterdeck, where a laurel wreath had been placed on the plaque marking the spot where Nelson fell. She stood for a moment in silent homage and then plucked a leaf from the wreath as a memento.[56]

Two years later, in 1846, another Trafalgar Day tradition was established when John Pasco, formerly the *Victory's* signal lieutenant who had organised the hoisting of Nelson's famous signal, 'England Expects Every Man Will Do His Duty', became the ship's captain. He held a dinner on board to which survivors of the battle were invited and, according to the report in *The Times* a toast to 'The immortal memory of Nelson and those who fell with him' was drunk immediately after the Loyal Toast.[57] At about the same time – the exact date is not known – the custom of dressing the *Victory* overall on Trafalgar Day was replaced with the tradition of hoisting the flags of Nelson's 'England Expects' signal. On the day of the battle, the signal had been sent two words at a time, in six separate 'hoists', but for the commemoration, a method was devised of flying the whole signal at once from every available yardarm.

All these customs continue to be practised on board the *Victory* on Trafalgar Day. The ship flies Nelson's signal throughout the day and wreaths are suspended between the masts. In the morning the Royal Navy holds a special service on board, during which Nelson's prayer is read out and a laurel wreath is laid on the quarterdeck plaque by the senior admiral present. In the evening, a formal dinner is held in Nelson's cabin at which the toast to 'The Immortal Memory' is still drunk. Indeed, the custom, of holding a special Trafalgar Dinner has now spread to all ships and shore establishments in the Royal Navy – and even to foreign navies, and civilian organisations as well.

So, by 1850, all the main components of the Nelson Legend were in place: enshrined in influential books, made visible through famous paintings and monuments and sacramentalised in formal ceremonies.

IV

At about 2.30 in the afternoon of 21 October 1805, Captain Thomas Hardy paid the first of two visits to the dying Nelson in the *Victory*'s cockpit. Having given some operational instructions, then Nelson asked his friend to come closer and whispered, 'Pray let my dear Lady Hamilton have my hair and all other things belonging to me' (see Plate 12).[58] Even in death, Nelson was still subverting the rules – in this case the rules of inheritance. While it was fair enough to ask Hardy to give Emma his hair, strictly speaking 'all other things belonging to me' should have been handed over to his legal heir, his elder brother William. In fact Hardy obeyed his chief's instructions and delivered all Nelson's personal belongings to Emma – including the uniform coat that he had been wearing when he was shot. The young son of a Merton neighbour of Emma Hamilton's, Lionel Goldsmith, was taken to see her shortly after the news of Trafalgar reached England and he remembered seeing her in bed with Nelson's letters strewn around her, and the coat lying on the bed beside her, 'the hole where the bullet passed through stiffened with congealed blood'.[59] There ensued an unseemly wrangle with Earl William, who recognised the coat's importance as a relic and wanted to have it to display in the grand house that he eventually purchased with a grant from parliament. But Emma clung on to it and eventually it passed to another of her neighbours, Alderman William Smith in settlement of some of her debts.

In 1844, Sir Nicholas Harris Nicolas heard of its existence and opened negotiations with Smith's widow with a view to acquiring it for the nation. He was about to launch a public appeal to raise funds to purchase the coat when the matter came to the notice of Prince Albert who advanced the £150 required out of his own pocket and presented it to the Greenwich Hospital.[60] It was placed in the Naval Gallery in the Painted Hall, where it at once became the star attraction and it has remained on public display almost constantly ever since, becoming, in the process the most iconic of all the Nelson relics (see Plate 25). In 1891 it was lent to the great Naval Exhibition in Chelsea, where it once again proved one of the most popular items on display[61] and it also featured in a special centenary exhibition in 1905. In 2005, from July to November, it will be one of the central items in the National Maritime Museum's special bicentenary exhibition, *Nelson & Napoléon* reunited, briefly, with the bullet that made the neat hole in the left shoulder, which is now in the Royal Collection.

So, we can see the same process at work that we traced with Nelson's prayer. Nelson (assisted by Emma) ensures that the Trafalgar coat survives; the Establishment recognises its importance and elevates it to the status of holy relic and it then becomes a cornerstone of the Nelson tradition and a talismanic centrepiece at celebratory events.

In January 1804, Nelson wrote to Count Waltersdorff, a Danish diplomat whom he had met and befriended during the 1801 Baltic campaign: 'If we have talents we have no right to keep them under a bushel, they are ours for the benefit of the Community.'[62] Certainly he did not hide his talents – nor did his contemporaries and, together, they created a Legend that has indeed been of great 'benefit to the Community' in the past. As we stand at the beginning of the bicentenary year, it is appropriate for us carefully to examine, and fully to understand, how the Legend has evolved, so that it can continue to be of benefit to our community, both now and in the future.

Notes

1. For facsimiles of both versions of the prayer, together with a discussion of their provenance, see O. Warner, *Nelson's Last Diary* (London: Seeley Service, 1971).
2. The coat is now in the collection of the National Maritime Museum.
3. The phrase 'The Nelson Legend' was first coined by me in an unpublished public lecture at the Royal Naval Museum in September 1994, 'The Immortal Memory: the development of the Nelson Legend.' It was subsequently examined in more depth in 'The Immortal Memory' in my *Nelson Companion* (Stroud: Sutton, 1995). Hereafter cited as White, *Companion*.
4. For a fuller discussion of Nelson's leadership style, see my *Nelson – the New Letters* (London: Boydell and Brewer, 2005). Hereafter cited as White, *Letters*.
5. See, for example, T. Coleman, *Nelson* (London: Bloomsbury, 2001), p. 320. Hereafter cited as Coleman.
6. Nicholas Harris Nicolas, *The Dispatches and Letters of Lord Nelson* (London, 1844/6), vol. VII, p. 349. Hereafter cited as Nicolas.
7. T. Pocock, *Horatio Nelson* (London: Bodley Head, 1987), p. 242.
8. Nelson to Spencer, 19 July 1799. British Library: Add Mss 75832 f. 40.

9. Dudley Pope, *The Great Gamble* (London: Weidenfeld and Nicolson, 1972).

10. See White, *Letters*.

11. Nelson to Locker, 21 February 1797. Nicolas, II, pp. 354/5.

12. For a fuller discussion of Nelson's account of St Vincent, and the controversy it caused, see my *1797: Nelson's Year of Destiny* (Stroud: Sutton, 1998).

13. Nelson to Fittler, 15 October 1802. Nelson Museum, Monmouth, E123.

14. Nelson to Buttersworth, 1802. British Library: Add Mss 34902.

15. Nelson to Thomas Forsyth, 2 February 1802. Quoted in Richard Walker, *The Nelson Portraits* (Portsmouth, 1999), p. 248.

16. The article appears in Volume III of *The Naval Chronicle* (January–June 1800), pp. 157–88.

17. Nelson to Captain Sneedorf, 12 April 1801. Printed in *The Naval Review*, 1951, p. 243.

18. Nelson to Emma Hamilton, 4 June 1805. Nelson Museum, Monmouth, E167.

19. James Harrison, *The Life of Horatio Lord Viscount Nelson of the Nile* (London, 1806), vol. II, p. 458.

20. For a fuller analysis of Emma's role as curator, see my 'Emma Hamilton and the Making of the Nelson Legend', *The Trafalgar Chronicle*, 5 (1995).

21. Royal Naval Museum, 1957/84. The christening cup is also in the museum's collection (1957/60).

22. Marianne Czisnik, 'Nelson and the Nile: The Creation of Admiral Nelson's Public Image', *Mariners Mirror*, 88 (2002).

23. For an examination of the reasons for Nelson's appointment see my 'The Public Order Book of Vice Admiral Lord Nelson', in M. Duffy, *The Naval Miscellany*, vol. VI (Navy Records Society, 2003).

24. For a full description of the funeral ceremonies, see my 'The Immortal Memory', in White, *Companion*. The music and words of the service have been recorded by Portsmouth Cathedral Choir and issued on CD by Herald. Herald HAVPCD 232.

25. T. Jenks, 'Contesting the Hero: The Funeral of Admiral Lord Nelson', *JBS*, 39 (2000).

26. J.S. Clarke and J. M'Arthur, *The Life of Admiral Lord Nelson*, 2 vols (London, 1809).

27. This reconstruction of the controversy is based on the papers of John M'Arthur, now in the Rosenbach Library in Philadelphia. Msf 1073/12.

28. Frances Nelson to John M'Arthur, December 1806. Rosenbach Library, Msf 1073/12.

29. The process was started by Coleman and has been ably continued, and greatly expanded, by John Sugden in *Nelson: A Dream of Glory* (London: Jonathan Cape, 2004).

30. West contributed two paintings; Pocock six and Westall five. All are now in the National Maritime Museum.

31. These are: Encounter with a polar bear; Boarding a captured ship; The capture of the *San Nicolas*; The boat action at Cadiz and Nelson wounded at Tenerife.

32. From the title page of the first edition.

33. The Nelson Letters Project was commissioned by the Royal Naval Museum in 1999 and has continued in partnership with the National Maritime Museum

since 2001. Its aim is to locate and transcribe all unpublished Nelson letters. To date 1,400 letters have been located, of which some 900 have been transcribed. For a full report on the Project, see my article, 'The Nelson Letters Project', *Mariners Mirror*, 89 (2003).

34. See: White, *Letters*. The original letters are now in the British Library (Add Mss 46356), the National Maritime Museum (AGC/27) and the private collection of Mr Clive Richards.
35. Nelson to Clarence, 4 April 1801. BL: Add Mss 46356 f. 37.
36. Nelson to Clarence, 26 May 1797. NMM: AGC/27/ 24.
37. Huntington Library: HM 34181.
38. For an excellent exposition on Southey's shortcomings, and corrections of his main mistakes, see the edition edited by G. Callender (London, 1922). See also: D. Eastwood, 'Patriotism Personified: Robert Southey's *Life of Nelson* Reconsidered', *Mariners Mirror*, 77 (1991).
39. I am indebted to my colleague Pieter van der Merwe for drawing my attention to the Naval Gallery. For more details about the Gallery's formation and contents see, P. van der Merwe, 'The Naval Gallery of 1824–1936 and the Greenwich Hospital Art Collection', *Maritime Art Greenwich* <www.nmm.ac.uk/mag>.
40. The public ones were at: Portsmouth, Glasgow, Edinburgh, Liverpool, Dublin, Great Yarmouth, Birmingham, Hereford, St Paul's Cathedral, The London Guildhall, Montreal and Barbados. For a full examination of the design and construction of these, and details of the privately erected monuments, see, Flora Fraser, 'If You Seek His Monument', in White, *Companion*.
41. C. Oman, *Nelson* (London, 1947), p. xv.
42. For example by E. Vincent, *Nelson: Love & Fame* (New Haven: Yale University Press, 2003) who lists Nicolas among the 'Primary Sources' in his bibliography.
43. For a full analysis of Nicolas's omissions, see White, *Letters*.
44. Devon Records Office: 152M/C1803/ON33.
45. Nelson to Horatio Nelson (undated). BL: Add Mss 34988 f. 356.
46. BL: Add Mss 30260.
47. Danish State Archive, Copenhagen: D/173.
48. Royal Naval Museum (Admiralty Library): MS200.
49. Danish State Archive: D/173.
50. General Sir Ralph Abercrombie, to whom Wilson had been second in command in the Egyptian campaign of 1801. Abercrombie was killed in action at the Battle of Aboukir on 8 March 1801.
51. Nelson to Sir Robert Wilson, 23 December 1802. BL: Add Mss 30114 f. 1/2.
52. They are BL: Add Mss 34950–34960.
53. So, for example, some of the new material in the pressed copy books relates to intelligence and diplomacy – including secret letters relating to Nelson's dealings with the supposedly neutral Kingdom of Sardinia.
54. For an examination of the development of the square as a centre for public events see, R. Mace, *Trafalgar Square, Emblem of Empire* (London: Lawrence and Wishart, 1976).
55. For an examination of the *Victory*'s transformation into a symbolic relic, see K. Fenwick, *HMS Victory* (London: Cassell, 1959) and A. McGowan, *HMS Victory – Her Construction, Career and Restoration* (London: Chatham, 1999).

56. Fenwick, *HMS Victory*, p. 348.
57. White, *Companion*, p. 17.
58. 'Narrative of the Death of Lord Nelson', by William Beatty, quoted in Nicolas, VII, p. 248.
59. Quoted in Flora Fraser, *Beloved Emma* (London: John Murray, 2003), pp. 317–18.
60. See Nicolas, VII, pp. 347–52.
61. Huw Lewis-Jones, 'Displaying Nelson: Navalism and the Exhibition of 1891', *Trafalgar Chronicle*, 14 (2004).
62. Huntington Library: HM 23793.

6

Nelson Entombed: The Military and Naval Pantheon in St Paul's Cathedral

Holger Hoock

Shortly before 1 o'clock in the afternoon of 9 January 1806, infantry bands and cavalry trumpets heralded the imminent arrival of Admiral Lord Nelson's funeral procession at St Paul's Cathedral in the City of London (see Plate 26).[1] Here was to end the journey of Britain's pre-eminent naval hero, who had travelled from the vicarage of his lowly clergyman father in the Norfolk village of Burnham Thorpe to the triumphant victories of the Nile, Copenhagen, and Trafalgar. From there, Nelson's body, preserved in a large cask filled with brandy, had made its way on the admiral's flagship the *Victory* via Gibraltar, where it was embalmed, to the Painted Hall at Greenwich. The body lay in a coffin made from pieces of the mainmast of the French flagship at the Battle of the Nile, *l'Orient*, encased in further coffins of lead and elm. An outer coffin of mahogany was covered in black Genoa velvet and divided by countless double-gilt nails into several compartments containing designs of Grief, Fame, Nelson's crests, a sphinx, and a crocodile. Over three days, 100,000 mourners filed past Nelson in the vast, heavily ornamented mourning chamber.

On 8 January, with muffled drums and pipes playing the dead march from Handel's *Saul*, a two mile procession of black-draped boats, rowing against a strong south-westerly gale, escorted the coffin underneath a canopy topped with ostrich feathers in one of the king's barges up the Thames, past St Paul's and to the Whitehall Stairs, whence it was taken to the Admiralty for the night. The following morning, polite spectators filled the windows in the Strand; a solemn crowd of several tens of thousand lined the streets from Whitehall to Ludgate Hill. Minute-guns boomed as 'a formidable army'[2] of some ten thousand troops – together with Greenwich Pensioners, seamen and marines of the *Victory*, thirty-one admirals, one hundred captains, cabinet ministers, the Lord Mayor of London, noblemen, and seven royal princes, led by the heir to the throne, accompanied Nelson's funeral car to St Paul's. In a striking alteration of heraldic protocol, Sir Peter Parker, Admiral of the Fleet, instead of a member of Nelson's family, had been chosen chief mourner, to signify the Navy's importance to the state and continued British naval superiority. Since 11.00am, the tiers of seats in the dome and choir area of the Cathedral had been filled by ticket holders (see Plate 27). At the end of the four-hour-long burial service, as night was falling over wintry London, the Garter King at Arms proclaimed the style, titles, and dignities of the deceased peer, ending, unusually and dramatically, with the exclamation: 'the Hero, who, in the moment of victory, fell covered with immortal glory'. After the choirs of St Paul's, Westminster Abbey, the Chapel Royal, and St George's Chapel, Windsor, had sang *His body is buried in peace* (G.F. Handel, adapted by T. Attwood), at 5.33pm a concealed lift lowered the coffin into the crypt. There it would be laid in an extravagant Renaissance sarcophagus of black marble, originally designed for Cardinal Woolsey and later intended for Henry VIII. Nelson's coronet was placed on top of the sarcophagus, which rested on a pedestal also taken from Woolsey's tomb-house at Windsor. Below, within a base of coarse masonry, the coffin was enclosed (see Plate 28).

Three weeks after the funeral, parliament decided to erect a monument to Nelson in St Paul's (Fig. 6.1). In John Flaxman's massive pyramidical design, a larger than life-sized figure of Nelson, dressed in the pelisse which the admiral had received from the Grand Signor, leans on an anchor, with a coil of rope beside.[3] Beneath, on his right, Britannia directs the attention of two young seamen to the great example of Nelson. On the left, the obligatory, crouching British lion guards the monument. The figures on the pedestal represent the North Sea, Nile, and Mediterranean. The names of Nelson's greatest battles – COPENHAGEN, NILE, TRAFALGAR – are inscribed on the cornice. The main inscription reads:

ERECTED AT THE PUBLIC EXPENSE

TO THE MEMORY OF

VICE-ADMIRAL HORATIO VISCOUNT NELSON, KB

TO RECORD HIS SPLENDID AND UNPARALLELED ACHIEVEMENTS

DURING A LIFE SPENT IN THE SERVICE OF HIS COUNTRY,

AND TERMINATED IN THE MOMENT OF VICTORY BY A GLORIOUS DEATH

IN THE MEMORABLE ACTION OFF CAPE TRAFALGAR,

ON THE XXI OF OCTOBER MDCCCV.

Figure 6.1 *Monument to Lord Nelson* John Flaxman, 1808–18, Conway Library, Courtauld Institute of Art, London.

Nelson was the only British war hero who fell in the French and Napoleonic wars to be granted a state funeral. But when he was buried in St Paul's in January 1806, he joined a rapidly growing pantheon of naval and military officers. Since the outbreak of hostilities with France in 1793, a rage for heroes had taken hold of the British national imagination. It was now fast filling St Paul's with monuments. By the time Flaxman's Nelson monument was finally unveiled in 1818, parliament had commissioned over thirty monuments at St Paul's. These included some of Nelson's fellow officers in the amphibious West Indian operations of the mid-1790s and at St Vincent, Aboukir, Copenhagen, and Trafalgar, as well as statues of outstanding army officers. In this chapter I will put Nelson's funeral, his tomb, and monument into the context of the histories of national commemoration and the cult of the hero in the French Revolutionary and Napoleonic period. In particular, I will examine the discrepancies between the wider discourse about heroic Nelson and the concepts and practices underlying the St Paul's pantheon, as well as the tensions and ambiguities inherent to building a military pantheon in the Cathedral.[4]

I

When the Secretary of State for War, Castlereagh, proposed the monument to Nelson in the House of Commons, he stressed Nelson's importance as an example: whilst alive, he had inspired his fellow officers. As a dead hero, he provided a 'model for his profession to study', a model whose life and achievements 'would continue to animate the British navy to the end of time'.[5] The end of time. Nelson's funeral was a terminus, but it was also a catalyst, at once marking his mortality and consecrating him as an immortal, great man: 'His body is buried in peace, but his name liveth evermore', sang the choir, just before the coffin was lowered into the crypt. Nelson's natural, mortal body was buried. His social body, his place in society, his name, were to live on in the collective memory of the nation. The monument in St Paul's not only marked Nelson's burial place, but it also, and perhaps more importantly, balanced the ephemeral, transient nature of the funereal spectacle. It was to preserve the image of Nelson's social body, his example and reputation, for eternity.

Since antiquity, the contemplation of the images of exemplary men had been central to the formation of moral communities, particular veneration being reserved for those who sacrificed themselves for the public good, especially military leaders. By the eighteenth century, the term 'pantheon' had come to refer to a collection of 'great', exemplary men of a society or nation, and the physical site of their representation. A pantheon was thus a particularly potent manifestation of the national monument. This seeks to perpetuate a moment in a nation's history, an event, a person or group of persons, and thus to encapsulate national identity in a permanent symbol.[6] In the case of the St Paul's pantheon, the hope was that by highlighting patriotic, heroic, and chivalric values, public sculpture commemorating naval and military achievements would foster emulation. Sculpture was considered the pedagogically most effective form of public art: the solid marble promised eternity; the medium forced the artist to focus on one single expressive gesture; as a three-dimensional form sculpture was more life-like than painting; and monuments were easy to set in scene in ceremonies staged around them.

But was it not in Westminster Abbey where the nation buried and commemorated its great men – prime ministers and warriors, explorers and men of science, composers and poets? In fact, among the scores of eighteenth-century monuments in the Abbey, only five were voted by parliament as truly national monuments of naval, military, and political worthies, including the elder Pitt, Earl of Chatham, and General Wolfe. The vast majority even of the naval and military monuments were privately commissioned; many in fact commemorated officers who had seen little or no active service at all, and died away from the battlefield. The Dean and Chapter allocated monumental spots as part of their social patronage and were often accused of being unworthy of representing the nation in composing a national pantheon.[7]

St Paul's Cathedral meanwhile, a city church, not a royal peculiar like Westminster Abbey, was also a public space at least in the sense that it was included in London tours and charged twopence each for the view of specific sights such as the Great Model or the Geometrical Staircase.[8] Between the victories at Blenheim and Trafalgar, it also became 'the setting of choice for the celebration and commemoration of national events'.[9] For theological reasons, St Paul's was initially devoid of monuments or decoration, apart from Sir James Thornhill's scenes from the life of St Paul, barely visible high up in the cupola. It was only when Westminster Abbey became overcrowded with monuments, and with theological objections to certain kinds of art in churches subsiding, that in 1791 the Cathedral authorities finally decided to admit statues into St Paul's as well. Within two years of the outbreak of war with France in 1793, the state appropriated St Paul's to create an official British naval and military pantheon.[10]

This was a completely different affair from monument building by private individuals in Westminster Abbey: the new pantheon reflected and fostered changing attitudes of the state to commemoration, heroism, and public art. Now the state sponsored a national programme of commemoration, carried out by native artists, with the Treasury insisting that national monuments 'should be the best Testimonies of the Taste of the age in which such works are executed'.[11] National military monuments became part of Britain's war-effort – the pursuit of war by different means, 'the cheap defence of nations', as the *Monthly Magazine* put it.[12] The St Paul's pantheon thus represents a unique and coherent effort on the part of the British state at the Napoleonic-era peak of fiscal-military expansion to sponsor a site of loyalist national commemoration, and to inculcate notions of patriotic dedication and sacrifice, both in the armed forces and the wider public.

In contrast to the indiscriminate cluttering of Westminster Abbey, state control meant that this new group of monuments could be developed as a spatially coherent ensemble of eventually thirty-two in all, commissioned by parliament in 1794–1823 at a total cost of some £110,000.[13] To that end, the Royal Academy of Arts, in tense collaboration with a Treasury-appointed connoisseurial Committee of Taste, organised competitions, selected designs, and chose positions for the monuments. Initially at least, military rank dictated the value of a commission: admirals and generals were worth 6,000 guineas, captains 4,000 guineas. All monuments were erected in the north and south transepts and the entrance to the choir – largely maintaining symmetries both of military rank and of type of monument, both within and across the transepts. The highest-ranking officers, Nelson and Cornwallis, were allocated the most prominent spaces against the two great piers on the north and south sides of the great eastern arch between the dome and the choir. In a juxtaposition of Trafalgar casualties, they were overlooked by Nelson's captains Cooke and Duff.

II

We have already encountered a range of officers pantheonised in St Paul's. But what were the criteria by which they were chosen? We can reconstruct these by relating battle histories and reports of the circumstances of the deaths of military personnel to the parliamentary debates about monumental honours. First, commanding officers dying at the moment of victory were honoured with monuments to commemorate their leadership, strategic skills, or cautious foresight, and their function as role models for subordinate officers, crews, and troops: Abercromby, Nelson, Cornwallis, Moore. Commanders who survived important battles and died either peacefully, whether in active service or in retirement, or in later, less important action, were honoured with monuments as lifetime achievement awards, such as Admirals Rodney and Howe. The highest ranking junior officers killed in a significant battle often received a monument if all superior commanders survived, and very rarely alongside their fallen commanders. On 1 June 1794, the highest ranking casualty was Captain James Montague of HMS *Montague*, whilst

Admirals Bowyer and Pasley only lost one limb each.[14] This first group of monuments was thus an extension of the traditional system of honours and promotions awarded by the crown and government. As with peerages and medals, reward here was a function primarily of military rank, and only secondarily of the specific merit of the individual honoured.

A second group of monuments commemorates the spectacularly brave, gallant, (and often recklessly suicidal) actions of individuals, especially young captains, who managed to fall 'in the moment of victory'. Whilst increasingly organised warfare placed simple obedience over individual heroism, these monuments reflect a more general revival of militaristic and chivalric ideals among the British elite. It was fed by a public school education emphasising competitive physical hardiness, aggressive manliness, and a classical curriculum (instilled with the birch rod), which glorified the heroic and patriotic achievements of men of rank. With this second category of monuments the male elite in parliament (with a significant naval and military element amongst them) adopted a muscular pose and admitted individual military bravura into the pantheon.

Several topoi were common to both groups – to exemplary commanders-in-chief *and* reckless frigate captains – notions such as precise heroic timing, defeating a numerically superior enemy, and bodily sacrifice. In all of this, Nelson was an archetype. The topos of commanding officers dying 'at the moment of victory' relates the St Paul's pantheon to an important trope in the code of the warrior hero. Though mortally wounded, he would continue fighting, in an almost super-human fashion, to present an example and leadership to his men. If eventually he had to die, this was only after witnessing the victory he had delivered. Nelson's death 'at the moment of victory' was referred to with unrelenting repetition in the proclamation of his titles at the funeral, parliamentary resolutions, the inscriptions on his many monuments, and his early memoirs.[15] The American traveller Benjamin Silliman, who was in the Admiralty in London when he heard the news of Trafalgar, recorded stereotypically: 'He lived to hear victory declared, expressed his resignation to death, sent his farewell to Admiral Collingwood, and expired.'[16] The poet Robert Southey further dramatised the hero's prolonged death:

> Once, amidst his sufferings, Nelson had expressed a wish that he were dead; but immediately the spirit subdued the pains of death, and he wished to live a little longer; – doubtless that he might hear the completion of the victory which he had seen so gloriously begun. That consolation – that joy – that triumph, was afforded him. He lived to

know that the victory was decisive; and the last guns which were fired at the flying enemy, were heard a minute or two before he expired.[17]

The pantheonised officers – admirals and captains, generals and brigade commanders – were further connected by the notion of accumulated bodily sacrifice, heroically sustained. Admiral Collingwood defined pension prospects in the Navy in terms of bodily loss: no man received a pension unless he had lost a limb or 'knock'd off many from his enemy'.[18] The model of the cumulatively mutilated body was again Nelson's.[19] Attention to the wounds and disfigurements which Nelson suffered was one of the main motifs in terms of which his life was understood, both during his life – as Kathleen Wilson shows in her chapter – and after his death.[20] Poets rhapsodised on Nelson's 'nobly mutilated form', his 'mangled form', his body 'Lopp'd, batter'd, and broke'.[21] A footnote in the anonymous publication *Victory in Tears; or, The Shade of Nelson* of 1805 considered Nelson's body as a site of interaction between the hero and his audience, the nation:

> his countrymen beheld his wounds with grateful reverence; they considered him, like a defensive tower on the frontiers of their safety, which long exposed to the blasts of war, had suffered in its outworks, and been somewhat dismantled by the storm; the security it had afforded, endeared to them its dilapidations; it derived a new character of interest from every injury; and with the most depressing emotions of gratitude and regret, they have seen it at length shaken to its foundations, and leveled to the ground.[22]

Nelson's perseverance was seen to be encouraging officers, marines, and sailors, who identified specifically with the admiral's body. Anecdotes abound – most of them highly formulaic tales in newspapers, memoirs, and plays – of the horrifically wounded, brave patriotic 'sons of Neptune', waiting for their turn at the surgeon's and merrily singing *Rule Britannia* during amputations of arms and legs. A seaman on the *Victory* was reported to remark while his arm was being amputated: 'Well, this by some would be considered a misfortune, but I shall be proud of it, as I shall resemble the more our brave Commander in Chief.'[23] Association by amputation was only surpassed by simultaneous death. James West, a fore-mast man onboard HMS *Britannia* reported the deaths of several messmates to relatives at home: 'Pray, inform their poor friends of their death, and remind them that they died at the same time as Nelson, and in the moment of glorious victory!'[24] Here was a tar using the same language that parliament deployed in honouring the heroic timing of officers. Indeed, contemporary battle accounts, prints, and ballads made much of the heroic mind-set and actions of ordinary fighting men and presented victory as a triumph of British valour shared by all ranks (in the armed forces and society at large).

Even the President of the Royal Academy, Benjamin West, fostered this trend. West displayed *The Death of Lord Nelson* allegedly to thousands of people at his house during 1806, and certainly to some sixty thousand at the Royal Academy in 1811 (Plate 29). The painting includes portraits of ordinary seamen, some of whom are identified in an engraved key which accompanied the publication of James Heath's engraving of the picture in 1811: no. 8, it says, 'James Berkan, Seaman'; no. 53, 'Drummond, a Seaman'; no. 58, 'Sanders, a Powder Boy'; and no. 25, 'Saunders, a seaman', seen very prominently in the right foreground kneeling before Nelson and laying a Spanish flag at his feet.

But if we revisit Nelson's national monument: there is no acknowledgement of heroic tars, of ordinary sailors' participation in the hero's achievement, nor even tars witnessing his deeds – only the next generation, the two young midshipmen, being brought to learn from the now dead hero's example. Nelson's statue in this sense is no exception in St Paul's. The heroic was never admitted into the pantheon below the rank of captain and, in the army, major-general. Only half a dozen out of the over thirty Napoleonic-era monuments in St Paul's include representations of ordinary soldiers or sailors. These all stand in a position subordinate to the genteel officer heroes. The wounded General Abercromby, for instance, falling from his horse, is caught by a Highland foot soldier who stands in a literally supportive and hierarchical relationship to his genteel equestrian officer. Similarly, several other monuments to officers include mourning Tars and Tommies as exhortative figures: they appeal to an inclusive community of addressees, and acknowledge the ordinary serviceman's presence, though without elevating him to the status of the hero. For example, in the monument of Captain Duff a bare-chested, kneeling tar is sobbing over the captain's tomb.[25] Maria Hackett in her *Popular Account of St Paul's* identified the male figure helping to lay General Sir John Moore to rest in Charles Rossi's monument as a Spanish soldier. Another author however thought it represented Valour. The confusion or conflation of ordinary servicemen with allegorical figures neatly reflects the insecure status of the former.[26]

Even the occasional inclusion of soldiers and sailors in these monuments marks a departure from earlier commemorative practice. It may reflect the notion that a leader's relationship with his men increasingly counted towards his status as a public hero. Captain Duff had a reputation for being regarded with particular affection by his crew; this had apparently prevented them from joining the mutiny in 1797.[27] Similarly, many accounts stressed Nelson's paternal care for his crew.[28] Nevertheless, there are no isolated figures of ordinary servicemen in St Paul's, neither did parliament ever move before 1815 to approve a general war monument to all the fallen and veterans of any battle, as they were being built in Revolutionary France and even in Prussia and Habsburg Austria. In Britain, the ruling orders clearly remained uneasy about the political ambiguities that general battle honours and a more democratic commemorative culture might have been seen to carry, and which could have been exploited by those like Major Cartwright who demanded political participation for all fighting men. An expanded concept of the state's acknowledgement of the heroic still extended only so far.[29]

III

It will have become clear by now that there are significant discrepancies between the wider discourse about heroic Nelson, and the concepts and practices underlying the St Paul's pantheon. I want to pursue some more of these discrepancies. I have made much of the corporeal heroism which served contemporaries as a framework within which to conceptualise Nelson. But if we look again at Nelson's monument in St Paul's, the sculptor almost ignored the admiral's progressive mutilations. Flaxman created a noble portrait, the slight proportions of the admiral heightened and broadened, the fur-lined cloak over the shoulder concealing the amputated arm, and both eyes intact, with the pupils incised. Nelson is presented as an idealised hero, recognisable enough, but made, or made to look, perfect.[30]

The discourse on the heroic ideal vs. historical verisimilitude had divided artists and connoisseurs ever since Benjamin West had adapted the pietà formula to a supposedly historically correct representation of the death of General Wolfe in 1771. As long as Sir Joshua Reynolds had been alive and President of the Royal Academy, he had ensured that most public sculptures with which the Academy was associated wore classical drapery or nudity rather than modern dress. By the early nineteenth century, however, modern dress was gaining ground – you will have noted the dress and attributes of naval warfare in Flaxman's Nelson. The sculptor's portraits are usually idealised. But when working on the St Paul's Nelson, Flaxman had argued the importance of faithfully portraying Nelson as lifelike and, in the interest of general accessibility, of discarding allegory:

'Divine attributes, moral virtues or national characteristics, represented by allegory, are addressed to the speculation of the philosopher, or the imagination of the poet – but ... general feelings are more gratified by the likeness of the man.'[31]

We can begin to understand Flaxman's approach by looking at a major row which had erupted over one of the earlier naval monuments in St Paul's. This was Thomas Banks' Captain Rundell Burgess, a casualty of the battle against the Dutch fleet at Camperdown in 1797 (see Fig. 6.2). The monument consists of a larger than life-size figure, with a portrait head on top of a nude body, scantily draped. The strange naked man is greeted by a winged Victory handing him a sword over a hefty cannon between them. One London guidebook of 1807 commented:

an *English* Captain of a man of war, suffering with fortitude, dying at the moment of victory? Obliterate the inscription; and who is he? Not a Briton. We have no *naked naval Captains*. If a man would redden with shame and indignation at barely being asked to enter a friend's house stripped, how is it that we dare prophane the house of God with such indecent representations? ... These *Roman* fancies are absurd to the last extreme ... in the name of propriety, let future statues for St Paul's be Britons in their features, their actions, and their habits.[32]

Alan Cunningham, biographer of British artists, was also outraged: 'every-day noses and chins must not be supported on bodies moulded according to the godlike proportions of the Greek statues ... no British warriors go naked into battle'. The lack of decency was problematic even after Banks conceded to clerical delicacy an extra handbreadth of drapery: among the ladies visiting 'the flutter of fans and the averting of faces was prodigious'. Cunningham was also concerned with the intelligibility of monuments: 'That Victory, a modest and well-draped dame, should approach an undrest dying man, and crown him with laurel, might be endured – but how a well-dressed young lady could think of presenting a sword to a naked gentleman went far beyond all their notions of propriety.'[33] Contemporary psychology taught that the power of association was the greater, the lesser the distractions from the connections between ideas: Cunningham made his point by (deliberately) confusing allegory and realism in captain and goddess.

In brief, realistic portrait busts and statues were at odds with the aesthetic demand for works embodying the qualities of classical Greek sculpture. Half-naked representations of modern man in a church were considered indecent by many. Realistic sculpture at least ensured

Figure 6.2   Monument to Captain Burgess, St Paul's Cathedral, London Thomas Banks R.A., 1798–1802, Conway Library, Courtauld Institute of Art, London.

that the wider public could more easily recognise their heroes by their appearance and specific physical characteristics. The mixture of realistic and idealising elements à la Burgess stood the risk of being dismissed as both aesthetically unsatisfactory and didactically ineffective. Flaxman, it seems, sought a different compromise between the realistic and the ideal, avoiding any classical nudity or allegory in the main figure, but idealising Nelson by making his mutilated body 'whole' again.

There is one other route by which can we approach the design. Since the mid-eighteenth century, artists and writers in Britain had conflated military manliness and sensibility. Representations of British soldiery and imperialism often emphasised decorous manly sentiment, compassionate battlefield clemency, and magnanimity in victory, rather than aggressive and bombastic virility.[34] Kathleen Wilson rightly argues in her contribution to this collection that the living Nelson represented a masculine, aggressive, conquering patriotism. But the ideal of the humane, compassionate British warrior also survived the return of those more aggressive militaristic notions in the 1790s. Wordsworth's 'Happy Warrior' – composed around the time of Nelson's funeral, and published in 1807 – was strong and brave, yet selfless, gentle, and compassionate, transmuting the horrors of war to 'glorious gain'.[35] So, there was a tradition of *not* representing corporeal heroism and the horrors of battle in eighteenth-century British martial imagery. But then, other images of Nelson did of course acknowledge his mutilations and his death in bloody battle. Denis Dighton's *The Fall of Nelson, Battle of Trafalgar, 21 October 1805*, painted in the 1820s, shows the 'fin' and some blood, while the fin is also prominent in Sir Richard Westmacott's monument in Birmingham.

To explain Flaxman's Nelson we need to look again more closely at its site, St Paul's, and the other monuments there. It seems that in their designs for Cathedral monuments, sculptors were generally reticent in depicting naval battles (otherwise not uncommon in eighteenth-century monuments), as well as bodily mutilation. Among the fairly exceptional representations, in St Paul's, of army officers dying in battle are Sir Richard Westmacott's vivid General Abercromby and Francis Chantrey's relief commemorating General Bowes being shot in the heat of the storming of Salamanca.[36] But by and large the darker sides of naval battle and of heroic death are mostly avoided. In brief, it seems that Flaxman's design was shaped and constrained by British conventions in depicting heroes, by the pitfalls of the mixing of styles, and by the particular demands of the site.

IV

Similar ambiguities are evident in the religious contexts of the cult of the hero. Religion was both a unifying and a potentially divisive factor in British public life, in the forging of a national identity, and in the politics of national commemoration. Both supporters and opponents of the war against Revolutionary France argued from religious doctrine.[37] On Thanksgiving and Fast days, the government 'displayed its concern to benefit from both the propaganda potential of the vast network of loyalist preachers across the country, and the public legitimation of the war which theology could provide'.[38] The majority of established church ministers accepted the inevitability of war and provided theological readings in terms of divine providence protecting God's elect nation, war as a fact of life after the fall, and the need for national repentance. Clerics urged congregations and readers to conduct themselves in faith and with virtue, valour, and patriotism. Stressing that the purpose of the war was not (or not so much) personal gain and glory, but rather the protection of English or British religion, liberties, national independence, and the rights of civil society, they called for national unity and loyalty to king and country.[39] Political and spiritual opposition to the French Revolution – fear of domestic insurrection and anxiety over Church and State – fuelled their preaching. Unlike thanksgiving services and sermons, which could equally be used by dissenters to assert their loyalty, Nelson's funeral was an opportunity to assert Anglican hegemony and to stress the boundaries of the British state.[40] In any case, more dissenters than Anglicans thought that war signified divine chastisement of Britain and Europe. Some objected to war because they considered it to be evil or in opposition to liberty. Dissenters also played an important role in the wider anti-war movement.

Religious thinking both enhanced and set limits to the process of heroisation. To start with, there was strong evangelical and Methodist resistance to the celebration of earthly heroism in monuments sited in churches. James Hervey, in his widely read *Meditations among the Tombs*, showed distaste for 'bribing the vote of fame, and purchasing a little posthumous renown' for the expeditious death of a mortal in the necessary service of his country, since this was dwarfed by Christ's voluntary death for his enemies.[41] However, because there was 'sufficient common ground between the ethics of patriotic example and Christian theology', it seems that at least in wartime the formation of a naval and military pantheon within a church was tolerated.[42] In fact, when George III brought the French military banners to St Paul's for a Thanksgiving in 1797 to testify to God's protection of Britain, he was seen as imitating David laying the spoils of victory before the Temple at Jerusalem.[43] From the admission of the first monuments in 1791, some even expressed their satisfaction that the British Temple of Fame had the 'additional sanction of religion'.[44] The tension between the marble warriors and their religious receptacle was eased by the figure of the British Christian warrior, pious and humane, fielded by a free Protestant nation against, first, atheistic, barbaric, Revolutionary, and then against militaristic, Napoleonic France. Sermons preached onboard battle ships and during thanksgiving services on shore, private battle accounts, and parliamentary rhetoric commonly emphasised the 'national humanity' of British sailors saving their defeated, drowning enemies.[45] In the Trafalgar debate, Lord Castlereagh praised not only the British seamen's bravery in battle, but also the 'generous spirit of self-devotion to the benefit of their fellow-creatures, those exalted principles, which it had been the glory of ancient France to cultivate, and which it has been the endeavour of modern France to extinguish'.[46]

The darkest image of war in St Paul's was indeed of the French Revolutionary enemy, especially in John Bacon's design for the monument of Major-General Dundas, a light infantry commander who died of yellow fever on Guadeloupe in June 1794 (see Fig. 6.3). Britannia pays tribute to Dundas, accompanied by Sensibility, and 'a boy presenting an olive branch, indicating that the only just object of war, is the attainment of lasting and honourable peace'. On the plinth, the figure of Liberty flies to Britannia, to be protected by her against Anarchy, who holds a human head in one hand, and a flaming torch in the other. Anarchy is aided by Hypocrisy, whose smiling mask partly conceals a ferocious countenance.[47] The drawing also shows a sarcophagus with the General's feet protruding – a hint at the monument's raison d'être. For, within six months of Dundas's burial in Fort Matilda, the French had recaptured Guadeloupe, ordered Dundas's body to be disinterred and 'given as prey to the birds of the air', and marked his burial place by a monument: 'This ground', it said, 'restored to liberty by the valour of the Republicans, was polluted by the body of Thomas Dundas, Major-General and Governor of Guadaloupe for the bloody George III.'[48] Dundas was the only British officer who had neither died in battle, nor been a supreme commander, to enter the St Paul's pantheon: French desecration was his claim to fame.

Demonising the barbaric French enemy made it easier to glorify military action in a British church. The contrast further empowered the notion of the humane British Christian warrior. Nelson's family background and his piety were seen to reflect on the values of the British polity and nation.[49] Nelson had been 'swifter than an eagle, and stronger than a lion', possessing 'all the quickness, the force, and the boldness of these noble animals without their fierceness, tempered by humanity ... reason and wisdom'. He had displayed 'the greatest degree of courage', the 'highest sense of honour', but also a 'manly civility, urbanity of manners, and a mildness of disposition; ... his piety too was as conspicuous as his valour ... truly devout, without any tincture of enthusiasm'. Thus Richard Lendon, preaching in Pentonville, St James's, Clerkenwell, on Nelson's death, summed up the qualities of the British Christian warrior.[50] Nelson himself had promoted his image as a Christian hero. The day after the Battle of the Nile, he had given thanks to God on the quarterdeck of the *Vanguard*, then still a highly unusual public display of religion in a battle fleet.[51] Immediately before the engagement at Trafalgar, Nelson had prayed: 'May the Great God, whom I worship, grant to my Country, and for the benefit of Europe in general, a great and glorious Victory; and may no misconduct in any one tarnish it; and may humanity after Victory be the predominant feature in the British fleet.'[52]

Again, the sculptural language of Nelson's monument does not correspond readily with the wider discourse. There is no Christian iconography. Nelson is shown as if still in command on deck, in naval uniform and boat cloak – not at the moment of death or in a scene of apotheosis. In other depictions of the death of British heroes, the rituals and paraphernalia of Christian martyrdom were transferred to heroic iconography: in Benjamin West's pietà of the *Death of General Wolfe*, probably the most frequently reproduced British image of the eighteenth century; Joseph Wilton's Westminster Abbey monument of Wolfe, with the figure of a winged Fame visiting from heaven to crown Wolfe and the naked general evoking Christ at the deposition; West's design *The Apotheosis of Nelson*, virtually an altar piece, originally conceived for St Paul's, combining the three academic arts of architecture, sculpture, and painting in a tripartite allegorical memorial, with two groups of mourners – British seamen, and on the right, representatives of England, Scotland, and Ireland (see Plate 14); and the same painter's *Immortality of Nelson*, with Neptune draping the dead son over Britannia's knees, published in 1809 as the frontispiece to Clarke and M'Arthur's *Life of Nelson*, and then adapted to become the sculpted decoration on the portico of the King William block of the Royal Naval College, Greenwich; Richard Westmacott's intricate monumental apotheosis of Nelson in Liverpool, with an ungainly, 'aggressively unidealized' Nelson;[53] Arthur William Devis's *Death of Nelson*, resembling a Renaissance religious scene, with Nelson on the beam/cross, covered by a sheet/shroud, and bathed in golden light (Plate 12); and, finally, Legrand's *Apotheosis of Nelson* – showing Nelson, mourned by men on the deck of a boat and Britannia, and being received into immortality amid the gods on Olympus, among them Mars, Hercules, Minerva, and Jupiter (Plate 13).

Figure 6.3   Monument to Major-General Dundas for St Paul's Cathedral, London. John Bacon, design drawing, c.1798. National Archives.

In St Paul's itself, there are virtually no scenes of apotheosis, Captain Westmacott's monument being possibly an exception. Most monuments employ retrospective imagery, celebrating the achievements and virtues of the officers, rather than depicting death as a moment of birth, and deploying prospective imagery looking forward to an afterlife. With a sense of the horror or promise of death largely missing, the St Paul's pantheon – as a concept and in its iconography – negotiated the tensions between the different notions of a pantheon: the religious, or quasi-religious, and the secular.[54]

V

The cult of Nelson certainly assumed quasi-religious qualities. Even during his lifetime, he had been revered as a cult-figure, often described as a Greek heros occupying a position between gods and mortal man. Lord Minto declared after the Battle of St Vincent that Sir John Jervis was 'immortalised and Commodore Nelson a hero beyond Homer's' – like a Greek heros occupying a position between gods and mortal man.[55] Some poets even referred to 'godlike Nelson'.[56] On Nelson's departure from Portsmouth to join the fleet which would eventually bring him to Trafalgar, local people reportedly knelt down and blessed the admiral as he passed.[57] Receiving the Trafalgar news, Lord Minto tried to overcome his grief by reminding himself of the heroic code: 'such a death is the finest close, and the crown, as it were, of such a life; and possibly, if his friends were angels and not men, they would acknowledge it as the last favour Providence could bestow and a seal and security for all the rest'.[58]

In an age which saw the separation of churches and cemeteries, the interment of a national hero in the main Cathedral of the established church created a place of pilgrimage; the crypt with Nelson's tomb was immediately included in the cathedral tour and became one of the key sites of the British Christian empire (see Plate 28). Nelson relics were displayed at various other locations and entrepreneurs exhibited copies of the coffin and funereal decorations. Indeed, heroic martyrdom had considerable commercial potential. In the weeks before the funeral, the virgers at St Paul's had capitalised on the Nelson cult by adding the hero's future burial place to the traditional paid tours of the Cathedral. All aspects of Nelson's funeral, as well as of course of his last battle, were soon depicted on commercially produced ceramics, glasses, and silver-rimmed horn beakers, on enamel boxes, pendants, brooches, and on funeral fans. Such commemorative objects mediated visitors' experience of the pantheon, and served as aides-mémoires. There were also glass paintings of Nelson's death and funeral, and a plethora of prints, especially of the funeral car, which merged the popular genre of pasteboard ship models on the London stage with heraldic art.[59] The funeral car itself was to be preserved at Greenwich Hospital 'as a Monument'.[60] In spring 1806, Westminster Abbey installed Catherine Andras' life-sized wax figure of Nelson as a rival tourist attraction to the tomb in St Paul's.

Not everyone agreed with the commercialisation of the hero. In the poem *Nelson's Ghost*, published in 1806, Nelson's ghost returns to exhort his countrymen to leave the body in peace.

> ... a mercenary crew
> Expose my lonely tomb to view
> And, by the thirst of gain misled,
> Invade the quiet of the dead;
> And he, who in his country's cause,
> Fought to protect its rights and laws,
> And in the glorious conflict fell;
> O dire disgrace! and shame to tell,
> Serves, by a lucre-seeking throng,
> To make a show of when he's gone,
> Who crowds admit the live-long day,
> To view the place in which I lay.

The ghost then tells the narrator to announce his complaints to the world:

> ... that my spirit restless roams,
> Around these consecrated domes
> Till that my tomb, from curious eye,
> Is kept in constant privacy,
> And thus not made a thing for shew,
> By a rapacious dark-rob'd crew.[61]

But the tomb did become a site of (commercialised) pilgrimage. From around 1808 it was shown by the ghostly light of lanterns handed down in procession from virger to virger. Even for those who could not visit, its presence as an embodiment of the nation put its stamp on the public image of the site. The pantheon as the burial place of the national hero combined the Christian custom of burying a saint's body inside a sacred monument, with the Enlightenment's need to preserve the individual's memory among the living.[62] The notion of immortality implied in the stories of the St Paul's heroes is not the Christian notion of an afterlife, but the memory of future generations; as Sheridan's inscription on Nelson's monument in the Guildhall put it: 'THE PERIOD TOl NELSON'S FAMEl CAN ONLY BEl THE END OF TIME'.[63] Yet, the process of example was prone to description in religious terms and the personal cult of Nelson exemplifies the transfer of Christian terminology and ritual to nationalism. The limits of appropriating St Paul's as a pantheon of mortal warriors seemed reached when some proposed to erect Nelson's monument under the centre of the dome, directly above the tomb, making the monument the focal point of the church. The sculptor Flaxman, for one, objected: this was bordering too closely on unacceptable idolatry.[64]

In continental Europe, national pantheons, whether of statesmen and military officers, or philosophes and scholars, were commonly endowed with a quasi-sacred character by housing them in temple-like structures, often removed from conurbations and placed on an elevated site, such as Klenze's Walhalla, first conceived in the 1800s. The concepts and structures of the mausoleum, the pagan pantheon, and the modern museum merged in those shrines to national worthies. Germans were erecting purpose-built secular pantheons. In Paris, Ste Geneviève had been converted from a church into the Panthéon. St Paul's in London, a functioning cathedral of the established church, a prominent national Christian space, accommodated a secular pantheon. It celebrated the earthly heroism of officers who during their lifetime and in death were often idolised in a quasi-religious fashion as Christian heroes.[65]

VI

Contests over the relevance and meanings of this set of monuments continued well into the nineteenth century. On the one hand, it was incorporated into a system of official monumental sculpture and inspired further commemorative art, including Nelson's column in Trafalgar Square.[66] Regency and Victorian war literature – fiction, martial memoirs, and campaign accounts – reaffirmed the pantheon's aristo-military code and the centrality of the French wars to the British self-image and consciousness.[67] On the other hand, Sir William Napier's hugely popular Romantic history of the Peninsular War, published from 1828 in the spirit of a modern Froissart's *Chronicles*, cultivated a kind of bottom-up military history which challenged the officers' commemorative monopoly.[68] After the Crimean War, the first regimental monuments were erected in St Paul's.

This was also the decade when access to the Cathedral was widened. Until the mid-nineteenth century, only during some twenty hours of services a week access was gratis. The print *The Sailor's Monument*, published in 1806, shows Jolly Jack Tar standing sulkily in his backyard looking at his own crude memorial to Nelson. The caption says: 'I'll be no twopence customer at St Paul's' (see Plate 30).[69] Under increasing pressure from parliamentary committees wanting to improve public taste, spread historical understanding, and impart religious impressions, the Cathedral authorities removed barriers on the floor. This, the Dean and Chapter promptly claimed, converted the Cathedral 'into a lobby for fashionable loungers', resembling more 'a promenade in a ball-room than a congregation in the house of God'. The noise of idle loungers and fashionable ladies talking and walking disturbed those attending divine service. Free access at all times, they continued, would turn St Paul's into a 'Royal Exchange for wickedness'. Already there was the scandalous behaviour of women knitting, lunch parties, straying dogs, people urinating in pews, and tapping monuments with their sticks and scribbling on them. Admission fees were finally dropped only in the context of the Great Exhibition in 1851.[70]

Throughout the nineteenth century, Nelson's monument and tomb were represented as sites of pilgrimage – of remembrance for the old, and of inspiration for the young. An engraving after a lost painting by Millais shows veteran Greenwich pensioners, limbs missing, paying homage to the admiral (Plate 31). One imagines them listening to the stories of their commander-hero, and to their own, as in Andrew Morton's 1845 painting *The United Service* (Plate 32), of army and navy veterans viewing the Naval Gallery in Greenwich Hospital, including on the left Arnald's *Destruction of the l'Orient at the Battle of the Nile*. Among the principal group of men are soldiers and sailors who had fought in at least seven of the battles commemorated in the St Paul's pantheon. Nine of the Greenwich pensioners had once served with Nelson, who is present in a copy of Hoppner's full-length portrait on the wall behind. While the men are recounting the stories of battle, the women represent a contrast to war, but also the link to the next generation of warriors, embodied by the male baby with blue ribbons. Beauty and nurture, and heroic armed force, were seen to be mutually dependent. Flaxman's allegory in the Nelson monument at St Paul's, of Minerva, the less aggressive variant of Britannia, leading two young midshipmen to a patriotic lesson (Fig. 6.4), was re-enacted by poets and pamphleteers:

> The mother there shall lead her child to con
> The deed engraven on the sculptur'd stone!
> The boy shall turn a hero from the pile,
> And rise the future Nelson of the isle![71]

Among the many nineteenth-century guidebooks to St Paul's is *London Scenes, or, A Visit to Uncle William in Town* – a guide for families with children. Uncle Will brings his country bumpkin nephews and nieces to show them Nelson's tomb and monument at St Paul's. When Miss Hastings asks how they could possibly remember all the heroes' names, Mr Beresford spontaneously composes a poem, incorporating the names of all the heroes in the national pantheon for the children to memorise:

> In monumental marble stand
> Nelson and Collingwood;
> Those brave defenders of our land, -
> The noble and the good.
> …
> Though Westcott's lost, except his name,
> And Miller's thread is cut;-
> With Hardinge they survive in fame,
> Like Burgess, Faulknor, Hutt.[72]

In 1852, the Duke of Wellington's state funeral appeared to complete the Napoleonic-era pantheon – at one stage, Wellington's coffin was appropriately, though precariously, suspended above Nelson's tomb. By the time Alfred Stevens' Wellington monument was completed in 1912, it came too late to blend easily into the Napoleonic-era pantheon. Since the later nineteenth century, the erstwhile coherent pantheon had been dismantled – more by neglect, and the moving around of monuments, including Nelson's, rather than by the Blitz. A marble head severed by a bomb could be reattached – but dispersing monuments had already destroyed the group and much of its layered meanings.

In 2002, Joan Bakewell, the then chair of the British Film Institute, had decided she would tell her grandchildren stories from Britain's history. Having shown them Nelson's bullet-pierced uniform at the National Maritime Museum, she wanted to show them Nelson's tomb. Alas, 'even with granny and grandson reductions' it would have cost £6 admission: 'Just one tomb, I pleaded. But no, you buy the tourist packet or nothing.' They went to see Tate Modern across the River Thames instead.[73] In fact, not only Nelson's tomb is now in the crypt, but many monuments have been moved there over time, some gathering in appropriate proximity to Nelson, others serried like bus queue generals and admirals. Many of the heroes have thus lost their positions in the narrative they once constituted

Figure 6.4 *Monument to Lord Nelson* John Flaxman, detail, 1808–18, St Paul's Cathedral, London, Conway Library, Courtauld Institute of Art, London.

– the story, in marble, of Britain's epic struggle with Revolutionary and Napoleonic France. But at least Joan Bakewell and her grandchildren could have seen some of them free of charge: Nelson's band is once again all the rage – guarding the public lavatories and posing as crypt cafeteria captains.

Notes

1. For the funeral see T. Jenks, 'Contesting the Hero: The Funeral of Admiral Lord Nelson', *JBS* 39 (2000), 422–53; J. Fairburn, *Fairburn's Second Edition of the Funeral of Lord Nelson* (London: Fairburn, 1806); T.O. Churchill, *The Life of Lord Viscount Nelson ... Illustrated by engravings of it's most striking and memorable incidents* (London: Bensley, 1808).
2. Unidentified press-cutting in BL 10815.dd.1 [A Collection of Cuttings from Newspapers, containing Memoir of Lord Nelson, account of his funeral, official papers relating to the battle of the Nile, etc.]
3. National Archives [PRO], T27/60.153, Henry Wellesley, Treasury Chambers, to Mr. Westmacott, Jun., Mount St, 4 Sept. 1807. Flaxman was asked to adopt part of the design, or 'the sentiment', of his rival Westmacott, but Flaxman insisted that the *'composition of the figures* will be his own'. K. Garlick, A. Macintyre and K. Cave (eds), *The Diary of Joseph Farington*, 16 vols (New Haven and London: Yale University Press, 1978–84), VIII, 2993 (24 March 1807).
4. This chapter does not explore the political and partisan history of the St Paul's pantheon, for which see Jenks, 'Contesting the Hero', and my 'The British Military Pantheon in St Paul's Cathedral: The State, Cultural Patriotism, and the Politics of National Monuments, *c*.1790–1820', in M. Craske and R. Wrigley (eds), *Pantheons: Transformations of a Monumental Idea* (Aldershot: Ashgate, 2004), pp. 81–105, and forthcoming work on the politics of commemoration.
5. *Parliamentary Debates from the Year 1803 to the Present Time*, vol. VI (21 Jan. to 26 May 1806) (London: Hansard, 1812), 28 Jan. 1806, cols. 97–107, at 102.
6. T. Nipperdey, 'Nationalidee und Nationaldenkmal in Deutschland im 19. Jahrhundert', *Historische Zeitschrift* 206 (1968), 529–85; A. Ben-Amos, 'Monuments and Memory in French Nationalism', *History & Memory* 5,2 (1990), 50–81.
7. M. Craske, 'Westminster Abbey 1720–70: a public pantheon built upon private interest', in Craske and Wrigley (eds), *Pantheons*, pp. 57–79.
8. By 1785, the full tour cost 14 pence per person: J. Mazzinghy, *The New and Universal Guide through the Cities of London and Westminster* (London, 1785), p. 230.
9. N. Aston, 'St Paul's and the Public Culture of Eighteenth-Century Britain', in D. Keene, A. Burns and A. Saint (eds), *St Paul's. The Cathedral Church of London 604–2004* (New Haven and London: Yale University Press, 2004), pp. 363–71, at 363.
10. *Journals of the House of Commons*, vol. 49, 738, 740, 744; vol. 50, 428f, 444f, 490, 513.
11. National Archives [PRO], T29/78.486–8 (quotation fo. 487). For the new role of the state vis-à-vis the arts from c.1790 see my *The King's Artists. The Royal Academy of Arts and the Politics of British Culture, 1760–1840* (Oxford: Clarendon Press, 2003), part III.
12. *Monthly Magazine*, 20 (1 Jan. 1806). For totalitarian French Revolutionary use of the arts see J.A. Leith, *The Idea of Art as Propaganda in France, 1750–1799: A Study in the History of Ideas* (Toronto: University of Toronto Press, 1969); *Space and Revolution: Projects for Monuments, Squares, and Public Buildings in France 1789–1799* (Montreal: McGill-Queen's University Press, 1991).

13. For a list of all monuments, with sculptor, date and value of commissions, and a plate showing their original positions in St Paul's, see my *King's Artists*, table 2 and plate 9.1.

14. National Maritime Museum COL/14, Collingwood to Rev. Dr. Carlyle, 10 June 1794.

15. For examples see *Journals of the House of Commons*, vol. 61, 16 (28 Jan. 1806); BL Add. MSS 28333, fo. 6, Admiralty to Lady Nelson, 6 Nov. 1805; Anon., *Brief Memoir of the Life and Heroic Achievement of Horatio Nelson* (Gateshead: J. Marshall, 1806), p. 12.

16. B. Silliman, *A Journal of Travels in England, Holland and Scotland* (New York, 1810), vol. II, p. 207.

17. R. Southey, *The Life of Nelson*, 2 vols (London: Murray, 1813), II, 267–8. Captain Hardinge's heroic timing was less than perfect, as Parliamentarians acknowledged in stating that he had died 'in the path to victory'. As if by way of compensation, together with the hero's name the word 'VICTORY' is set in larger letters than the rest of his monument's inscription. For Abercromby as an army counterpart to Nelson see BL Add. MSS 38759, fos. 85f; R. Wilson, *History of the British Expedition to Egypt*, 2 vols, 2nd edn (London, 1803), II, p. 304; *Gentleman's Magazine*, vol. 71, 480f; [An Officer], *The Life of Sir Ralph Abercromby* (Ormskirk: Fowler, 1806), preface, n. p.

18. National Maritime Museum COL/14/22, Adm. Collingwood to Rev. Dr. Carlyle, 25 Jan. 1801.

19. Anon., *Brief Memoir*, title-page; W. Beatty, *Authentic Narrative of the Death of Lord Nelson* (London: Cadell, 1807), pp. 68–71. For Capt. Harvey's successive mutilations on 1 June 1794 see N. Tracy (ed.), *Naval Chronicle*, consolidated edn (London: Chatham, 1998–99), I, p. 107.

20. The best discussion is T. Jenks, '"Naval Engagements". Patriotism, Cultural Politics, and the Royal Navy, 1793–1815' (unpublished Ph.D. thesis, University of Toronto, 2001), pp. 265–90 with further references. For visual culture, shown in the Nelson Lecture, see the print *The Hazards of War; or, Nelson Wounded* (published in 1798 by J. Fairburn, NMM, PAD4244) and the anonymous portrait of Nelson wounded at the Nile, returning on deck to see *l'Orient* on fire (see Plate 11, this volume) (NMM, BHC2903).

21. Poems quoted in Jenks, '"Naval Engagements"', p. 266.

22. Anon., *Victory in Tears; or, The Shade of Nelson. A Tribute to the Memory of That Immortal Hero* (London, 1805), footnote on p. 20 to line 269, 'Though shook by toil–though shatter'd by the storm'.

23. *Naval Chronicle*, XIV, 478f. See M. Lincoln, *Representing the Royal Navy: British Sea Power, 1750–1815* (Aldershot: Ashgate, 2002), p. 32, on the endurance of physical pain as part of gender training and on admiration for seamen bearing amputation without complaint.

24. *Naval Chronicle*, consol. edn III, p. 235, 'Naval History of the Present Year', 1806 [XV, 158–60].

25. Bacon also included a common sailor in the monument to Captain James Cook in Westminster Abbey.

26. G.L. Smyth, *The Monuments and Genii of St Paul's Cathedral and Westminster Abbey*, 2 vols (London, 1826), II, p. 676.

27. *Journals of the House of Commons*, vol. 61, 17, 20 (28 and 31 Jan. 1806); Smyth, *Monuments*, II, p. 634 note. See also, on Abercromby, Duncan, Brock, Le

Marchant, Craufurd, Hay, McKenzie, and Picton: Wilson, *History of the British Expedition to Egypt*, pp. 75f; M. Hackett, *A Popular Account of St Paul's Cathedral* (London, 1830), p. 31; W. Wood, *Select British Documents of the War of 1812*, 3 vols (Toronto, 1920–28), I, p. 14; D. Le Marchant, *Memoirs of the Late Major General Le Marchant* (London, 1841), p. 305; J.V. Page (ed.), *Intelligence Officer in the Peninsula: Letters and Diaries of Major the Hon. Edward Charles Cocks 1786–1812* (New York: Hippocrene; Tunbridge Wells: Spellmount, 1986), p. 166, diary entry for 26 Jan. 1811; J.A. Hall (ed.), *History of the Peninsular War*, vol. 8, *The Biographical Dictionary of British Officers Killed and Wounded, 1808–1814* (London: Greenhill, 1998), pp. 268, 373; *Gentleman's Magazine*, 84,2 (1814), 517; H.B. Robinson, *Memoirs of Lieutenant-General Sir Thomas Picton*, 2 vols, 2nd. rev. edn, (London: Bentley, 1836), II, p. 401.

28. Southey, *Life of Nelson*, I, p. 231.

29. Plans for a more inclusive honours system which would have exploited Nelson's meritocratic associations and extended honours right down to midshipmen were abandoned after quite detailed drafting in 1805–06: National Archives [PRO], Pitt Correspondence, 30/8/143, fos. 84–91; 30/8/144/1, fos. 7–12. Jenks, 'Contesting the Hero', 431–3.

30. Nelson's head is based on a life-mask made in Vienna around 1800, which was used to make a bust by Ransom and Thaller, which in turn stood model for Flaxman's monument.

31. BL Add. MSS 39790, fos. 28–9, John Flaxman to the Rev. William Gunn, Sept. 1814, quoted in M. Busco, *Sir Richard Westmacott, Sculptor* (Cambridge: Cambridge University Press, 1994), p. 45.

32. J.P. Malcolm, *Londinium Redivivum; or, an Ancient History and Modern Description of London*, 4 vols (London, 1802–07), III, pp. 124ff.

33. A. Cunningham, *Lives of the Most Eminent Painters and Sculptors*, 6 vols (London: Murray, 1829–33), III, pp. 101, 102.

34. Cf., for the Seven Years War, M. Craske, *Art in Europe 1700–1830. A History of the Visual Arts in an Era of Unprecedented Urban Economic Growth* (Oxford and New York: Oxford University Press, 1997), pp. 263f; D. Solkin, *Painting for Money. The Visual Arts and the Public Sphere in Eighteenth Century England* (New Haven and London: Yale University Press, 1993), ch. 5; D. Bindman and M. Baker, *Roubiliac and the Eighteenth-Century Monument* (New Haven and London: Yale University Press, 1995), pp. 147ff, 172, 189, passim.

35. W. Wordsworth, 'Character of the Happy Warrior', in T. Hutchinson (ed.), *Wordsworth. Poetical Works with Introduction and Notes edited by Thomas Hutchinson. A new edition, revised by E. de Selincourt* (Oxford, 1974), pp. 386f.

36. The code of the dying warrior was rehearsed by Parliamentarians and writers: *Journals of the House of Commons*, vol. 56, 427, 444; Smyth, *Monuments*, I, p. 10. A few other monuments depict the modern warrior as critically wounded or dead: Baily, Ponsonby; Westmacott, Brock; Chantrey, Cadogan.

37. E. Vincent Macleod, *A War of Ideas. British Attitudes to the Wars against Revolutionary France 1792–1802* (Aldershot: Ashgate, 1998), chs 1, 3, 5, 6.

38. Ibid., p. 137.

39. [Church of England], *Form of Prayer and thanksgiving ... for the victory obtained over the French Fleet* (London, 1798), pp. 7f; [Church of England], *Form of Prayer, 29 Oct. 1797* (Duncan's victory 11 Oct. 1797). On providential intervention

in a variety of discursive contexts see Anon., *Eulogy on the Illustrious Admiral [Duncan]; Parliamentary Debates*, XX, 511–14, 524.

40. Jenks, 'Contesting the Hero'.
41. J. Hervey, 'Meditations among the Tombs', in *Meditations and Contemplations. To which is prefixed the Life of the Author* (London: Rivington, 1818), pp. 46ff; see also E. Young, 'The Complaint Night I. On Life, Death, and Immortality', in *Night Thoughts* (London, 1798), pp. 1–15. See my 'The British Military Pantheon in St Paul's Cathedral', with further references to counter-traditions to the heroic.
42. M. Craske and R. Wrigley, 'Introduction', in Craske and Wrigley (eds), *Pantheons*, pp. 1–10, at p. 5.
43. *Form of Prayer ... used in all Churches upon the nineteenth of December next, being the Day appointed by Proclamation for a general Thanksgiving* (London, 1797), p. 6; Macleod, *War of Ideas*, pp. 143ff. The introduction of statues to St Paul's had also been eased by the fact that the first was to John Howard, the prison reformer and philanthropist, who during his lifetime had humbly rejected the idea of a monument to him, and was now represented as a charitable Christian: *Gentleman's Magazine*, 66,1 (1796), 179–81, with plate facing 179.
44. *Public Advertiser*, 4 April 1791, 3; see also under the same date *World*, 3, and *Times*, 3; *Public Advertiser*, 25 April 1791, 2; 3 March 1792, 3.
45. For examples see *Parliamentary History ... to 1803* (1818), 'Debate in the Commons on the Vote of Thanks to Lord Howe', 16 June 1794, 906–7. *From A Narrative of my Adventures (1790–1839) by Sir William Henry Dillon, K.C.H., Vice-Admiral of the Red*, ed. by M.A. Lewis, in D. King and J. Hattendorf (eds), *Every Man will do His Duty: Anthology of Firsthand Accounts from the Age of Nelson, 1793–1815* (London, 1997), p. 31; National Maritime Museum HIS/35/10.
46. *Parliamentary Debates*, vol. VI (21 Jan. to 26 May 1806), 28 Jan. 1806, cols. 97–107. See also J.S. Clarke and J. M'Arthur, *The Life of Admiral Lord Nelson*, 2 vols (London: Cadell & Davies, 1809), II, pp. 455–6, for an extension of the contrast to Spanish gallantry, French lack of humanity, and British humanity.
47. P. Hoare (ed.), *Academic Correspondence, 1803* (London: Cadell, 1804), p. 28. When the monument was unveiled in 1806, *The Times* stressed that Hypocrisy's real features were 'expressive of the most ferocious and horrid barbarity'. *Times*, 7 Jan. 1806.
48. *Gentleman's Magazine*, 2nd ser., 20 (1843), 155–60, 249–56, at 255, quoting the notorious republican commissioner Hugues. See also BL Add. MS 39781, 10–13, Major F[rederick] Maitland to Charles Dundas, 12 June 1794, esp. 11v.
49. Jenks, '"Naval Engagements"', p. 252.
50. R. Lendon, *Public Tokens of Sorrow due to brave Men who fall in the Service of their Country* (London: Bye and Law, for the benefit of the Patriotic Fund, 1805), pp. 13–15. Lendon's colleague at Bedford, Charles Abbott, stressed that Christians should 'cherish the memory' of Nelson primarily because 'he was a pious man' who knew 'that earthly palms and victory's dear-bought laurels are only the precursors of an eternal, a brighter and a heavenly recompense': C. Abbot, *A Sermon preached in the parish church of St Mary, Bedford, on Sunday, November the 10th, 1805* (Bedford: Webb, 1805), pp. 14–16.

51. For the neglect of religion in the eighteenth-century Royal Navy and its revival in the 1790s see Lincoln, *Representing the Royal Navy*, p. 118.
52. Quoted in E. Vincent, *Nelson. Love & Fame* (New Haven and London: Yale University Press, 2003), p. 571.
53. Busco, *Westmacott*, p. 50.
54. For the terminology see W. Panofsky, *Tomb Sculpture. Its Changing Aspects from Ancient Egypt to Bernini*, ed. H.W. Janson (London: Thames & Hudson, 1964); Bindman and Baker, *Roubiliac*, ch. 3.
55. Countess of Minto (ed.), *Life and Letters of Sir Gilbert Eliot, First Earl of Minto from 1751 to 1806*, 2 vols (London: Longmans, Green and Co., 1874), II, p. 378.
56. *True Greatness; or, Tributary Stanzas to the Glorious Memory of Lord Viscount Nelson, dedicated to the Committee of the Patriotick Fund* (London, 1806), p. 13.
57. Southey, *Life of Nelson*, II, p. 230.
58. Minto, *Life and Letters*, II, p. 373.
59. Modelled in imitation of the hull of the *Victory*, with the coffin imagined as the quarterdeck, it displayed the figure of Fame or Victory, the English Jack flown at half-mast at the poop, the names of the four principal ships Nelson had taken, and traditional funerary accoutrements: ostrich feathers, a black velvet fringe, and heraldic escutcheons. National Archives [PRO] LC2/40, 37–8.
60. The College of Heralds and Lord Chamberlain had disputed the right to present the car to Greenwich Hospital: National Archives [PRO] LC2/4, fos. 10–18, 20, 23, 28, extracts from Chapter Meeting, College of Arms, 10 Jan. 1806.
61. E. Montagu, *The Citizen: A Hudibrastic Poem in Five Cantos. To which is added, Nelson's Ghost. A Poem in Two Parts* (London: Hughes, 1806), pp. 6, 9.
62. My discussion is informed by Ben-Amos, 'Monuments and Memory in French Nationalism'.
63. *Gentleman's Magazine*, 81 (1811), part 1, 390; see also Lendon, *Public Tokens of Sorrow*, p. 16
64. 'A Sinnot', *Gentleman's Magazine*, 75 (1805), part 2, 1119–20, recommended a Nelson monument (by subscription as already opened) in St Paul's in the centre of the dome over the site of the vault, so it could be seen from all points in the Cathedral.
65. See with further references my 'British Military Pantheon', p. 96.
66. J.M. Crook and M.H. Port, *The History of the King's Works*, VI (London: HMSO, 1973), pp. 293–302; Busco, *Westmacott*, pp. 57–64. National Art Library, R.C. V.13, British Institution Minute Books, vol. III, n.p. [meetings on 20 Feb., 3 April, 18 July 1815, 8 and 25 April 1816]. C. Lloyd, *The Royal Collection. A Thematic Exploration of the Paintings in the Collection of Her Majesty The Queen. Foreword by HRH The Prince of Wales* (London: Sinclair-Stevenson, 1992), pp. 166–74.
67. W. Matthews, *British Autobiographies. An annotated Bibliography of British Autobiographies published or written before 1851* (Berkeley and Los Angeles; London: University of California Press, 1955); P. Krahé, 'Admiral Nelson in der englischen Literatur: Wandlungen eines patriotischen Leitbildes', *Archiv für Kulturgeschichte*, 66 (1984), 315–45; S.H. Myerly, *British Military Spectacle. From the Napoleonic Wars through the Crimea* (Cambridge, Mass. and London: Harvard University Press, 1996), pp. 146–50.

68. Sir William F.P. Napier, *History of the War in the Peninsula and in the South of France, from the Year 1807 to the Year 1814*, 6 vols (London, 1828–40).

69. Cf. the discussion in A. Yarrington, *The Commemoration of the Hero, 1800–1864. Monuments to the British Victors of the Napoleonic Wars* (New York and London: Garland, 1988), pp. 66–7.

70. *Parliamentary Accounts and Papers* (London: Hansard, 1837), 119, XXXVI.447, 'Correspondence between the Secretary of State and the Dean and Chapter of St Paul's'. J.T. Smith, *Nollekens and His Times*, 2 vols (S.l.: Henry Colburn, 1829), I, pp. 376f. Cf. my 'Reforming Culture. National Art Institutions in the Age of Reform', in A. Burns and J. Innes (eds), *Rethinking the Age of Reform: Britain 1780–1850* (Cambridge: Cambridge University Press, 2003), pp. 254–70.

71. W. Turton (ed.), *Luctus Nelsoniani. Poems on the Death of Lord Nelson* (London, 1807), p. 147. For children as authors of commemorative culture see *Nelson's Death, the Words by a Young Lady, Eight Years of Age, The Music Composed by S. Ball, Organist Ipswich* (London, n.d.).

72. Anon., *London Scenes, or, A Visit to Uncle William in Town* (London: Harris, 1824), pp. 26f.

73. Joan Bakewell, *New Statesman*, 18 Nov. 2002, <http://www.findarticles.com/p/articles/mi_m0FQP/is_4614_131/ai_95764229>.

7
Nelson Goes Global: The Nelson Myth in Britain and Beyond

John M. MacKenzie

Trafalgar Day[1] remains a resonant date in the calendar, commemorated in many places in the Anglophone world. The continuing significance of this day, remembered annually in so many places for almost two hundred years, is ample evidence of the mythic status of the action it commemorates and the most famous actor at the centre of that victory. Indeed, the legendary status of Horatio Nelson is probably the greatest of all the heroic myths created by the British to explain the essence and uniqueness of their history. In the nineteenth century, the mythic hero became a central instrumental device for British social cohesion. In explaining the history of a nation whose unity was only a recent creation it also performed vital economic and strategic roles. When Thomas Carlyle wrote in *Heroes and Hero Worship* (1841) that 'No great man lives in vain. The history of the world is but the biography of great men' he produced a manifesto for the teaching of history in the Victorian age and for the preparation of the countless books of heroes published in those years.[2]

I

A myth is not of course an untruth. It constitutes a heightening and embroidery of truth in order to create a grander conception of some central moment that observers take to be a crucial turning point. The myth emerges from a key event upon which a great counterfactual structure can be built. 'We would all now be speaking French' is the most common formulation in this context. Furthermore, the central figure of

144

this cultural and political superstructure invariably comes to explain and justify qualities of national character associated with the rise of the state, and helps to create the core to which the components of national identity can be bolted. As well as personifying national greatness, he offers an example of self-sacrificing service to a current generation, and acts as the instrument of pressure groups and interests in the formulation of policy. He becomes a key element in youth training, as well as an exemplar and touchstone for those who follow in a similar service. Indeed, the mythic figure becomes a guiding ancestor, developing such popular potency that he could be used to whip up agitations to influence governments that were often as much reactive as active. In the history books and compendia of heroic biographies that were such a feature of the late Victorian era, such figures mainly inhabited three heroic ages: first the Elizabethan period; second, the sequence of wars against the French in the eighteenth century, culminating in the Napoleonic; and third the imperial age. Figures like General James Wolfe, David Livingstone, Henry Havelock and Charles Gordon emerged in both high and popular culture as exemplars of heroic action to match those of the earlier golden age of the later sixteenth century.[3]

If we analyse what makes these heroic myths, we find a number of common characteristics. First, the myth cannot of course be made out of a man of straw. The central figure requires a combination of clearly perceived and extraordinary abilities, an indomitable will, almost superhuman physical stamina, and a religious (or quasi-religious) passion in the attainment of near-miraculous objectives. This involves an unassailable conviction of rectitude. Second, the truly mythic figure requires martyrdom fully to achieve its status. Wolfe, Nelson, Livingstone and Gordon all shared this and their mythic power was much more potent as a result. Third, the myth requires a striking and moving icon, invariably the moment of martyrdom: Wolfe dying on the Heights of Abraham; Nelson's drawn-out death on the deck of *Victory*, surrounded by his officers; Livingstone kneeling in prayer in Central Africa, discovered by his faithful black followers; Gordon standing at the top of the stairs at the palace in Khartoum patiently awaiting the Dervish spears.[4] This promotes the central figures to the status of secular saints, complete with relics, miracles of a sort, and groups of acolytes. Fourth, and following on from this, the icon needs to be endlessly reproduced and promoted by a fervently supporting faction which brings the name of the hero constantly to public attention. This is all the more significant if there is a spontaneous upsurge of commemorative activity promoted in many places around the land. This latter characteristic is very much true of

Nelson. And finally, the martyrdom and the icon have to reflect the manner in which the hero faces a formidable foe and overcomes it in the very moment of death: Wolfe the French empire in Quebec; Nelson the French and Spanish fleets; Livingstone the slave traders and the environment of Africa; Gordon the alien passion of the Mahdi. We might add that heroes like to establish a sort of apostolic succession. Nelson regarded Wolfe as his own great hero, invoked his memory at moments of attack, and was a great admirer of Benjamin West's death scene.[5]

The exemplary life is thus also an envisioned life, and one which is visualised through a death which is laden with meaning. Such iconic representations mould and colour both individual and collective memory. They simplify through careful arrangement the complexities of history, omitting much, while creating a sense of historical coherence out of the chaotic mish-mash of past events. In this respect, representation and memory operate in much the same way as oral evidence, selecting, clarifying and shaping the past to a particular form. The heroic and exemplary life ties together beliefs and practices in such a way that individuals are bound to community, and nationality is defined by forms of historical faith. Yet the creation of key historical prototypes also serves in the promotion of stereotypical images which ultimately begin to control the actions and beliefs of succeeding generations. In doing so, these myths are never static. They are malleable, constantly manipulated for the requirements of the age. The Nelson myth was repeatedly massaged to satisfy the requirements of the British in respect of their relations with Europe and the world. It was bent to strategic imperatives and to the needs of imperial power. It was appropriated by white communities across what is increasingly known as 'the British World', mainly represented by the territories that used to be known as the white dominions. Above all, logically and naturally, Nelson's reputation was central to the needs of the Royal Navy and the training of its recruits. He was invoked to protect the Navy's budget and to sell related products.[6] To work in advertising an icon has to be immediately recognisable.

That Nelson's myth is among the greatest of them all, at least in the Anglophone world, is well attested by the quite extraordinary numbers of streets that were named after him in cities and towns up and down the land. He has a town in Lancashire, customarily called Nelson after the pub which changed its name in his honour after Trafalgar. Another Nelson, and its surrounding district, in the South Island of New Zealand was named in the early 1840s as a conscious effort by the New Zealand Company to match the commemoration of Wellington in the future capital to the north.[7] British Columbia boasts the town of Nelson in the Okanagan, as well as two small communities, Nelson Forks and Fort Nelson in the far north. Manitoba also has a Nelson and a Nelson Lake, while the Nelson River runs into Hudson Bay. Victoria in Australia has a town of Nelson and also a Cape. There are a number of other Nelsons in the world (including, for example, a strait in Chile). Yet it is a fact that there are more Wellingtons in the world, just as there are more streets named after Wellington in London.

But Nelson is much less of a mouthful than Wellington. Maybe that is why it is said that boys in the West Indies were named after him, certainly in the period before 'Winston' became popular. And when young Rolihlahla Mandela went to school in the Transkei, his missionary teachers had trouble pronouncing his name. So they followed the well-established custom of calling their pupils after British heroes. Mandela got Nelson, which his mother promptly and rather charmingly Africanised into Nelisile.[8] In such a fashion did one iconic figure become assimilated into another who was to become one of the most celebrated figures of the late twentieth and early twenty-first centuries. A half nelson is of course a one-armed wrestling grip, and I well remember once playing, on a Rhodesian (as it was then) tobacco farm a quite revolting game known as Nelson's eye. Thus were his physical disabilities engrossed into popular pastimes, but with the effect of maintaining the visibility of his name.

But such geographical and cultural representations are not enough to sustain the power of the myth. The intention here is to illustrate what may be called its functionality, for myths do not float in some cultural ether. They perform key functions in the economic, social and, above all, strategic life of a dominant imperial power or of colonies as nascent nations. This is well illustrated by the manner in which the Nelson myth operated in the further binding of Scotland into the Union. Nelson helped, in other words, to confirm Scots as 'Britons'.[9] A century later, the myth becomes highly significant in the emergence of a new naval power, Japan, proud of its rapid westernisation, not least under the naval tutelage of the United Kingdom. At the same time the Nelson myth is resurrected and re-emphasised in the territories of white settlement of the British empire, taking on further social and strategic meaning. By those years, a century after the formulation of the myth, there may be evidence that its role in Scotland was experiencing some decline.

II

It is through monuments that Nelson's legendary status is most clearly expressed, and the social mores and stylistic modes associated with these monuments are replete with meaning. Wellington is always commemorated in the rather grand equestrian statue, larger than life, wearing the eponymous boots, and looking forward keenly as though observing and plotting the Battle of Waterloo. Nelson was associated with masts and therefore with height, with visibility over the horizon, with the sending of signals, both literal and metaphorical. The Nelson monuments are uniformly tall, lofty tributes to a short man with a towering reputation to match or even exceed his well-known vanity. Such memorials strikingly echo the heroic myth itself. They stand as a fixed element in an urban or even rural landscape which is constantly changing, being transformed as new buildings are constructed, new road layouts are arranged, as trees grow higher, the noises of the countryside change, and different kinds of vehicles appear upon the roads. Above all the people also change, the small and ordinary people who scuttle about at the base of these towering symbols, changing not only through the generations, but through migrations, ideologies, and beliefs. With some of these monuments the viewer looks upwards, almost blinded by the brightness of the sky and of the reputation there displayed. Others can be ascended, and the visitor reaches a viewpoint, like a ship's crow's nest, from which he or she can scan the surrounding countryside, as though embracing the land that Nelson saved from foreign rule. Thus the monuments become (in appropriate metaphors) anchors or masts of memory, sometimes vilified as well as revered. Colin White has listed and described many of these monuments, but this chapter will focus on a few that are lesser known.[10]

We should be clear that these monuments come at a key cultural turning point. The Romantic Age was creating a new type of hero, the individual posed against almost insurmountable odds. And with this reification of the hero came a desire to display his (and at this point it is generally his) attributes to all around. There are some precedents for this. The great gardens of Lord Cobham at Stowe featured a Temple of the Worthies dating from as far back as 1733, containing the busts of a succession of Whig heroes including King Alfred, Walter Raleigh, William Shakespeare, Isaac Newton and Alexander Pope. The statuary of the period mainly concentrated on kings and these were always displayed in classic guise, usually wearing the Roman toga. The gardens at Stowe boasted a fine obelisk, over one hundred feet high, which was later significantly rededicated to commemorate General Wolfe after his Quebec victory of 1759. He had dined with Earl Temple's family just before he sailed for Canada.[11] This is interesting in that it represents a crucial shift from the 'worthies' to a new type of hero, military and now usually connected with the empire. What has happened is that the sense of heroism located in the past, often the classical past by which heroes are judged, has now been translated to a global imperial context. The distance of past times has been replaced by the remoteness of distant climes. History painting accommodates this. A genre that used to illustrate a former age (though inevitably commenting on the present in the process) becomes associated with astonishing events of a new heroic, and contemporary, period. Benjamin West's 1771 painting of the death of Wolfe on the Heights of Abraham at Quebec is the first celebrated example.

One of the most surprising of the early monuments has been described as 'a hidden treasure', a 'formidable landmark in red sandstone'.[12] It is a 23-feet-high statue of William Wallace in the Borders of Scotland, dressed in a toga, with a saltire shield and a massive two-handed sword. He stands in the landscape as the Guardian of the nation. Yet its history is intriguing. The Earl of Buchan who commissioned it originally wished to celebrate Burns, a very eighteenth-century concern with the literary figure. But when he saw the medium, a huge block of red sandstone, he realised that only a martial subject would be appropriate, and the commission was changed to Wallace. It was erected on a magnificent site in 1814 and is not, of course, to be confused with the striking Wallace Tower, a late Victorian creation, near Stirling.

It was indeed in Scotland that the first ideas for the commemoration of Nelson seem to have emerged. And it is their spontaneity which is so surprising. The very first, reputedly, came from the workers at the great iron furnace at Bonawe in Argyllshire. When they heard of the victory of Nelson at Trafalgar, they took a large prehistoric standing stone and re-erected it on a hilltop above Loch Etive. They carved on a small stone the legend 'To the memory of Lord Nelson, this stone was erected by the Lorn furnace workers, 1805'.[13] Now this suggests a number of interesting conclusions. First, the name of Nelson was already exceptionally well known, even to the ironworkers of Argyllshire. They would, no doubt, have heard of his earlier victories. He was a living hero before he became a dead one. This was a literate society where newspapers would have been common currency and all would have heard celebratory sermons from the pulpit.

The second intriguing factor is that it is Scotland. Nelson was quintessentially English. This was no Caledonian hero in the mould of Bruce or Wallace or Burns. But those iron workers now had a sense of being Britons and were aware of a national, British, struggle against the French. And to this one can add the obvious factor that their livelihoods depended upon the very circumstances that Nelson had created. To understand the voluntary actions of these iron workers, you have to realise that the iron which they smelted came from Cumberland. It was shipped up the Irish Sea and Hebridean waters to be landed at a jetty just below their great furnaces. Nelson kept those seas open and consequently preserved their jobs.

While the iron workers of Argyllshire were producing their spontaneous response, major cities, particularly those dependent on trade, were preparing their tributes. A meeting took place in Liverpool as early as 15 November, not much more than a week after the news of the victory and Nelson's death reached the city.[14] The astonishing sum of £4,500 was promised almost immediately, including £1,000 from the Corporation, £750 from the Committee of Lloyds, and £500 from the Chairman of the West Indies Association. This was to fund a monument to Nelson to be erected in the central area of the New Exchange Buildings. The monument is now in Springfield Park. In Edinburgh, a meeting took place on 22 November and the committee appointed for managing the fund comprised many of the leading aristocracy, lawyers, judges, and politicians in the city.[15] In Glasgow, an anonymous letter first appeared in *The Glasgow Herald* on 15 November 1805 suggesting that it has become 'the policy of enlightened nations to commemorate by substantial symbols departed excellence and to rouse national emulation with the view of the prolonged honours that attend distinguished patriotic zeal and intrepidity'. The letter went on to point out that the citizens of Glasgow were prevented by distance from attending the funeral, but could still evince 'the liberality for which they are pre-eminent'. After all, it concluded 'we have shared largely in the benefits consequent on his ability' and the resulting security of the oceans.[16]

No doubt the news from Liverpool, reported in *The Herald* of 22 November, acted as a spur, for there was often a competitive edge of civic pride involved in these matters. The Glasgow meeting took place in the Town Hall on 6 December, and pledged itself to create a monument 'in grateful remembrance of Nelson's eminent services' and 'to rouse the youth of succeeding generations'. In Glasgow, unlike Liverpool, there were no large institutional donations. All subscriptions were personal. They were far from being private. The subscription lists were opened in a number of shops and the name and amount of each subscription was published in *The Herald*. There must have been some soul-searching about the extent of individual munificence. This extended from £100 from the Marquis of Douglas, fifty guineas from a number of other members of the quality, such as Lord Archibald Hamilton, right down to a guinea from quite a number of citizens. In the end there were some two hundred subscribers contributing more than £2,000.[17]

Throughout this period, the name of Nelson was kept constantly before the public. There were advertisements for biographies of Nelson and of prints of famous paintings of the great man, including the Beechey portrait. Moreover, other calls were being made upon pockets at the time. There was of course the Patriotic Fund, made up of quite considerable donations from collections at the doors of parish churches. Later, there was a subscription list for a statue to Pitt the Younger, who died in 1806. Perhaps as a result some correspondents were unhappy with the idea of a monument. One suggested that the money should be given to the widows and orphans of sailors. Another proposed that the money should go towards the building of a 'naval seminary' as a better substitute for the erection of pillars and obelisks. Such a college would be, it was suggested, more suitable to the character of the deceased hero and would produce more permanent benefits. The correspondent further suggested that graduates should receive the distinction FNTC, Fellow of the Nelson Trafalgar College, which would be a flattering passport to success.[18] (Presumably the idea was that there would be more Scots officers in the Royal Navy.)

But the truly interesting thing about the list of subscribers is the fact that it is, in effect, a roll call of the great Glasgow merchants of the day, men who had made fortunes from the tobacco and other trades of North America and the West Indies, like Henry Glassford, Robert Dennistoun, and Kirkman Finlay. The laying of the foundation stone was set for 1 August 1806, an appropriate date, it was thought, because it represented the anniversary of the Battle of Aboukir Bay (or the Battle of the Nile). This was of course the victory which had firmly secured the heroic reputation of Nelson in the minds of the British public. In the months up to that date there was a quickening of interest in the local papers. There were reports of the meetings of subscribers, of the appointment of the architect and mason, and of the choice of a prime site at the very centre of the Glasgow Green. Summonses were issued to all the Masonic lodges to prepare to attend. In April 1806, *The Herald* published a poem with no fewer than 110 lines with sentiments like:

> 'He sunk 'mid radiance like the setting sun
> When first he rose his country hail'd the sight
> Now millions worship his departing life.'
> 'And well may Nelson's hovering spirit claim
> From realms his valour saved a deathless fame,
> For England's shores her matchless hero's praise
> And freedom's altar burns with brighter blaze.'[19]

There are some echoes here of the reception accorded at least in visual imagery of the death of Captain Cook, particularly 'hovering spirit' and 'deathless fame', but there is also something new, the emphasis on a setting sun and the hallowing of freedom's altar. This is heroism on a fresh and major scale, sufficient to fire the imaginations of Southey, Coleridge, Wordsworth and Byron.[20]

The service, procession and laying of the foundation stone were clearly one of the biggest things to happen in Glasgow for a long time. The service took place in the High Kirk, now better known as the cathedral. The collection was to go to increasing the height of the monument, so height was clearly important to the pride of the city. The procession was said to be more than a mile long, featuring the Glasgow Volunteer Light Horse, the 71st Regiment, civic dignitaries, subscribers, grand masters and masons of twenty-three lodges. The procession formed up into a hollow square at the site and the stone was laid by Sir John Stuart of Allanbank, the Provincial Grand Master, with the usual Masonic rituals amid cheers from the immense crowds, said, perhaps incredibly, to number eighty thousand. Sailors knelt to kiss the stone. The streets were packed with the citizenry and people watched from all the windows of the route. The city congratulated itself that there were no incidents and of course the whole event was followed by dinner and the usual toasts.[21]

The monument so begun turned out to be a 143-feet-high obelisk, reflecting the fascination with Egypt of the times. The architect was D. Hamilton and the mason A. Brocket. But this monument was soon to be the site of a further celebrated incident. On Sunday 5 August 1810 there was a violent storm of thunder and lightning over Glasgow. The monument was struck by lightning and was, in the words of a contemporary, 'most materially injured'. It was torn open from the top for more than twenty feet and several stones were cast down. On the south side a rent was made in the column as far down as the pedestal. It became so dangerous that a military guard had to be placed to hold back curious, 'thoughtless and daring' spectators. A meeting of subscribers was called to consider the damage on 10 August, and Glaswegians no doubt had to dip into their pockets once more for the repairs. Moreover, the event was so celebrated that it was commemorated in paintings by the artist John Knox. At least three slightly different versions of this dramatic painting exist – one in the collection of the Hunterian Art Gallery of the University of Glasgow, one in the People's Palace on Glasgow Green and one in the possession of the Dundas family of Arniston House.[22]

If the Glasgow monument was purely ornamental, the canny Establishment of Edinburgh resolved that their monument would be useful. The foundation stone was laid on Trafalgar Day in 1807, though without any of the ceremony that occurred elsewhere. The council defended this on the grounds that such a ceremony would have been expensive and would, in any case, have led to 'the idleness and debauchery to which such events always give rise'.[23] It must be a pleasant surprise to Glaswegians that the Edinburgh populace was less trusted than in the sister city. After some trouble over funding, the monument on the key site of Calton Hill was completed in 1815 at a cost of £1,500.

It has to be said that if you compare the monument with the costs and style of those erected elsewhere, the Edinburgh public got a remarkable bargain. It can be seen from all over central Edinburgh and consists of a grand tower on a substantial base, with a cap house and a double bartizan, forming two lookouts, on top. There are several rooms within it which were supposed to be homes for retired sailors (they were never used for this purpose) and it was designed to fly government signals. In fact, it did signal the arrival of the mail boats in Leith and was also used for the drop of a time ball, controlled from the nearby Royal Observatory. In the nineteenth century the charge for admission to see the view was a shilling, quite a considerable sum, and in 1829, the rooms at the base were let to a vendor of soups and sweetmeats. It was clearly intended that it should be a place of leisure for the respectable general public.

Anglo-Irish sentiment followed quickly on that of the Scots. The adoption of the Nelson myth obviously performed similar functions: the Union had only just been declared in 1800 and Irish trade was clearly dependent upon Royal Naval dominance of the Irish Sea. Mindful of this, the Dublin elite set about creating a grand monument with construction starting in 1808. An immense structure, it stood 140 feet high and combined a viewing gallery with a plinth for a statue of Nelson. Entrance to it was threepence, and it became a favourite place of resort for Dubliners, a spot where lovers would arrange to meet. But it was also a striking symbol of British power and it was partially blown up by the IRA in 1966. The Irish government do not seem to have held it in much affection either, so they immediately sent in the army and demolished the lot. After the statue had fallen to the street, the head of Nelson was stolen by students, subsequently recovered, and is now displayed in the Dublin Civic Museum.[24] The new Dublin spire occupies the same site. English commemorations were numerous, but were often raised more slowly than those in Scotland and Ireland. The foundation stone for the Portsmouth monument was laid in 1807, but that at Great Yarmouth was not completed until 1819, at the considerable cost of £10,000.[25] In Wales, the visit of Nelson to Monmouth in August 1802 was commemorated in the creation of the naval temple and roundhouse, which Nelson himself saw, and the Nelson garden. Nelson sat in the summer house of this town garden and it has ever since been used as a memorial to the hero.[26] Even Captain, later Vice-Admiral, Hardy has his own monument, a pillar on Black Down hill in Dorset, erected in 1846.[27]

Liverpool and Glasgow were clearly going to benefit immensely from Nelson's victory; Edinburgh and Dublin were significant capital cities; while Portsmouth, Great Yarmouth and Monmouth had clear connections with the admiral. But some of the other commemorations are rather more difficult to explain. In the Morayshire town of Forres, a call for subscriptions was sent out announcing the intention of building a tower on the summit of Cluny Hill. This 'monument to departed heroism' would command a prospect of the richest part of Morayshire, a large part of the Moray Firth, and of seven surrounding counties. 'Exclusive therefore of answering the intended purpose, it will form a most agreeable object to every Traveller in the County at large, an useful Sea-beacon, an excellent Observatory, and a Commanding Alarm Post in the event of an Enemy's approach by Sea or Land' (capitals in the original). £300 was called for to complete the first proposal, but it was thought that this might be reduced because many men in the district proposed to offer materials. But another and grander plan had been submitted by the architect Charles Stuart and it was thought that this would cost 700 guineas.

The foundation stone for the grander version was laid on 26 August 1806 with all the usual ceremony. By then £619 had been raised, including a shilling from each of 269 less affluent subscribers. It took some time to raise the rest of the funds and, after additional appeals, it was duly completed between 1807 and 1810 and opened on Trafalgar Day in 1812. Two gentlemen, one in Forres and another in London, contributed two four-pounder cannon said to have been used by the fleet in the bombardment of Alexandria. The tower, still open as a museum, is indeed a striking structure, 70 feet high, with a diameter of 24 feet, with rooms on three floors connected by a spiral staircase and offering spectacular views from the top. It contains a grand bust of Nelson raised on a column in a niche surrounded by cannon balls.

But even more surprising than the appearance of this monument is the founding of the Forres Trafalgar Club on Trafalgar Day 1807. Local aristocrats and landowners like the Duke of Gordon, his son the Marquis of Huntly, and James Brodie of Brodie were closely involved with this. This club acquired a number of possessions including a punch bowl decorated with images of Napoleon and Nelson sitting across a table and eyeing each other in a menacing manner. A chamber pot with a bust of Napoleon inside was used at the social gatherings between 1815 and 1840. A grand silver cup was given by the Duke, a medal bearing a striking likeness of Nelson by the Rev. Gordon of Banff, a fine print of Nelson's dying scene by the Marquis. Donations were received for the Nelson bust which was duly unveiled in 1837. But already, the original enthusiasm was waning. The founders began to die out and the club virtually ceased to meet in 1840. All its possessions were handed over to Forres Town Council in 1851, and intriguingly, the Nelson snuff box continued to be passed around the councillors of the town council before each meeting, a tradition maintained until local government reorganisation in 1975.[28]

So why Forres? There is a local tradition that a number of the sailors on board *Victory* came from the area. It is also suggested that a surgeon did so, and he is buried in Cawdor kirkyard. The nearby coast has long been a nursery ground for sailors given the importance of fishing there. Its strategic situation was also frequently noted, even if seldom put to the test. Moreover, the Duke of Gordon had recently completely remodelled his grounds at Gordon Castle. The notion of a tower on a hill top surrounded by trees (now much grown) fitted romantic concepts of the picturesque and sublime, and the proposed functions as navigation beacon, signal tower, observatory, and alarm post seemed to give point to the whole conception.

Visibility is vital to legendary status, and in all the ways that I have described the Nelson myth was probably the most visible of all.[29] But just as the Trafalgar Club at Forres began to lose its momentum by the middle of the nineteenth century, so was there perhaps a dip in the power of the Nelson myth. It is true that the Nelson statue on its column in Trafalgar Square, described by Peel as 'the finest site in Europe', was erected in 1843 with Landseer's lions added as late as 1867, but there is some evidence that Nelson's reputation momentarily waned.[30] Just as the Victorians were uncomfortable with some of the bawdiness of Shakespeare's plays or with the sexual elements of Mozart's operas, so did they become anxious about the Nelson–Emma Hamilton relationship.

It is true that Queen Victoria visited *Victory* to imbibe its national significance, but naval heroes were now wanting, and heroism had been translated to more exotic locations. But towards the end of the century, the Nelson myth came back into its own, now constituting a vital call to naval arms. Interest groups began to promote the cause of the Royal Navy in the second half of the 1880s, culminating in the Naval Defence Act of 1889. The Royal Naval Exhibition at Chelsea in 1891 constituted a major turning-point in the public profile of the Navy, and much was made of the Nelson myth in its galleries and in its remarkable replica of *Victory*.[31] The same decade saw the founding of both the Naval Records Society (1893) and the Navy League (1894). The Nelson legend now had new and powerful champions.

III

This revival has been much commented upon, but what interests me is that the Nelson legend had become an imperial phenomenon. Nelson was appropriated by people in the empire and used to counter the anxieties and bolster the demands of the territories of white settlement, the dominions. This was not of course difficult to do, not least because Nelson himself had been an imperial figure. As well as the extraordinary Arctic expedition of 1773, when he had sailed on the same ship as the now celebrated former slave Olaudah Equiano, he had served on the India station as a midshipman, had called in at the Cape when it was still Dutch, and had visited and been involved in crucial engagements in the West Indies on several occasions. In the early 1780s, he had been in North America and had visited Quebec, Halifax, and New York. Above all, the Battle of Aboukir Bay was of course seen as frustrating Napoleon's designs on India. He was also well aware of his role as saviour of significant parts of the British empire. In 1805, he wrote to Lord Seaforth, the Governor of Barbados, that 'Your Lordship may rely that everything in my power shall be done to preserve the colonies.'[32]

Not surprisingly, then, Nelson monuments had sprouted in the empire too. After a dramatic announcement of the Trafalgar victory at the Assembly Ball in Montreal, a coadestone statue was commissioned and unveiled in 1808.[33] At Bridgetown, Barbados, a subscription opened as soon as news of his death reached the island and raised £2,500 within a few weeks, presumably from officials and wealthy plantation and slave owners. 'The Green' in the centre of town was purchased for £1,050 and renamed Trafalgar Square. A bronze statue of Nelson in admiral's uniform was unveiled there soon afterwards. At Port Royal, Jamaica, the area on the ramparts outside Nelson's quarters in Fort Charles became known as Nelson's quarterdeck and his arms were painted above the door with a suitably stirring inscription. Fig Tree Church near Charlestown on Nevis displayed the marriage certificate of Horatio to Mrs Frances Nisbet on 11 March 1787. It was later sent to London for the Colonial and Indian Exhibition of 1886 where it apparently excited a great deal of interest. Nearby was a spot known as 'Nelson's Watering Place', while a plaque to Nelson adorned the entrance gate of the ruins of Montpelier

House.[34] It was easy to portray Nelson as the saviour of the West Indies, and consequently of one of the significant bases of British imperial and economic power.

The naval base at Simonstown in the Cape still boasts its plaque commemorating the visit of Nelson there on his way back from India, while, almost inevitably, his bust was donated to the South African naval college to inspire its student cadets. The Mount Nelson Hotel stands on land named by the former owner. We have already seen how place names commemorated Nelson in the empire, and, as towns and cities grew, street names appeared everywhere. What is happening here is that the British World is expressing its cultural unity through a shared history, particularly a share in the heroic icons of the past. Even if imperial federation was never a practical policy, a sort of cultural federation was promoted in all sorts of ways.

All of this came to a great climax with the centennial celebrations in 1905. If the British empire had been only partially formed in 1805, it was now fully established with settlers everywhere eager to plug themselves into a more potent historical tradition. Strangely enough the centennial celebrations in Britain and the Navy itself were muted on the orders of the Admiralty, in order not to offend the new allies, the French (though there was still a good deal of activity, including a naval, shipping and fisheries exhibition at Earl's Court). But further afield, the celebrations seem to have taken similar forms throughout the empire. In the larger cities, often the quarterdeck of *Victory* was re-created in the largest hall available; salutes were fired, nearly choking the participants; Nelson's celebrated signal was flown; pieces of oak from *Victory* were displayed and revered; patriotic songs were sung and poems in honour of Nelson read.[35] Lengthy speeches were given by governors, prime ministers, mayors, bishops, chaplains and chairmen of the local branches of the Navy League. Schools had celebrations everywhere and smaller towns organised outdoor events, often associated with other notable civic occasions, like the inauguration of a park or bandstand (as at Gisbourne, New Zealand). The local newspapers carried a round-up of what was happening elsewhere, with a faintly competitive whiff to the descriptions. In Dunedin in the South Island of New Zealand, the *Otago Witness* produced a 'Centenary of Trafalgar' special issue with 32 pages 'exclusive of advertisements', 120 illustrations, and major articles, good value for sixpence, and warned its readers to order quickly since it would soon sell out, an accurate expectation as well as a marketing ploy.[36]

In the reports of the events and the speeches, a number of themes emerge: one is the extent to which the British empire had grown, an expansion which was ultimately built on Nelson's victories. Another was that Nelson took precedence over Wellington since if Napoleon's power at sea had not been broken first, then Waterloo would never have happened. A further notion was an internationalist one: that in breaking the power of France, Nelson had been the benefactor of all the nations. In 1905, it was suggested that even the French accepted this and French sailors everywhere acknowledged the significance of Nelson. In the South Island of New Zealand, the Governor of the Colony, together with the Attorney General, sailed on Saturday 21 October to the city of Nelson, triumphantly decorated for the occasion. His Excellency was driven down Trafalgar Street (all the main streets had been given Nelson-related names) to lay the foundation stone of a new building at Nelson College.[37]

In Melbourne, the celebrations were remarkable.[38] It should be remembered that at this point, Melbourne was the capital of the recently created Commonwealth of Australia. Australia had been a continental state for fewer than five years and it was looking for a national myth that would help to bind it. It was also aware, as New Zealand was, of its remote position dependent for its defence on the sea power of others. There was a considerable build-up to 21 October in the Melbourne papers, *The Age* and *The Argus*. The streets and shops, together with the ships at Port Melbourne and in the river, were almost universally decorated and comparisons were drawn with the comparatively recent and wild rejoicings at the lifting of the sieges in the Boer War. The main commemoration took place in the Town Hall, organised by the Royal Society of St George, and so many thousands of people besieged the building for admission that hundreds who had actually bought tickets in advance could not get in. The disappointed ones were described as 'wrestling manfully with the police'. The prime minister, Alfred Deakin, pointed out that those present were 'the possessors of a continent' which had been won by 'fathers and founders' owing much to the Navy and 'to Nelson as its embodiment', a sentiment met with prolonged cheering. Fears were expressed of the war to come, and of the desperate need for another Nelson.[39] Another speaker, Sir Philip Fysh suggested that Australia had 'inherited the blessings of British institutions' as a result of Trafalgar, while the Archbishop of Melbourne in the local St Paul's Cathedral suggested in his sermon that without Nelson the 'French flag would be flying over Australia and New Zealand'. Nelson was also hailed as a Protestant hero, whose predecessors had defeated the 'perverted Christianity of the Middle Ages' in defeating the Spanish Armada. But the moral problem of Nelson was confronted. The Archbishop merely said that Nelson had his faults, but these should be passed over in silence.[40]

The Argus blamed Lady Hamilton for having exerted, through her flattery, a perverse influence upon him.[41] But Bishop Langley, preaching at All Saints, Bendigo, struck the most powerful note of doubt: he could not, he pronounced with Knoxian fervour, 'refer to Nelson without condemning his moral character, for, while he was publicly a hero, he was privately a libertine'.[42]

Similar, if less judgemental, celebrations took place in Bridgetown, Barbados, under the auspices of the Navy League, in Nevis, in Gibraltar (where, in the classic paradox of the Rock, there was a commemorative mass), the Bermudas, Canada and Cape Colony, not to mention at the Victoria Club in Boston, Massachusetts.[43] At Halifax, Nova Scotia, the ceremonies took place at yet another St Paul's Church, where Nelson had worshipped when stationed there.[44] Despite the attempt to restrain them, the ceremonies in Trafalgar Square and St Paul's Cathedral in London were also, of course, imperial events, with high commissioners, agents general, and other representatives of colonies present. But interestingly, in Glasgow, fervour seemed to have waned. Although a service in the cathedral was well attended, the decorations in the city were disappointing as was the interest in an event in the St Andrew's Hall, while nothing happened at the monument on Glasgow Green. At the Cathedral, the minister may have offered a clue. Scots, he said, could still honour Nelson while adhering to their own heroes, such as Bruce at Bannockburn. *The Glasgow Herald*, just as it had done after the Relief of Mafeking, produced a Scotland-wide survey of events, starting alphabetically with my own Perthshire village of Alyth. It would appear that in many places the Scottish centennial celebrations were a little desultory.[45] It is clear that Scots, who had celebrated the Boer War Reliefs with massive patriotic fervour, had other things on their minds in 1905.

Nevertheless, two key events influenced the 1905 celebrations. One was the newly formed Entente Cordiale with France. Everywhere, reference was made to French sailors. Pieces of oak from the *Victory* were given to visiting French councillors and others. In Melbourne it was said that the more thoughtful citizens actually flew the Tricolor as well as the Union flag. The second notable event to have occurred was the Battle of Tsushima just a few months earlier and at this point the newly emergent empire of Japan seems to have appropriated the Nelson myth. The Anglo-Japanese treaty had been signed in 1902 and the Japanese victory over the Russians was hailed as the first great naval engagement since Trafalgar itself. In Boston, Commander Takashima, who it was said had been with Admiral Togo on his bridge, was present at the Nelson dinner. In London, a bust of Nelson made from the timbers of *Victory* was presented to the

Japanese naval attaché on behalf of Togo. (Togo cabled his 'heartfelt thanks'.)[46] The Japanese dimension, and the apparent security of the treaty, cannot have been lost in Australia and New Zealand too. Indeed the Melbourne *Argus* specifically referred to the significance of Tsushima as the battle of the centennial and also hailed the significance of the works of Alfred Thayer Mahan on the influence of sea power in history – which concluded before the Napoleonic period – as well as his biography of Nelson.[47]

Visitors to Togo's preserved flagship, the *Mikasa*, at Yokosuka near Yokohama, cannot fail to notice that the Nelson legacy is everywhere.[48] Togo saw himself as the inheritor of the Nelson touch. He was acutely aware of the significance of the centennial. Before the battle, he flew a signal which almost precisely imitated that of Nelson, 'Japan expects ....' His tactics at Tsushima were similarly innovative and it is not surprising that the London attaché said that Japan had an unbounded admiration for Nelson's heroic deeds. The *Mikasa*, built in Barrow-in-Furness, is a popular museum site and Japanese visitors are invited to see Togo as the inheritor of the Nelson mantle.

But if Togo had appeared to put paid to any Russian naval ambitions, the spectre of Kaiser Wilhelm's Germany became an increasing source of anxiety in the years that followed. This fuelled interest in the Navy League and its constant invocation of Nelson's legacy. In 1907, a bust of Nelson was presented to the Corporation of Ottawa with much ceremony.[49] In 1910 in Dunedin, the record of the Trafalgar Day celebrations in the Garrison Hall was issued as a pamphlet, featuring quotations about the significance of Nelson and the British Navy from Mahan as well as prime ministers Gladstone and Asquith. Lantern slides of Nelson at Trafalgar were shown and he was described as the 'greatest seaman since the world began'.[50] Two years later, a pamphlet was published in Auckland with the significant title 'The Battle of Trafalgar: Shall We Keep its Fruits?' Trafalgar was described as the naval victory which made New Zealand possible and Nelson was the genius who gave our countrymen the opportunity to build up a mighty empire. The agenda of New Zealand's Navy League branch, as this pamphlet made clear, was to protect the Nelson legacy not by joining Australia in what was contemptuously described as a 'baby fleet in the South Pacific', but in contributing more to an imperial navy which would protect the Trossachs as well as Toronto, Devonshire as well as Auckland and Sydney.[51]

It has been suggested that myths can also be millstones, that it was the myth of Nelson which contributed to so many of the failings of the Royal Navy in the First World War, notably the misplaced emphasis upon rate of fire.[52] But the Nelson myth was also an energiser: outside the British empire, it certainly had that effect upon Admiral Togo. Within the empire, it became a shared memory and a common cause. Whether mirage or miracle, it is apparent that Nelson and Trafalgar had a powerful resonance across the globe. As the newspaper accounts amply demonstrate, those who participated in events in Nelson, New Zealand or Trafalgar in Gippsland, Australia, or in the many larger centres in five continents were aware of participating in an extraordinary world-wide phenomenon. It is by these means that the nineteenth-century empire can be seen as a 'British World', a cultural entity bound together by appeals to history, to heroic myths and ancestral courage. Until the British World was to be transformed by migrants from elsewhere in Europe and Asia in the course of the twentieth century, settlers carried a simple message with them. The members of the colonial elite who organised events, delivered the speeches and wrote the pamphlets were playing upon a theme that was already well embedded in the consciousness of citizens of colonial territories. These uniting myths are often displayed in guide books, as well as school texts and more exciting juvenile material like novels and books of heroes.

IV

Thus are myths anchored in the strong ground of entwined economic and strategic interests. To be influential, a myth has to be instrumental. This is why the Scottish and colonial examples are so interesting. The monuments raised in Scotland and elsewhere in the early nineteenth century celebrated the security of trade and the opportunities for emigration (and immigration) which Nelson was seen to have protected. They also bore testimony to a belief in a united state and Scotland's position within it. By the early twentieth century, Scots seem to have been looking to other areas of instrumentality. A cultural and political revival, however tentative, had re-emphasised Scottish heroes. Participation in nineteenth-century imperial warfare had given the Scottish regiments a particular and ethnically identifiable aura, not possible in a navy which lacked such organisational sub-divisions. But by then the Nelson myth had real significance for a newly emergent naval power, Japan, basing itself on western models.

Meanwhile in the 'dominions' and other colonies, the myth remained potent for white societies which still felt relatively small and insecure. By the Edwardian era, the legendary status of Nelson seems to have been celebrated more in Dunedin than Edinburgh, Melbourne than

Glasgow. The people who wrestled with the police to gain access to Melbourne Town Hall were eager to re-affirm their identity through the celebrations taking place within, and they were also aware of the manner in which they clung to the fringe of a continent at the further edge of great oceans. As their speechmakers and newspapers amply indicated, the myth remained significant for them. Artists of the period liked to portray the apotheosis of great heroes, rising to the skies in death. But the true direction was not upwards, but outwards. The myth of Nelson became, for at least a hundred years, a global phenomenon.

Notes

1. The author is grateful to the following people and institutions for supplying information: Susan Ashworth of the Lancashire Museums Service; Anne Bennet of the Falconer Museum, Forres, Moray Council; Anne Dulau, Hunterian Art Gallery, University of Glasgow; Sally Birkbeck; Nigel Dalziel; Admiral Sir John Kerr; Huw Lewis-Jones; Dorothy Marsh, Edinburgh Museums and Arts Department; Montrose Museum, Angus Council; Nelson Museum and Local History Centre, Monmouth; Norfolk Museum Service; Lt. Cdr. F. Nowosielski of *Victory*; Finlay McKichan; Jeffrey Richards; Lisa Watson, administrator, National Trust, Stowe Garden; the Glasgow City Archives; the Mitchell Library, Glasgow; the Glasgow Museums Service (the People's Palace and Photo Library). Research visits were made to Glasgow, Edinburgh and Forres, as well as to the Archives of the Western Cape, Cape Town, the Nova Scotia Archives, Halifax, the Hocken Library, Dunedin, and the State Library of Victoria, Melbourne, where the help of archivists and librarians was much appreciated.
2. Carlyle recognised the heroic significance of Nelson and chose to write about him in an early stage of his career. Andrew Lambert, *Nelson: Britannia's God of War* (London: Faber, 2004), pp. 334–5.
3. For other analyses of imperial myths, see John M. MacKenzie, 'David Livingstone and the Construction of the Myth', in Graham Walker and Tom Gallagher (eds), *Sermons and Battle Hymns* (Edinburgh: Edinburgh University Press, 1990), pp. 24–42; MacKenzie, 'Heroic Myths of Empire', in John M. MacKenzie (ed.), *Popular Imperialism and the Military* (Manchester: Manchester University Press, 1992), pp. 109–38; MacKenzie, 'T.E. Lawrence: The Myth and the Message', in Robert Giddings (ed.), *Literature and Imperialism* (London: Macmillan, 1991), pp. 150–81; MacKenzie, 'The Iconography of the Exemplary Life: The Case of David Livingstone', in Geoffrey Cubitt and Allen Warren, *Heroic Reputations and Exemplary Lives* (Manchester: Manchester University Press, 2000), pp. 84–104, as well as other chapters in the same volume. For naval heroic myths, see C.I. Hamilton, 'Naval Hagiography and the Victorian Hero', *Historical Journal*, 23.2 (1980), pp. 381–98.
4. These iconic moments are generally themselves mythic, although the Nelson one was more accurately represented by at least some of the artists who depicted it. Those of Livingstone and Gordon (as in the celebrated painting

by G.W. Joy, recreated in the film *Khartoum*) are almost certainly pure fabrications.

5. A number of biographers have commented on Nelson's fascination with Wolfe. Sir N.H. Nicolas's *Dispatches and Letters of Vice-Admiral Nelson* (7 volumes, London, 1844–46) contain a number of references. Off Corsica in 1794, Nelson wrote 'What would the immortal Wolfe have done?' (quoted in Christopher Hibbert, *Nelson, a Personal History* (Harmondsworth: Penguin, 1995), p. 95). Nelson's celebrated encounter with Benjamin West at Fonthill in 1800 is fully recounted in Lambert, *Nelson*, p. 181, while Nelson's early sense of a death scene coming on, at the Battle of the Nile, is described on p. 128.

6. A good example is the well-known early twentieth-century image associated with Player's Navy Cut cigarettes.

7. A.W. Reed, *Dictionary of New Zealand Place Names* (Wellington: Reed Books, 2002), p. 333; A.H. McLintock (ed.), *An Encyclopaedia of New Zealand*, vol. 2 (Wellington: R.E. Owen, 1966), p. 643. Later the Nelson Lakes National Park was gazetted in the twentieth century.

8. Anthony Sampson, *Mandela* (London: HarperCollins, 1999), p. 7.

9. Linda Colley, *Britons: Forging the Nation, 1707–1837* (London: Yale University Press, 1992).

10. Colin White, *The Nelson Encyclopaedia* (London: Chatham, 2002), pp. 176–8.

11. I am grateful to Lisa Watson, the National Trust administrator at Stowe, for information on the various monuments there.

12. Charles Alexander Strang, *Borders and Berwick: An Illustrated Architectural Guide to the Scottish Borders and Tweed Valley* (Edinburgh: Rutland Press, 1994), p. 172.

13. This crudely carved stone has now been moved inside the furnace buildings at Bonawe.

14. The Liverpool meeting and the immediate institutional subscriptions were reported in *The Glasgow Herald*, 22 November 1805.

15. An account of this meeting can be found in *The Glasgow Herald*, 29 November 1805. The fortunes of the Edinburgh monument can be followed in the Edinburgh Town Council minutes, vols 149 (1814), 166 (1814), 166 (1818), 176 (1834) and many others. Accounts of the monument can be found in the City of Edinburgh Monuments Catalogue, and the Inventory of Monuments in Edinburgh.

16. The victory at Trafalgar was announced in *The Herald* on 11 November and the letter was published on the 15th. Information on preparations for planning and building the monument as well as material that kept Nelson's name and reputation before the Scottish public continued to appear throughout November and December. There are also interesting letters relating to Nelson in the Glasgow City Archives, TD 333/1 and TD 424.

17. A manuscript list of subscribers is in the Glasgow City Archives, TD 200/112. Lists of subscribers and their subscriptions appeared in *The Herald* from 16 December and carried on into January 1806.

18. *Glasgow Herald*, 30 December 1805.

19. *Glasgow Herald*, 25 April 1806.

20. Useful accounts of the responses of these poets can be found in Lambert's *Nelson*. Byron, who of course wished to slot himself into the 'apostolic

succession' of heroes, made frequent references to Nelson and coined the phrase 'Britannia's god of war' in *Don Juan*.

21. Notices to all Masonic lodges and public bodies were issued in *The Herald* in late July 1806. The account of the laying of the foundation stone appeared on 4 August 1806. Other accounts can be found in Robert Chapman, *The Picture of Glasgow or Stranger's Guide*, editions of 1806, 1811, 1818, pp. 178–9; also George MacGregor, *Glasgow Ancient and Modern* (Glasgow, 1872), vol. 3, pp. 593–4 and 1888 edition, p. 69. See, additionally, Elspeth King, *The People's Palace and Glasgow Green* (Glasgow, 1985) and Ray McKenzie, *Public Sculpture of Glasgow* (Liverpool: Liverpool University Press, 2002).

22. Chapman's *Picture of Glasgow*, 1811 edition carries an account on p. 58; information on the Knox paintings can be found in the records of the Hunterian Art Gallery, University of Glasgow, and the People's Palace, Glasgow Green (Glasgow Museums Service).

23. 'Nelson Monument', City of Edinburgh Museums Pamphlet No. 7.

24. Annaba Kilfeather, 'O'Connell Street Monument, Dublin', <www.mglarc. com/projects/oconnell.htm>, posted 15/08/00. A BBC Radio 4 programme on the monument 'Fallen Heroes' was broadcast on 19 August 2003.

25. Norfolk Museums service issue an information sheet on this monument and a number of press cuttings were sent by the staff of the service. There is also a useful website: <http://website.lineone.net/~d.bolton/misc/monument. htm>.

26. Monmouthshire County Council issues leaflets on the Nelson Garden and the Nelson Museum and Local History Centre.

27. A website on this monument can be found at <http://members.aol.com/ thardy1001/admiral.html>. In addition to all these commemorative structures, many towns acquired portraits of Nelson. One example hangs in the Ashton Hall at Lancaster Town Hall, a large canvas by the artist James Lonsdale probably depicting Nelson at the Battle of Copenhagen. It was presented to the city in 1806 and formerly hung in the council chamber. Information from Lancashire Museums Service.

28. Materials on the tower (including the manuscript call for subscriptions and list of subscribers), Cluny Hill, the ceremonies associated with the monument, and the Trafalgar Club, together with the artefacts of the Club can be seen at the Falconer Museum, Forres, Morayshire.

29. As well as the spectacular monuments described here, Nelson was also commemorated in a host of other ways, from a great range of paintings and their associated prints (still to be seen in the shops of Greenwich today) to countless ceramics, medallions and the extraordinary glass pictures which were published within six months of his death. See L.P. Le Quesne, *Nelson Commemorated in Glass Pictures* (Woodbridge: Antique Collectors Club, 2001). For some of the ceramics, see David Williams, 'Nelson Commemorated', *The Trafalgar Chronicle*, no. 14, 2004, 88–99. All forms of Nelson commemorative material can be found in the Nelson Gallery of the National Maritime Museum, Greenwich.

30. Margaret Baker, *London Statues and Monuments* (Princes Risborough: Shire, 1995), pp. 8–9. While John Ruskin, influenced by Southey, respected Nelson, he did not admire the columns erected to his memory.

31. Huw Lewis-Jones, '"Displaying Nelson": Navalism and "The Exhibition" of 1891', *The Trafalgar Chronicle*, no. 14, 2004, 53–86.

32. Nelson to Seaforth, 8 June 1805, Seaforth papers, National Archives of Scotland GD46/17/16. These papers contain a hitherto unknown small cache of Nelson letters.

33. White, *Nelson Encyclopaedia*, p. 177.

34. Sir Algernon Aspinall, *The Pocket Guide to the West Indies* (London, 1931), pp. 78–80, 229, 272, 230.

35. There is an echo here of a tradition established at the Royal Naval Exhibition in Chelsea in 1891.

36. An advertisement for this special issue appeared in the *Otago Daily Times*, 18 October 1905. Many advertisers also hitched their products to Trafalgar Day.

37. Accounts of Trafalgar Day events can be found in the *Otago Daily Times*, 21, 23, 24 October, with a lengthy discussion of the significance of Nelson and of Trafalgar in the same paper on Friday the 20th.

38. Accounts of the celebrations can be found in *The Argus* for 19, 20, 21, and 23 October and in *The Age* for 21 October.

39. *The Argus*, 23 October 1905.

40. *The Age*, 21 October 1905.

41. *The Argus*, 21 October 1905.

42. *The Argus*, 23 October 1905.

43. *The Glasgow Herald*, 23 October 1905 produced a round-up of imperial events and also a detailed description of the dinner at the Victoria Club in Boston.

44. See the accounts in *The Morning Chronicle* of Halifax and *The Halifax Herald*, 23 October 1905.

45. *The Glasgow Herald*, 23 October 1905, described the events in Glasgow and elsewhere as 'modest', while writing up the 'stirring scene' and 'remarkable spectacle' in Trafalgar Square.

46. *The Glasgow Herald*, 23 October 1905.

47. Alfred Thayer Mahan, *The Influence of Sea Power Upon History, 1660–1783* (London, 1890), and *The Life of Nelson, the Embodiment of the Sea Power of Great Britain* (London, 1897).

48. Personal observation on a visit to *Mikasa*, 21 September 1997.

49. *The Glasgow Herald*, 27 February 1907.

50. 'Trafalgar Day Demonstration', pamphlet 1910, Hocken Library, Dunedin.

51. 'The Battle of Trafalgar: Shall We Keep its Fruits?' An address by Mr. W.J. Napier, President of Navy League, Auckland Branch on Trafalgar Day, 1912.

52. Andrew Lambert in his BBC2 series *War at Sea*, February 2004.

8
Nelson Afloat: A Hero Among the World's Navies

John B. Hattendorf

The legacy of Horatio Nelson is something more than just that of a fleet commander who had won a famous victory and more than just that of a distinctively British naval hero. His legacy is different from that of a Marlborough or a Wellington, who are also seen as great commanders. Beyond that, Nelson is seen as the embodiment of key professional virtues for naval leaders that provides an enduring model. Within a century after his death, Nelson had become a hero among the world's navies and an icon of naval professionalism around the globe. The applications of Nelson's name in professional naval terms are remarkable and extend to the present day and to modern navies that no longer bear any physical resemblance to those of the age of fighting sail. If one excludes from examination here the distinctive views that may have developed in Nelson's own victorious Royal Navy and those navies that directly evolved from its traditions in British colonies and the Commonwealth and then if one adds to that number those that Nelson defeated, France, Spain, and Denmark, there are still nearly 150 of the world's navies to consider. In that wide field, one may turn to the navies of Germany, Japan, China, the Soviet Union, Latin America, and the United States as representative cases.

In the United States, for example, the currently serving civilian head of the United States Navy, the Secretary of the Navy, wears as his 'trademark' necktie one that features Nelson's famous flag hoist, 'England expects every man will do his duty.'[1] The same words are on a cast bronze plaque at the outside corridor entrance to his Pentagon office and, just inside the door, there is a framed print of Montague Dawson's painting of 'the Battle of Trafalgar'. Until recently, another Trafalgar scene dominated the Secretary of the Navy's official dining room in the Pentagon: an anonymous Dutch painting of the French ship *Achille* exploding at the end of the Battle of Trafalgar. Of course, these interconnected references in the Secretary's office to Trafalgar and 'England expects' are a humorous play on words, as this Secretary of the Navy's surname is England, the Honorable Gordon R. England.[2] Yet, the application is appropriate and it is instantly recognisable to everyone who serves in the US Navy as something that relates directly to the core values that the US Navy emphasises: 'Honor, Courage, and Commitment.'[3] These are the very values that Nelson's example as a naval warrior embodies and has come to represent as an ideal.

There are several phases in the growth of Nelson's image in navies around the world. In the history of nineteenth-century British culture, Nelson's image was part of a wider development of heroes which began in three stages over the century from the early development of a distinctive Victorian idea of a Christian hero, its heyday at mid-century, and then its distillation in the years leading up to the First World War.[4] While the image of Nelson takes its place in Britain in these years, it was somewhat different in the context of the professional naval world, where he was, first, a professional figure noticed in his own time; secondly, a figure within recent professional memory, and thirdly, a more distant figure in history and an historical example for emulation.

I

In the broader discussion of Nelson's image in the naval profession around the world, the United States Navy provides an interesting example, not only because of its present role as a superpower navy, but also because the US Navy dates only from Nelson's time and mention of Nelson's name and activities can occasionally be found in the official US Navy documents of that time as well as in the centuries that have followed as Nelson gradually became a more remote professional icon. The US Navy officially recognises 13 October 1775 as its founding date, yet following the end of the War for American Independence in the 1780s, the newly established American republic did away with its first naval force, called the Continental Navy. A decade later in 1794, Congress authorised the building of the first ships for a United States Navy, first within the War Department and from 1798 under the newly established Navy Department. While the US Navy was an infant service as part of the War Department, American diplomats in Spain reported that Nelson had protected American merchant ships from the French at Malaga in March 1797.[5]

The first US Navy ship went to sea in May 1798, USS *Ganges*, and she was soon followed by others. One of them was commanded by Captain James Sever, whom many had criticised for having trouble with his crew and for not chasing a privateer that had been more heavily armed than his own ship. Defending Sever's conduct to President John Adams in 1799, the first Secretary of the Navy, Benjamin Stoddert, used Nelson's reputation as an example and protested to the President that under the same circumstances Admiral Nelson, 'if his understanding is equal to his bravery, would have pursued the very course that Sever did'.[6] As the ships of the United States Navy began to make overseas deployments, they were concerned first with the Quasi-War with France in 1798–1801 and nearly simultaneously, between 1800 and 1807, with protecting American trade from the depredations of the Barbary States on the North African coast. In the context of both conflicts, the operations of the Royal Navy had an indirect influence on what the small American navy was doing to protect its neutral trade. Nelson's victory at Aboukir Bay had a long-term positive influence on American interests in the Mediterranean region. Reflecting the continuing image the victory left on the North African states, the American Consul in Algiers, Tobias Lear, wrote in February 1804, 'The heroic character of Lord Nelson, who commanded the fleet, forbids the idea of fear on the part of the British ....'[7]

One of the famous and dramatic incidents in the US Navy's wars with the Barbary powers involved the US frigate *Philadelphia*, which had run aground on an uncharted reef in Tripoli harbour. All the efforts failed to refloat her under gunfire from shore batteries and her officers and men surrendered and were imprisoned as hostages. *Philadelphia*'s Tripolitan captors quickly took charge of the ship and turned her guns outward to defend against the other American ships. The commander of the American squadron in the Mediterranean, Captain Edward Preble, organised a volunteer party of officers and men under Lieutenant Stephen Decatur in the ketch *Intrepid*, boarded the captured ship on 16 February 1804 and burned her at anchor. It is often repeated in modern American naval histories that Nelson is said to have called this 'the most bold and daring act of the age'.[8] An entirely undocumented quotation, this is nevertheless an example of the way in which another navy used and continues to use Nelson's appropration, real or imagined, as a means of giving some emphasis to its own naval heritage.

Within a decade after Trafalgar, Britain and the United States went to war in a conflict that occurred simultaneously with the final stages of the Napoleonic Wars in 1812–15. Even though the Royal Navy was the enemy in the war of 1812, American readers were widely interested in Robert Southey's recently published *Life of Nelson*. Several unauthorised editions of the book were printed in the United States in 1813–14[9] and these were probably the source for a growing wide-spread familiarity in America with events in Nelson's life, although these would certainly have been an event of recent memory. Among the many events that took place during that war, Nelson's influence seems to have been clear at the Battle of Lake Erie on 10 September 1813, when the American commander, the 28-year-old Captain Oliver Hazard Perry, USN, faced his 27-year-old opponent, Acting Commander Robert Heriot Barclay of the Royal Navy, who had been commended for his action at Trafalgar as a lieutenant in HMS *Swiftsure*. Perry's biographer, Alexander Mackenzie, wrote in 1843 that on the night before the battle, Perry's 'last emphatic injunction with which he dismissed them was, that they could not, in the case of difficulty, advise them better than in the words of Lord Nelson, "if you lay your enemy close alongside, you cannot be out of your place!"'[10]

A year later, one can find another prominent instance of Nelson's influence at the Battle of Plattsburg Bay on Lake Champlain on 11 September 1814. There, Captain Thomas Macdonough's small squadron of US naval vessels faced the squadron under Captain George Downie, RN. Preparing for the battle that played a key role in General Provost's decision to withdraw British forces from the area, Macdonough hoisted a signal on board his anchored flagship, the 24-gun corvette *Saratoga*: 'Impressed seamen call on every man to do his duty.'[11] Macdonough's alteration to Nelson's signal carried with it not only a reflection of current American foreign policy in denouncing British impressment of American sailors, but it also transmitted a sense of Macdonough's caring support and concern for the ordinary seaman. In preparing to fight British forces on Lake Champlain, Macdonough decided to fight with his squadron in a defensive formation at anchor. Clearly, Macdonough was aware of Nelson's successful tactics against an anchored enemy at the Nile in 1798 and at Copenhagen in 1801. Macdonough used descriptions of those battles to guide his defensive planning on Lake Champlain, so as to avoid the French and Danish weaknesses in those engagements and to better a British officer, whom Macdonough expected would use Nelsonian tactics.[12] Macdonough carefully guarded against having his anchored squadron doubled, as Nelson had doubled Bruey's anchored ships in Aboukir Bay. In an innovative approach, the American commander ensured that his ships could use capstans and kedge anchors with carefully submerged spring lines to their anchor cables to turn themselves and to maintain broadside fire against the attacking British.

By 1830, Southey's *Life of Nelson* was so well known that the author's name became part of the title in American editions to distinguish it from other Nelson biographical works.[13] Even before this appeared, a friend wrote to Southey to report that he had heard that the American government had produced an edition of the book for everyone in the US Navy. Southey was correct to reply to his correspondent that 'It is not likely that the American Government, which is as parsimonious as Mr. Hume would wish ours to be, should incur the expense ....'[14] No trace of such an official action has yet been found, but there is a widespread assumption that American naval officers in this era had read the book at one point or another in their early careers.

By the end of the 1850s, one begins to find the first suggestions that Southey's descriptions lacked technical accuracy. At this point, American naval professionals were beginning to wonder exactly how Nelson had won his great victories and, in this regard, much focus turned on the seamanship involved in the Battle of the Nile. A one-time midshipman in the US Navy and the author of its first history, James Fenimore Cooper, dismissed Southey's account of the Nile. 'The life of Nelson by Southey, in all that relates to this feature of the day is pure fiction, as, indeed, are other parts of the work of scarcely less importance.'[15] This was, perhaps, an ironic comment coming from the creator of the American sea novel.[16] In fact, it was a point he made in a preface to his 1842 book, *The Admirals*, an early naval novel that focused, as the author described it, on the movement of fleets. Cooper's leading characters in the novel, Sir Gervaise Oates and Sir Richard Bluewater, were respectively modelled on Collingwood and Nelson and in writing it Cooper had made extensive use of the published Collingwood papers.[17] As the most widely known commentator on American naval events of his own day, Cooper went on to note, 'Had Nelson led in upon an American fleet as he did upon the French at the Nile, he would have seen reason to repent the boldness of his experiment.'[18]

One of the first officers in the US Navy to cast a professional eye on this issue was James H. Ward. At the time that the United States Navy entered the Civil War in 1861, Commander Ward had the reputation of being the most scholarly officer in its service. As a lieutenant in 1845, he had become the first Commandant of Midshipmen at the newly established Naval Academy and one of the very first American line officers to teach a professional naval subject in the classroom. Some years later, while serving at sea on the West African coast, as he explained 'to beguile leisure and relieve the tedium of service in that horrid region', Ward wrote *A Manual of Naval Tactics* for the Academy's use that was published in 1859.[19] Two years later, he was the first combat casualty among US naval officers during the Civil War, but his *Manual* continued to influence American professional thinking for a decade to come.[20]

Designed to be a digest of the major theoretical works on naval tactics, Ward combined this work with his own insights gained from practical experience, an analysis of recent battles as well as his own understanding of how he imagined future battles might be fought. In this, an important appendix to the *Manual* was a section taken directly from Sir Howard Douglas's 1858 book *On Naval Warfare with Steam*.[21] Ward was careful to point out that he had examined some details of the historical accounts on Nelson for his volume that differed from Douglas's descriptions. Ward wrote:

> With great deference it is claimed that when the *Manual* varies from this [Douglas's] text, either as regards the distance apart of the French ships at the Battle of the Nile, the length of the French line, the number of columns in which Nelson's ships approached, the mode of anchoring the ships, etc., reliable authorities or seamanship will be found to sustain the *Manual*.[22]

In the context of a broader understanding of naval tactics, Ward attempted a critical analysis of tactical usage, noting in regard to Trafalgar, that 'with a different sort of adversary, Nelson's tactics might have been more circumspect'.[23] He concluded that the superior readiness of the British fleet was the critical factor that made Nelson's tactics successful and that they might not have been successful with a different enemy.

Between 1861 and 1865, the United States was plunged into civil war with the secession of its Southern States and the establishment of the short-lived Confederate States of America. In these years, one can find Nelson's name invoked from time to time in professional correspondence by American officers. As an example of this in September 1861, Commander S. Phillips Lee, commanding the sailing sloop USS *Vandalia* on close blockade duty off Charleston, South Carolina, had mistaken the sleek steamer HMS *Steady* for a blockade runner and had fired a gun, the shot of which passed half a mile off *Steady*'s quarter. Promptly apologising for the misidentification, Lee invoked British naval history when he wrote to her commanding officer to apologise for his error:

A smart steamer moving under false colors (which we know is done, and which your great naval authorities, Admirals Nelson and Collingwood, admitted an enemy has a right to use) bent on running the blockade, can slip by a sailing vessel, lying to without steam and near the bar.[24]

Similarly three years later, Lee, now an acting Rear-Admiral, invoked Nelson's name when he sought permission from Assistant Secretary Gustavus Vasa Fox for one of Lieutenant William Cushing's daring exploits. Cushing 'thinks that the fort on Bald Hill [North Carolina] may be surprised by the blockaders', Lee wrote:

Will you in any manner, even by a 'Go it Ned' (after the fashion of the Attorney and Lord Codrington), justify the attempt? The idea is taking and the thing is possible, though Nelson failed in such an effort. But I like enterprises and have always encouraged them.[25]

Just a month before, Commander George Henry Preble, lamenting the escape of the Confederate raider CSS *Florida*, wrote in an official dispatch, 'Nelson said the want of frigates in his squadron would be found impressed on his heart. I am sure the want of steam will be found engraven on mine.'[26]

On the Confederate side, Secretary of the Navy Stephen R. Mallory used the measure of Nelson and a range of other British commanders to condemn the performance of the US Navy under Rear-Admiral S.F. DuPont in its failed attempt to take Charleston in 1863. Mallory wrote in disparagement, 'If DuPont had but possessed a spark of that flame which animated Exmouth at Algiers, Nelson at Copenhagen, or Hope at the Pei-Ho, he might still have failed, but he could not have been disgraced.'[27] In a less direct way, others showed that Nelson's story had made a deep impression on their own professional conduct. Among them, Lieutenant Francis A. Roe confided in his private diary during Flag-Officer David Farragut's opposed passage past the Confederate forts at the mouth of the Mississippi River in 1862. At a critical point in the operation and on the brink of battle, Roe wrote,

... I look for a bloody conflict. These may be the last lines I shall ever write. But I have an unflinching trust in God that we shall plant the Union flag upon the enemy's forts by noon to-morrow. I trust in Almighty God for the results. If I fall, I leave my darlings to the care of my country.[28]

The Civil War was a conflict that brought with it many professional innovations and developments for the US Navy. One of them was the creation of the rank of admiral, a title never before used in the American service, but brought about by the practical need to divide the fleet into several operating squadrons. Initially given the title 'Flag Officer', David Glasgow Farragut was the first of nine officers, who were eventually commissioned as rear-admirals during the war. Soon, Congress created for Farragut the rank of vice-admiral in 1864, and, finally in July 1866, admiral. With his new rank, Americans quickly compared and contrasted Farragut to Nelson. At the end of the war in 1865, on the day that Farragut returned his flagship USS *Hartford* to her homeport and hauled down his flag, Assistant Secretary of the Navy Fox wrote to the hero of Mobile Bay and New Orleans, 'It is a source of very great happiness to me that you have come back with the laurels of Nelson without leaving any limbs or eyes ....'[29] The exiled French Prince de Joinville, an erstwhile French naval officer who had come to America to observe the Civil War, wrote to Farragut, 'Since the days of Nelson I don't know of any more brilliant actions, and the skill and bravery displayed is, if possible heightened by the simplicity and modesty shown by yourself and your gallant brothers in arms.'[30]

A younger American officer, Winfield Scott Schley, who would become one of the leading American admirals in the Spanish-American War of 1898, had served as a lieutenant under Farragut in the Civil War and reflected in his memoirs that Nelson and Farragut were much alike. He compared them favourably in their restless energy of purpose, bravery, and self-poise. Yet, in the American's opinion, 'Farragut's private life and high ideals ... gave him preeminence over his great English compeer.'[31]

From the end of the American Civil War, sixty years after Trafalgar, Nelson's image as a figure within living memory had faded. In the United States Navy, at least, mention of his name no longer carried the currency that allowed it to remain widely used in the context of general conversation, personal letters, or official correspondence. Of course, among the well-read and those who were aware of naval history, his name was never forgotten, but there seems to be a clear change by the late 1860s in the Unites States, coinciding with both the passing of the generations that knew of him in terms of contemporary memory and the arrival of modern naval technology and the age of naval warfare under steam.

II

The origins of the modern study of naval history as an academic and professional naval subject may be traced to the teaching of Professor

Montagu Burrows at Oxford[32] and to the work of Professor Sir John Knox Laughton at King's College, London.[33] For the world's navies, Laughton's 1874 lecture, published in the *Journal of the Royal United Services Institution* on 'The Scientific Study of Naval History'[34] had direct repercussions, not only through the subsequent historical work in Britain of Vice-Admiral Sir Philip Colomb, Sir Julian Corbett, and Admiral Sir Herbert Richmond, but also in foreign countries. Laughton pointed out the continuing relevance of Nelson, when he commented:

> It was indeed astounding; and even now, after the lapse of three-quarters of a century, to continental nations, in whose eyes an army which numbers by mere thousands is as a thing of naught, the name of Nelson is almost a synonym for England's greatness. Aboukir and Trafalgar the true epitome of England's glory.[35]

Turning to draw the attention of the modern serving naval officer, Laughton went on to say, 'History, properly studied, teaches the principles on which battles have been won, or not won – have been lost or not lost ....'[36] Following Laughton's 1874 initiative in Britain, naval historical studies also begin to develop for the professional use of navies, first in Germany and then in the United States. For professionals looking toward naval history in both countries, as in Britain, the Nelson era was the period of the last great world-wide, maritime war. More recent, smaller wars in Europe and in America suggested some lines of new naval technological and tactical development, but these examples had not reached the proportions that would allow their examples to answer completely all the broad issues about major wars at sea in terms of naval strategy and leadership.

In the Imperial German Navy, Kapitän zur See Alfred Stenzel began his work in 1875 as a teacher at the Marine-Akademie at Kiel – that is the higher educational institution that provided, on a voluntary basis, a three-year course of study for middle grade officers, not the Marine-Schule for cadets at the beginning of their careers. Assigned at first on a part-time basis to the Akademie from 1875 until 1881 as teacher in naval history and tactics, Stenzel later returned again to the Marine-Akademie on a full-time basis in 1894–96 to teach naval history.[37] In these years, naval history was one of the professional areas that German naval officer students could choose for one of their three major areas of concentration for their advanced studies.[38] Among those, who made this choice and were taught by Stenzel, three were officers who later made their names in the early twentieth century as naval historians: Vize-Admiral Curt

Freiherr von Maltzahn, Kontre-Admiral Rudolph Rittmeyer, and Vize-Admiral Hermann Kirchhoff.

At the present stage of scholarship, it is difficult to assess how Stenzel's historical thinking grew and developed. His first published work was an analysis of British fleet manoeuvres in 1888, which shows wide reading in English-language journals and leads one to speculate whether or not he may have read Laughton's writings as well as the works of other British and American naval historians. A further problem lies in the fact that Stenzel died in 1906, before his major work appeared posthumously in print in 1913. Although he is reported to have dealt with Nelson in his early lectures, it is difficult to ascertain with certainty what he said at the earliest stages of his lecturing and which of his thoughts he may have developed later on the basis of other influences. Nevertheless, one can get a sense of what he inculcated in his students from his conclusion that

> As the last and highest token of Nelson's esteem to consider is that, in modern times one understands his importance as entirely exceptional, [and] one must nurture the Nelsonian Spirit, and cultivate his ideas in order to achieve that greatness.[39]

In the United States Navy, the key person who directly transmitted Laughton's ideas about naval history was Rear-Admiral Stephen B. Luce and it was he who first tried to institutionalise them in the US Naval War College, when it was established in 1884. In creating this college to serve as the US Navy's highest level of professional military education and 'a place of original research on all questions relating to war and to statesmanship connected with war, or the prevention of war',[40] Luce placed naval history as one of the principal means for studying strategy, along with international law, war gaming of future operations, and military theory. At the opening address of the first session of the college in 1885, Luce laid out his concept for 'The Study of Naval Warfare as a Science'. In his concluding remarks, Luce said, '… let us confidently look for the master mind, who will lay the foundations of that science and do for it what Jomini had done for military Science'. Thirteen years later, Luce handwrote as a postscript on a printed copy of his earlier remarks: 'He appeared in the person of Captain A.T. Mahan.'[41] Luce laid out for Mahan what he was to do with his historical studies and suggested to him the kinds of principles that needed to be illustrated. In doing so, Luce mentioned among other examples, the achievements of Nelson. In particular, he stressed Nelson's use of superiority of force at the Nile and at Trafalgar[42] and the success that came through 'the continuous celerity of their movements, to their great energy governed by an intelligent directive force'.[43]

In another lecture in 1885 at the Naval War College, 'On the Study of Naval History as Grand Tactics', Luce contrasted Howe and Nelson, whom he considered to be the great exemplars of two different branches of tactics, Howe representing 'minor, elementary or evolutionary tactics' and Nelson representing 'Fighting or Grand Tactics or the Tactics of Battle'.[44] Nelson, he said was also a great naval strategist, but this, Luce pointed out, is a distinct professional branch from the grand tactics of fleet fighting. The point that Luce took from his general study of British naval tactics was that Nelson's victories demonstrated to modern officers of the 1880s that success was not to be found in the old tactical concept of close action, ship to ship. This, Luce said was 'a principle directly opposite to what Nelson and his school taught. His teaching and the teachings of all great captains, both on shore and afloat, is to put *two against one*.'[45]

Here, Luce reflected the practical application that he believed could derive from a study of naval history and this was the charge he gave to Captain Mahan, when he directed him to undertake for the Naval War College a series of lectures on naval history and tactics. Mahan, himself, was initially very sceptical of what Luce wanted to achieve from historical study. As he later admitted, 'I shared the prepossession, common at that time, that the naval history of the past was wholly past; of no use at all to the present.'[46] He recalled escorting a journalist through the college building at one point in 1886, a man 'of magisterial condescension which the environment of the Fourth Estate nourishes in its fortunate members', who noticed a plan of Trafalgar hanging on the wall. '"Ah," he said, with superb up-to-date pity, "you are still talking about Trafalgar;" and I could see that Trafalgar and I were henceforth on the top shelf of fossils in the collections of his memory.'[47] Nevertheless, despite such initial reactions, Mahan went on to produce the historical study that the admiral had ordered. In the process of writing the first set of lectures delivered in the years 1886 through 1888, Mahan discovered the wisdom behind Luce's directive and went on to become Luce's immediate successor as President of the Naval War College as well as the most successful and most widely-read early promoter of the historical approach to understanding naval strategy. After publishing his first set of lectures in 1890 under the title *The Influence of Sea Power Upon History, 1660–1783*,[48] Mahan returned to the Naval War College for his second period as college president in 1892–93.

Even before he had completed his first *Influence* book, Mahan planned a sequel and a second series of lectures at the Naval War College to continue the theme. This volume appeared under the title *The Influence of Sea Power Upon the French Revolution and Empire, 1793–1812*, a volume devoted to the Nelson era.[49] In the preface to the new two-volume work, Mahan gave specific credit to the Naval War College as a place 'instituted to promote such studies'.[50] At the same time, he expressed his thanks to Admiral Luce 'for guiding him to a path that he would not himself have found'.[51] These references proved invaluable to the institution and they were largely responsible for saving it in the eyes of Secretary of the Navy Hilary Herbert, who had been bent on abolishing the college. On leaving an inspection visit to the college, Secretary Herbert wrote 'This book alone is worth all the money that has been spent on the Naval War College .... I had fully intended to abolish the college; I now intend to do all in my power to sustain it.'[52]

The story of Nelson's battles was clearly a part of Mahan's second sea power book and an analysis of Nelson's strategy and tactics had, thus, played a role in the US Navy's intuitional history as well as a continuing role in the curriculum of its highest professional educational institution. In this volume, however, Mahan had sublimated his narrative of Nelson's detailed operations to a wider analysis that focused at the higher level of political, political-economic, and governmental issues. Here he showed how Britain was able to counter and to neutralise the maritime threats from France and Spain and to eliminate secondary threats from The Netherlands and Denmark. In this, Mahan argued that the victory at Trafalgar removed the possibility of serious maritime challenge, secured the British blockade of the Continent, and the safety of overseas commerce. Together, Mahan showed that the effect was to secure Britain's commerce and, thus, her economic foundation.[53]

In coming to these broad conclusions, Mahan could see that the pattern and results of the wars of the French Revolution and Empire had not been inevitable. Through this analysis, Mahan understood that the individual leadership and decisions by those in key naval positions of responsibility had made a real difference to the course of events. This further consideration led him five years later in 1897 to publish a biography, *Nelson: The Embodiment of the Sea Power of Great Britain*, a work by a professional officer to guide other naval professionals as well as to interest the public.[54] In this large, two-volume study, Mahan repeated many of the things he had already said in his similarly sized *Influence of Sea Power* volume, but he placed these in the background as he focused at the forefront on his examination of Nelson as a naval commander. Here, most importantly was the message he wanted to give to naval officers. He saw in the naval officers of Nelson's time what he felt was a 'too common, almost universal, weakness, which deters men from a bold initiative, from assuming responsibility, from embracing opportunity ....'[55] Nelson stood out from these others by his conviction in seeking a decisive victory over the French. But, Mahan underscored his fundamental professional point that battles should not be fought with blind fury and that Nelson was not merely the embodiment of an aggressive warrior. In contrast, Mahan characterised Nelson's leadership at the Battle of the Nile as 'an instructive combination of rapidity and caution, of quick comprehension of the situation, with an absence of all precipitation; no haste incompatible with perfect carefulness, no time lost, either by hesitation or by preparations postponed'.[56] Nelson's intelligent use of what Mahan saw as military principles in fighting as well as Nelson's resolution in seeking his goals were the key attributes that made for sound military thinking. But, Mahan argued, those features also needed to be merged with another critical factor that Nelson characterised: moral courage.[57]

Five years later, in 1902, Mahan wrote another book on the same period of the Age of Sail, but this one did not become one of his famous works and it lay outside the 'Influence of Sea Power' theme. Entitled *Types of Naval Officers Drawn from the History of the British Navy*, Mahan's representative types were Hawke, Rodney, Howe, Jervis, Saumarez, and Pellew. Reviewing that list, 'The question may naturally be asked,' Mahan wrote in his preface,

> Why, among types of naval officers, is there no mention, other than casual, of the name of Nelson? The answer is simple. Among general officers, land and sea, the group to which Nelson belongs defies exposition by a type, both because it is small in aggregate numbers, and because of the eminence of the several members, – the eminence of genius, – so differentiates each from his fellows that no one among them can be said to represent the others .... Such do not in fact form a class, because, though a certain community of ideas and principles may be traced in their actions, their personalities and methods bear each the stamp of originality in performance; and where originality is found classification ceases to apply. There is a company, it may be, but not a class.[58]

Mahan's writings on Nelson are those of a professional naval officer interested in teaching the essential elements of high command and they reached a large range of professional naval officers as well as a much wider public readership. For years, Mahan's biography of Nelson was recognised within navies for its value as a work of professional naval importance. Through it, Mahan's interpretation had a clear influence on the way in which Nelson's image was presented in the context of American naval training and education over the next half century.[59] In a similar way, the biography had a direct effect on professional naval education in Japan[60] and in Sweden,[61] where the biography was translated for use in those navies.

III

Mahan's sea power books influenced naval thinking about naval leadership outside Britain, but his historical information also quickly merged with the growing number of works that were appearing in Britain leading up to and following the 1905 centenary of the Battle of Trafalgar. Several key books, read both in English and in translation, had a wide influence in navies outside of Britain and appeared in the years between the first edition of Mahan's *Nelson* in 1897 and the publication of Julian Corbett's *The Campaign of Trafalgar* in 1910.[62] German naval historians, beginning with Alfred Stenzel, were among the first to look at this topic, as far back as the mid-1870s and their interest soon paralleled and was influenced by naval works published in Britain and America. Following Stenzel's work, two other German naval writers made important contributions to studies on the Anglo-French naval wars.[63] These were Vice-Admiral Curt Freiherr von Maltzahn,[64] who had been a student of Stenzel's, and Vice-Admiral Eberhard von Mantey, who in turn had been a student of von Maltzahn.[65] In 1906, just following the Trafalgar centenary, von Maltzahn published a detailed study of the battle in the professional naval journal, *Marine Rundschau*[66] that summarised current understanding of the battle, while von Mantey went on to lecture to naval cadets and officers on similar subjects.[67]

In England, Joseph Conrad had clearly sensed the trend in his 1905 collection of essays, *The Mirror of the Sea*, when he wrote that the Nelsonian tradition, 'Like a subtle and mysterious elixir poured into the perishable clay of successive generations, it grows in truth, splendour, and potency with the march of ages.' From a narrowly British perspective, Conrad was correct in going on to say that

> In its incorruptible flow all round the globe of the earth it preserves from the decay and forgetfulness of death the greatness of our great men, and amongst them the passionate and gentle greatness of Nelson,

the nature of whose genius was, on the faith of a brave seaman and distinguished Admiral, such as to 'Exalt the glory of our nation.'[68]

Certainly the preservation of the memory of a British hero was one effect of this, but it was not this distinctively British patriotic and sentimental attraction that interested a number of professionals serving in foreign navies around the world. For them, interest in Nelson was motivated by two overlapping approaches. On the one hand, a number of naval professionals around the world shared a desire to penetrate, to analyse, and to elucidate the characteristics that made Nelson such a successful naval leader and tactician in history and to apply these practical findings to the education and training of officers and men in their own naval services. On the other hand, there was a desire for navies to share with one another in the larger body of inspirational naval heritage. These two aspects are quite different, yet overlapping, in their applications. Both share in the distinctive and age-old belief that mariners of every nation, serving in ships under every flag, share a fundamental commonality with one another. Naval men, whether officers or ratings, deal with similar equipment, share professional competencies in navigation, gunnery, and ship handling, have similar lives, develop similar standards, and include among their highest challenges the ability to face the caprice of the basic natural elements found in the 'boundless deep' of the world's oceans.

Research has so far found little distinctive interest in Nelson in Chinese professional naval literature during the nineteenth or for most of the twentieth century. By contrast, there was a very large interest in the Imperial Japanese Navy,[69] which seems to arise from the personal experience of Count Heihachiro Tōgō, the Japanese admiral who had commanded the fleet in the Russo-Japanese War, bombarded Port Arthur, and defeated the Russians at Tsushima in the centenary year of Trafalgar on 29 May 1905. His initial training had been spent in England as a cadet on board the training ship HMS *Worcester* in 1871–74. On the sixty-eighth anniversary of Trafalgar in October 1873, Tōgō observed a commemorative ceremony that deeply influenced him and reputedly led him to pattern himself on Nelson.[70] Through Tōgō, Nelson became a key part of Japan's naval heritage. This was most dramatically echoed in the Battle of Tsushima, when Tōgō ordered the 'Zed' flag hoisted, meaning: 'The country's fate depends upon this battle: let every man do his utmost.'[71]

One of the most important theorists for the development of Japanese strategy was Satō Tetsutarō and his idea of oceanic defence.[72] Sent to Britain and the United States for research in 1899–1901, Satō studied the relevance of British maritime experience to Japan's similar geographical position. A massive two-volume work, *On the History of Imperial Defense*,[73] which was soon cited as a classic after its publication in 1908–10, played a prominent role in Japanese naval thinking in the decades leading up to the Second World War. Although some have assumed that Satō was reflecting the ideas of Mahan in his work, a close examination of the text[74] reveals that he was most highly influenced by Vice-Admiral Sir Philip Colomb and the quite different emphases in his 1891 work on *Naval Warfare*[75] and his subsequent volume of *Essays on Naval Defence*.[76] In the broad context of Satō's work, Nelson's name appears only rarely, but when it does it is in a quite different light than British or Americans saw. In the 440 pages of the first volume, Satō makes a passing reference to Nelson, but attributes his victory at Trafalgar to the adoption of the idea that 'the true national defence is not to let the enemy set foot on national territory'.[77] In the second volume, Satō devotes only two pages to Nelson, where interestingly he highlighted the relative inferiority in numbers of the British fleet facing the combined Franco-Spanish fleet. With a quite different twist, the lessons that Satō interpreted here emphasised Nelson's need to do his *own* duty and for his captains to absolutely obey *his* orders.[78]

Just a year after Satō's work appeared, Ishihara Todatoshi wrote a more popular non-academic study in 1911. Entitled *Nelson and Napoleon*,[79] the book had no footnotes or bibliography making it difficult to determine its sources, but it contained a distinctive interpretation which may have been designed to inspire those contemplating a career in the Imperial Japanese Army or Navy. Published in the wake of two victorious wars over larger opponents, China in 1894–95 and over Russia in 1904–05, Ishihara's book emphasised some of the concepts of *bushidō* and reflected some traditional Japanese values that were being applied in a modern way to instil military values that could be useful to nineteenth- and twentieth-century Japanese forces.[80] In particular, Ishihara emphasised Nelson's personal determination to overcome his many illnesses, his bravery, and his ability to stand up against an enemy alone under adversity. Most importantly, Ishihara stressed Nelson's honourable death in battle and contrasted it to the dishonour and tragedy of Napoleon's death in exile.[81] Thus, Ishihara contributed a distinctively Japanese view and interpretation of Nelson.

Continuing the tradition of British connections through today, the former Imperial Naval Academy building at Etajima, built of red-bricks imported from England, still stands and is now the Officer Candidate School for the Japanese Maritime Self-Defense Force. A 1936 building with a Doric-style portico houses the school's purpose-built museum, where one may find Nelson's portrait still in a place of honour near the entrance and a lock of Nelson's hair acquired as recently as 1981 (apparently replacing an earlier lock of hair given soon after the Russo-Japanese War), which complements a similar lock of Admiral Tōgō's hair.

If Japanese interest in Nelson follows a tradition that is more than a century old, Chinese interest seems to be much more recent. Lin Xiangguang published a 120-page *Nelson Biography* only as recently as 1961,[82] based largely on the works of Robert Southey, A.T. Mahan, and Sir Geoffrey Callender. It is a fairly straightforward factual account that does not make any distinctive China-related interpretation of its own. In 1999, however, the Chinese People's Liberation Army-Navy published a western-style *Chinese Naval Encyclopedia* that contained two entries relating to our subject, one on Nelson and another on Trafalgar. These both extolled Nelson for his courage in battle, trail-blazing spirit, flexible leadership, rapid concentration of forces, well-conceived tactical planning, and for breaking away from the yoke of traditional naval tactics.[83]

When the flurry of interest in Nelson had settled following the centenary celebrations and the spate of books that appeared through 1910 had been absorbed by the reading public, views of Nelson in Europe and America settled down into the context of calmer historical study and reflection on broad historical narratives of the naval wars under sail and studies of the history of naval tactics. In Weimar Germany, Eberhard von Mantey included the battles of St Vincent, Aboukir, and Trafalgar in his 1928 illustrated atlas for students of naval history and tactics.[84] Similar studies looking at Nelson in the context of the broader development of naval tactics appeared in many navies, usually at the entry level of cadet or midshipman. Typical of these were locally produced reading materials by Gaetono Bonifacio used at the Italian Naval Academy from 1930 to 1958, succeeded by a series by Emilio Francardi, in use from 1959 to 1980, and then the published books of Alberto Santoni, used since 1981.[85] Former naval cadets who studied at the Italian Naval Academy before and during the Second World War, when Mussolini's Italy was fighting against Britain, recall that, despite the fascist propaganda against Britain their civilian and uniformed instructors in naval history taught them that Nelson was a very intelligent, audacious, courageous, charismatic leader, with an open mind for using new tactics. Similar reminiscences were expressed by former Italian cadets in the immediate post-Second World War era.[86]

In the late 1920s and early 1930s, there was apparently a momentary waning of professional interest in Nelson, both in the Royal Navy and elsewhere. As the battleship HMS *Nelson* prepared for her first commission in 1927, her commander requested Admiral Mark Kerr, RN, to prepare a series of lectures on the 'godfather' of the ship for the edification of the ship's company. By 1931, a typescript copy of these lectures reached the US Naval War College and came to the attention of its President, Rear-Admiral Harris Laning.[87] Struck by the professional relevance of what Kerr had written, Laning apparently promised to reproduce the lectures and send them to every ship in the US fleet. Although no documentary evidence has yet been found to show this actually happened, Kerr credited Laning's and the US Navy's deep interest in Nelson as the key source of stimulation that led to their publication in 1932.[88]

More commonly in the United States, Nelson was dealt with in the context of the broader history of naval tactics. The US Naval War College's Department of Intelligence made an early attempt to prepare a broad outline of the development of naval tactics under sail and their overview of the subject was first delivered as a series of lectures in 1927–28.[89] A more in-depth study did not appear in the US Navy for many years. Finally in 1942, Admiral S.S. Robison's general history of naval tactics from the Armada to 1930 was published and widely used.[90] It was superseded in 1960 by *Sea Power*, a naval history textbook for the US Naval Academy, edited by E.B. Potter and Fleet Admiral Chester W. Nimitz.[91] All of these place Nelson in the context of larger developments and highlight his importance as an innovative tactician and inspiring naval leader.

In contrast to what was going on in the United States, there was much less mention of Nelson in other navies, for example, in the Soviet Union. The old Tsarist Navy had been highly influenced by the works of both Vice-Admiral Philip Colomb and Mahan and had absorbed their views of Nelson in the process. The leading Soviet naval theoretician of the immediate post-1917 period, Professor Boris Gervais continued to propound the old Mahanist theory for a battleship navy to dispute command of the sea, but these views were heavily attacked in the 1920s and 1930s. Julian Corbett's views, in particular, were strongly criticised as allegedly ignoring the lessons of the Spanish-American and Russo-Japanese wars. The new trend in Soviet naval theory was to argue that the old ideas that Nelson represented in terms of general fleet engagements and blockade were no longer valid for modern naval thought.[92] However, in the years between 1946 and 1953 Soviet naval attitudes seemed to have modified and begun to accept Corbett's understanding of a 'fleet-in-being' strategy in the way that Corbett had attributed its understanding to Nelson in the Mediterranean in 1796: 'an inferior fleet kept actively in being' in order to exploit its 'general power of holding such command [of the sea] in dispute'.[93]

Following on from these precedents in Soviet naval thinking, Admiral of the Fleet of the Soviet Union Sergei Gorshkov criticised western naval theory. In 1972–83, Gorshkov wrote a series of articles that appeared in the Soviet naval journal *Morskoi Sbornik*[94] that were eventually republished in book form under the title *The Sea Power of the State*. On a single page, Gorshkov summarised his understanding of the wars of the French Revolution, which had been organised by 'the English bourgeoisie, seeking to gain a complete hold on the colonial possessions still left to France'.[95] In this struggle, the weakness of the French fleet played a fatal role for France. Napoleon's Egyptian expedition had been initially saved by Nelson's 'chain of errors' that delayed his attack on the French squadron in Aboukir Bay by two and a half months. Trafalgar, Gorshkov believed, 'like the role of the English fleet in the struggle with Napoleon, has been enormously exaggerated by Anglo-American ideologists'. Clearly making a point that could be translated into Cold War context and the need for the Soviet Union to develop a strong navy, he noted that it was Russia's victory on land over Napoleon that had provided the most decisive effect on European politics; but at the same time

> Trafalgar showed the total inability of France to wage war at sea against the more sophisticated English fleet consisting of better-quality ships manned by better trained crews and employing tactics new for that time. England and her colonies became practically invulnerable to strikes from the sea. This untied the hands of the English bourgoisie to organize and finance new alliances for continuing the struggle ....[96]

In contrast to the Soviet interpretation, a survey of the way in which Nelson has been understood and valued today in modern Latin American navies[97] reveals a number of points that are shared with many other navies around the world. The Argentine Naval War College, for example, published its own evaluation of Nelson in 1940. Dealing with many aspects of Nelson's life, it became the focus for a number of student papers written by mid-career officers.[98] In Argentine naval history, the Irish-Argentine naval leader Admiral Guillermo Brown is described as having 'the Nelson Touch'.[99] There were direct connections, too, with one of Nelson's opponents at Trafalgar being the last Spanish Viceroy of the River Plate. The man against whom the colonists fought for their independence from Spain was Rear-Admiral Báltasar Hidalgo de Cisneros, who had flown his flag in *Santissima Trinidad* at Trafalgar. In the struggle for Chilean independence and in Chilean naval history from 1818, Lord Cochrane plays an important role. Cochrane's 1798 meeting with

Nelson and Cochrane's understanding of Nelson's injunction, 'Never mind the maneuvers, always go at them',[100] has had an influence in Cochrane's career and has endured in his reputation in Chile. As in other navies throughout the world, currently serving officers in the Mexican and Uruguayan navies emphasise the tradition and heritage aspects of Nelson's contribution to their navies, particularly in terms of uniforms. Typically, one may mention: the blue colour on a seaman's uniform that has three white stripes, reputedly commemorating the battles of the Nile, Copenhagen, and Trafalgar; the black tie on seamen's uniforms, believed to be a sign of mourning for Nelson's death; the curl on the upper stripe of the gold braid on an officer's uniform, in many navies, that is attributed to Nelson's loss of his right arm in 1797; the standard usage of leaving unbuttoned the upper button of the frock coat, a usage reportedly used by Nelson to hold his empty right sleeve by way of the curl.[101]

IV

Nelson's legacy as a hero among the world's navies is a complex one that stretches not only around the globe but through a wide variety of applications. It ranges from historical actions by Nelson himself that had a direct or an indirect influence on foreign navies, to the slow development over two centuries, of invoking his name and attributing wide professional naval values to it. A close examination of this phenomenon shows both parallel development and tension as historical insight has developed and as traditional, heritage values have been applied as navies became increasingly professionalised during the two centuries since 1805.

Finally, there is a further dimension that has not yet been widely analysed, but which will be seen in practice in June 2005, when ships from the world's navies participate in the International Fleet Review in the Solent at Spithead. Such an occasion is perhaps the most public culmination of what is usually a more low-key and almost imperceptible use that combines naval tradition, naval history, and naval heritage as a tool of diplomatic engagement and professional cooperation between navies. Participation and exchange of information with other navies, and the presence, displays, and exchanges of portraits of historical leaders, such as Nelson, and paintings of battles, such as Trafalgar and the Nile, join with the tradition of the annual Trafalgar Night Dinners, where one joins in drinking the toast to 'the immortal memory.' All these serve to create a basis for a shared naval heritage, which navies have traditionally used to create the ambiance within which to discuss and to develop the most modern and advanced multilateral or bilateral relations on issues unconstrained by the past. For the navies of the world, Nelson's legacy is that of a hero who represented the highest values of professional competence for the world and therefore, a shared icon in world naval heritage. At the same time, continuing historical research goes on in naval history, reaching beyond the icons of tradition and heritage, to continue to deepen professional naval understanding of Nelson and his age.

Notes

1. Dallas-Fort Worth, Texas, *Star Telegram*. 11 August 2002. <www.dfw.com/mld/startelegram/3841477.htm>, accessed 2 September 2004.
2. Gordon R. England (1937–), served in the administration of President George W. Bush as the 72nd Secretary of the Navy from 24 May 2001 to 23 January 2003, when he became the first, Deputy Secretary of the Department of Homeland Security. After eight months in that office, he returned to the Navy Department as the 73rd Secretary of the Navy on 26 September 2003 and was serving as of 14 October 2004. His tenure is distinctive as being only the second person in US naval history to serve twice as the civilian leader of the US Navy–Marine Corps team and the first to serve in two consecutive terms.
3. 'Core Values of the United States Navy', <www.chinfo.navy.mil/navpalib/traditions/html/corvalu.html>, accessed 3 September 2004.
4. C.I. Hamilton, 'Naval Hagiography and the Victorian Hero', *The Historical Journal*, 23, 2 (1980), pp. 381–98.
5. Dudley W. Knox (ed.), *Naval Documents Relating to the Quasi War between the United States and France* (Washington, D.C.: Government Printing Office, 1935), vol. 1, p. 26: Letter from Samuel Sewell to Secretary Timothy Pickering, 27 December 1797. Compare with Sir Nicholas Harris Nicolas (ed.), *The dispatches and letters of Vice Admiral Lord Viscount Nelson, with notes* (London: H. Colburn, 1845–46), vol. II, p. 379.
6. Quoted in Michael A. Palmer, *Stoddert's War: Naval Operations During the Quasi-War with France, 1798–1801* (Columbia: University of South Carolina Press, 1987), p. 203.
7. Dudley W. Knox (ed.), *Naval Documents Related to the United States Wars with the Barbary Powers* (Washington, D.C.: Government Printing Office, 1941), vol. 3, p. 434. Tobias Lear to Robert Montgomery, 19 February 1804. Other passing references to the Battle of the Nile and its effect on American trade may be found in Knox (ed.), *Naval Documents Relating to the Quasi War*, vol. 1, pp. 467, 480, 481, 484, 507.
8. Among recent uses of this quotation, see, for example, E.B. Potter and C.W. Nimitz (eds), *Sea Power: A Naval History* (Englewood Cliffs, N.J.: Prentice Hall, 1960), p. 202; *The Dictionary of American Naval Fighting Ships* (Washington, D.C.: Government Printing Office, 1970), vol. 5, p. 282. A detailed description of the action, without the quotation, may be found in Christopher McKee, *Edward Preble: A Naval Biography, 1761–1807* (Annapolis: Naval Institute Press, 1972), pp. 189–99.

9. Originally published in London in 1813, American editions were quickly published at New York by Eastburn, Kirk, & Co., and at Boston by William Wells in 1813. Another edition was published in Hartford (Conn.) by B & J Russell for Oliver D. Cooke in 1814; there was another printing at Boston: E.G. House, 1814; and yet another at Hartford: W.S. Marsh, 1814.

10. Alexander Slidell Mackenzie, *The Life of Commodore Oliver Hazard Perry* 5th edition (New York: Harper & Brothers, [1858]), vol. 1, p. 222. I am grateful to Dr David Skaggs for this reference.

11. David Curtis Skaggs, *Thomas Macdonough: Master of Command in the Early US Navy* (Annapolis: Naval Institute Press, 2004), p. 127; William R. Folsom, 'The Battle of Plattsburg', *Vermont Quarterly*, 20 (October 1952), p. 253.

12. Skaggs, *Macdonough*. See also, Charles E. Brodine, Jr., Michael J. Crawford, and Christine Hughes, *Against All Odds: U.S. Sailors in the War of 1812* (Washington: Naval Historical Center, 2004), p. 59.

13. Beginning with the edition by Harper Brothers in their 'Family Library' series; New York: J. & J. Harper, 1830.

14. Letter from Robert Southey to Grosvenor C. Bradford, 8 December 1828, in Rev. Charles Cuthbert Southey (ed.), *The Life and Correspondence of Robert Southey* (London: Longman, Brown, Green, and Longman, 1850; facsimile reprint: St Clair Shores, Michigan: Scholarly Press, 1969), vol. V, p. 335 and footnote.

15. James Fenimore Cooper, 'Preface to the second edition [1851]', in *The Two Admirals: A Tale*. Historical Introduction by Donald A. Ringe. Text established by James A. Sapperfield and E.N. Feltskog. The Writings of James Fenimore Cooper Series. (Albany: State University of New York Press, 1990), p. 8.

16. Thomas Philbrick, *James Fenimore Cooper and the Development of American Sea Fiction* (Cambridge, Mass.: Harvard University Press, 1961).

17. G.L. Newnham Collingwood (ed.), *A selection from the public and private correspondence of Vice-Admiral Lord Collingwood: interspersed with memoirs of his life*. First American edition from the 4th English edition. (New York: G. & C. & H. Carvill, 1829).

18. Cooper, 'Preface', p. 9.

19. James H. Ward, *A Manual of Naval Tactics: together with a brief critical analysis of the principal modern naval battles* (New York: D. Appleton & Co., 1859), p. 6.

20. Later editions of *A Manual of Naval Tactics* were published in 1865, 1867, and 1870.

21. Sir Howard Douglas, *On Naval Warfare with Steam* (London: John Murray, 1858).

22. Ward, *A Manual of Naval Tactics*, footnote on p. 180.

23. Ward, *A Manual of Naval Tactics*, p. 6.

24. Letter from Commander S. Phillips Lee, USN, to Commander Henry Grant, RN, 28 September 1861. Professor Edward K. Rawson and Robert H. Woods (eds), *Official Records of the Union and Confederate Navies in the War of Rebellion* (Washington: Government Printing Office, 1897), Series I, vol. 6, *The Atlantic Blockading Squadron*, p. 294.

25. Letter from Acting Rear Admiral S.P. Lee, USN, to Assistant Secretary of the Navy G.V. Fox, 4 April 1864. Prof. Edward K. Rawson and Charles W. Stewart (eds), *Official Records of the Union and Confederate Navies in the War*

of Rebellion (Washington: Government Printing Office, 1899), Series I, vol. 9, *North Atlantic Blockading Squadron, 1863–1864*, pp. 583–4.

26. Letter from Commander George Henry Preble, USN, to Secretary of the Navy Gideon Welles, 1 March 1864. Richard Rush (ed.), *Official Records of the Union and Confederate Navies in the War of Rebellion* (Washington: Government Printing Office, 1895), Series I, vol. 2, *The Operations of the Cruisers 1863–64*, p. 622.

27. Letter from Confederate Secretary of the Navy S.R. Mallory to Commander James D. Bulloch, CSN, 7 May 1863. C.C. Marsh (ed.), *Official Records of the Union and Confederate Navies in the War of Rebellion* (Washington: Government Printing Office, 1921), Series II, vol. 2, *Navy Department Correspondence, 1861–65, with Agents Abroad*, pp. 417–19, quote from p. 418.

28. Extracts from the diary of Lieutenant Francis A. Roe, US Navy. Charles W. Stewart (ed.), *Official Records of the Union and Confederate Navies in the War of Rebellion* (Washington: Government Printing Office, 1904), Series I, vol. 18, *West Gulf Blockading Squadron, 1862*, p. 768.

29. Quoted in Chares Lee Lewis, *David Glasgow Farragut: Our First Admiral* (Annapolis: Naval Institute Press, 1943), p. 315.

30. Ibid., p. 530.

31. Winfield Scott Schley, *Forty-Five Years under the Flag* (New York: D. Appleton & Co., 1904), p. 51.

32. John B. Hattendorf, 'The Study of War History at Oxford', in Hattendorf and Malcolm H. Murfett (eds), *The Limitations of Military Power: Essays Presented to Norman Gibbs on his Eightieth Birthday* (New York: St Martin's Press, 1990), pp. 5–7.

33. Donald M. Schurman, *The Education of a Navy: The Development of British Naval Strategic Thought, 1867–1914* (Chicago: University of Chicago Press, 1965); Andrew Lambert, *The Foundations of Naval History: John Knox Laughton, the Royal Navy, and the Historical Profession* (London: Chatham Publishing, 1998); Andrew Lambert (ed.), *Letters and Papers of Professor Sir John Knox Laughton, 1830–1915*. Publications of the Navy Records Society, vol. 143 (Aldershot, Hants; Burlington, Vt.: Published by Ashgate for the Navy Records Society, 2002).

34. J.K. Laughton, 'The Scientific Study of Naval History', *Journal of the Royal United Services Institution*, vol. XVIII (1874), pp. 508–27.

35. Ibid., p. 522.

36. Ibid., p. 523.

37. 'Alfred Stenzel', in Hans H. Hildebrand and Ernst Henriot (eds), *Deutschlands Admirale, 1849–1945* (Osnabrück: Biblio Verlag, 1990), Band 3 *P-Z*, pp. 380–2; Hermann Kirchhoff, 'Einführung: Stenzels Leben and Werke', in Alfred Stenzel, *Kriegführung zur See: Lehre vom Seekriege*, ed. Hermann Kirchoff (Hannover und Leipzig: Hansche Buchhandlung, 1913), pp. xiii–xxxi.

38. James Russell Soley, *Report on Foreign Systems of Naval Education*. U.S. Senate. 46th Congress. 2d Session. Ex. Doc No., 51 (Washington: Government Printing Office, 1880), pp. 190–3.

39. 'Als letzte and als höchste Ehrung Nelsons ist wohl anzusehen, daß man in der neuesten Zeit wiederum seine Bedeutung ganz besonders hervorgehoben und erkannt hat, man müsse den Nelsonchen Geist wieder aufleben lassen, ihn hegen und seine Ideen pflegen, um das Größte zu erreichen.' Alfred

Stenzel, *Seekriegsgeschichte in ihren wichtigsten Abschnitten mit Berüchsichtigung der Seetaktik* (Hannover und Leipzig: Hahnsche Buchhandlung, 1911), p. 344.

40. Stephen B. Luce, 'An Address Delivered at the United States Naval War College..., 1903', reprinted in John D. Hayes and Hattendorf (eds), *The Writings of Stephen B. Luce* (Newport: Naval War College, 1975), pp. 39–40.
41. Quoted in editors' introduction to ibid., p. 47.
42. Ibid., pp. 61–2.
43. Ibid., p. 63.
44. Stephen B. Luce, 'On the Study of Naval History (Grand Tactics)', reprinted in Hayes and Hattendorf, *The Writings of Stephen B. Luce*, pp. 73.
45. Ibid., p. 92.
46. A.T. Mahan, *From Sail to Steam; Recollections of a Naval Life* (New York: Harper Brothers, 1907; reprinted: New York: Da Capo Press, 1968), p. 275.
47. Ibid.
48. A.T. Mahan, *The Influence of Sea Power Upon History, 1660–1783* (Boston: Little Brown, 1890).
49. A.T. Mahan, *The Influence of Sea Power Upon the French Revolution and Empire, 1793–1812*, 2 vols (Boston: Little Brown, 1892).
50. Ibid., vol. 1, pp. v, vi.
51. Ibid.
52. Quoted in Hattendorf, B. Mitchell Simpson III, and John R. Wadleigh, *Sailors and Scholars: The Centennial History of the Naval War College* (Newport: Naval War College Press, 1984), p. 35.
53. Jon Tetsuro Sumida, *Inventing Grand Strategy and Teaching Command; The Classic Works of Alfred Thayer Mahan Reconsidered* (Washington, D.C.: The Woodrow Wilson Center Press; Baltimore, MD, and London: The Johns Hopkins University Press, 1997), pp. 34–5.
54. A.T. Mahan, *Nelson: The Embodiment of the Sea Power of Great Britain*, 2 vols (Boston: Little, Brown, and Company, 1897).
55. Mahan, *Nelson*, vol. 1, p. 452.
56. Ibid., p. 347.
57. Sumida, *Inventing Grand Strategy and Teaching Command*, pp. 36–9. See also, the comparison between Nelson and Farragut on this point in A.T. Mahan, *Admiral Farragut* (New York: Appleton, 1892), pp. 308–9.
58. A.T. Mahan, *Types of Naval Officers Drawn from the History of the British Navy* (London: Sampson Low, Marston & Company, 1902), pp. xiii–xiv.
59. See for example, Lieutenant Commander Leland P. Lovette, USN, *Naval Customs, Traditions and Usage* (Annapolis: US Naval Institute, 1939), p. 15.
60. A.T. Mahan, *Eikoku Suishi Teitoku Neruson Den*. Translated by Sadamasu Oshima for Kaigun Jioiku Honbu [The Educational Headquarters of the Imperial Japanese Navy] (Tokyo: Kaubunkan, 1906).
61. A.T. Mahan, *Lord Nelson: Grundläggaren av Storbritanniens Herravälde över Haven*. Bemyndigad översättning av D. [Axel Daniel] Landquist, Underlöjnant vid K. Flottan (Stockholm: Norstedt & Söners Förlag, 1913).
62. Julian S. Corbett, *The Campaign of Trafalgar* (London: Longmans, Green, 1910).

63. See Hattendorf, 'The Caird Lecture: The Anglo-French Naval Wars (1689–1815) in Twentieth Century Naval Thought', *Journal of Maritime Research* (June 2001) <www.jmr.nmm.ac.uk>.

64. Hildebrand and Henriot (eds), *Deutschlands Admriale 1849–1945*, band 2, H-O: Curt Freiherr von Maltzahn (1849–1930), pp. 425–6.

65. Ibid., Dr. Phil h.c. Eberhard von Mantey (1869–1940), pp. 432–3.

66. Curt Freiherr von Maltzahn, 'Nelson und die Schlacht von Trafalgar', *Marine Rundschau* (1906), pp. 259–73. See also, von Maltzahn, *Der Seekrieg: Seine geschichtliche Entwicklung vom Zeitalter der Entdeckungen bis zur Gegenwart* (Leipzig: Druck und Verlag von B. G. Teubner, 1906).

67. Lectures in 'Kopien aus dem Nachlass des vizeadmrials a. D. Eberhard von Mantey (1869–1940), Band 1'. I am grateful to Dr Werner Rahn for providing me with photocopies of these materials.

68. Joseph Conrad, 'The Heroic Age', in *The Mirror of the Sea* (New York: Harper Brothers, 1906), pp. 328–9.

69. I am most grateful for the assistance and advice of Dr Bruce A. Elleman, Maritime History Department, Naval War College, for his translations from Chinese and Japanese sources cited.

70. Vice-Admiral Viscount Nagayo Ogasawara, *Life of Admiral Togo* (Tokyo: The Seito Press, 1934), p. 57; Georges Blond, *Admiral Togo* (New York: The Macmillan Co., 1960), p. 48.

71. E. Stuart Kirby, 'Heihachiro Togo: Japan's Nelson, (1848–1934)', in Jack Sweetman (ed.), *The Great Admirals: Command at Sea, 1587–1945* (Annapolis: Naval Institute Press, 1997), pp. 327–48.

72. David C. Evans and Mark R. Peattie, *Kaigun: Strategy, Tactics, and Technology in the Imperial Japanese Navy, 1887–1941* (Annapolis: Naval Institute Press, 1997), pp. 135–41.

73. Satō Tetsutarō, *Teikoku kokubōshi ron* (two vols, originally published 1908, 1910, reprinted Tokyo: Hara shobo, 1979).

74. For which, I thank Dr Bruce Elleman, and also advice from Dr Mark Peattie, Hoover Institution, Stanford University.

75. Satō refers to him throughout his work as 'Co-ro-mu'; P.H. Colomb, *Naval Warfare: Its Ruling Principles and Practice Historically Treated* (Originally published, London, 1891; reprinted in The Classics of Sea Power series, with an Introduction by Barry M. Gough; Annapolis: Naval Institute Press, 1990).

76. P.H. Colomb, *Essays on Naval Defence* (London, 1893; second edition, London, 1896).

77. Satō, *Teikoku kokubōshi ron*, vol. 1, p. 211.

78. Ibid., vol. 2, pp. 105–6.

79. Ishihara Todatoshi, *Neruson to Naporeon* (Tokyo: Keiseisha Publishers, 1911).

80. See the cautions on the use of this often misapplied term in Evans and Peattie, *Kaigun*, pp. 543 note 4; 609 note 46.

81. Ibid., pp. 2, 10, 29, 30, 419, 448.

82. Lin Xiangguang, *Na'erxun zhuan* (Taipei: China Cultural Publications, 1961).

83. *Zhongquo Haijun Baike Quanshu* (Beijing: Sea Tide Publishers, 1998–99), a column and a half entry for the Naval Battle of Cape Trafalgar:

'Telafa'erjiajiao Haizhan', vol. 2, pp. 1673–4, and a one column entry on H. Nelson: 'Na'erxun, H.', vol. 2, p. 1366. The latter includes a not altogether flattering portrait, as Nelson is shown at a slight angle with a huge nose, perhaps suggesting the fact that the Chinese often refer to foreigners as 'Da Bizi' which means 'Big Noses'.

84. Eberhard v. Mantey, *Seeschlachten-Atlas: Eine Einführung in die Lehre vom Seekriege* (Berlin: E.G. Mittler & Sohn, 1928; Second edition, 1937).

85. Gaetono Bonifacio, *Lezioni di Storia Navale* (Livorno: Tipo-Litografia R. Academia Navale, 1930); Emilio Francardi, *Appunti di Storia Navale* (Livorno: Poliigrafico dell'Accademia Navale, 1959); Albero Santoni, *DA Lepanto ad Hampton Road* (Milano: Mursia, 1991); Alberto Santoni, *Storia e Politica navale dell'Età Moderna* (Roma: Ufficio Storico della Marina Militare, 1998). I am grateful to Dr Marco Gemignani of the Italian Naval Academy for providing me with photocopies of the Nelson-related materials from these publications.

86. I am grateful to Dr Marco Gemignani, who interviewed surviving former cadets from these periods, and provided me with this information, 27 August 2004.

87. Naval War College Archives. RG 28: President's File: Laning. Letter from Admiral Mark Kerr to Laning, 22 January 1931. The original typescript is in the Naval Historical Subjects file, Naval Historical Collection, Naval War College. For Laning's career, see Harris Laning, *An Admiral's Yarn*, edited with an introduction by Mark Russell Shulman (Newport: Naval War College Press, 1999).

88. Mark Kerr, *The Sailor's Nelson* (London: Hurst & Blackett, Ltd, [1932], p. 9). I have not yet found any evidence that Laning actually did circulate copies of the typescript to the US fleet, although the published book seems to have found its way into key US naval library collections ashore: Navy Department Library in Washington, Naval Academy Library in Annapolis, and two copies at the Naval War College Library in Newport, Rhode Island.

89. US Naval War College. Edward C. Kalbfus, *A Review of the Naval History of the Eighteenth Century*, 2 vols reproduced for local use in typescript (Newport: Naval War College Department of Intelligence, 1929).

90. S.S. Robison, *A History of Naval Tactics from 1530 to 1930; the evolution of tactical maxims* (Annapolis: Naval Institute Press, 1942).

91. E.B. Potter, and C.W. Nimitz (eds), *Sea Power: A Naval History* (Englewood Cliffs, N.J.: Prentice Hall, 1960). With numerous factual historical errors, the best direct corrective was a revised edition published in German by Jürgen Rohwer, *Seemacht: Ein Seekriegsgeschichte von der Antike bis zur Gegenwart* (München: Bernard & Graefe, 1974).

92. Robert W. Herrick, *Soviet Naval Theory and Policy: Gorshkov's Inheritance* (Newport: Naval War College Press, 1988), pp. 12–13, 202–3, 206–7.

93. Ibid., p. 188, and also 225, 270; Julian S. Corbett, *Some Principles of Maritime Strategy*, edited with an introduction by Eric Grove, Classics of Sea Power series (Annapolis: Naval Institute Press, 1988), pp. 223–4. Corbett's comments are based on Nelson's letter to the Duke of Clarence, 19 August 1796. Nicolas (ed.), *Letters*, vol. III, p. 246.

94. Translated and published with western commentary in Sergei G. Gorshkov, *Red Star Rising at Sea* (Annapolis: Naval Institute Press, 1974; reprinted 1978). See pp. 7–8 for comments on Nelson.

95. Sergei G. Gorshkov, *The Sea Power of the State* (Annapolis: Naval Institute Press, 1980), p. 65.
96. Ibid., pp. 65–6.
97. I am grateful to Captain Guillermo Montenegro, Argentine Navy (ret.), who provided detailed information on Argentina and coordinated additional responses for me on this subject from Captain Carlos Tromben, Chilean Navy (ret.); Lieutenant Commander Ramiro Lobato Camacho, Mexican Navy; Captain Jorge Ortiz Sotelo, Peruvian Navy (ret.); and Commander Diego Rombys, Uruguayan Navy (ret.).
98. G.J. Montenegro, 'Nelson's Figure in the Argentine Navy', unpublished paper, 2004. Eloy S. Soneyra, *Ideas Estratégicas del Almirante Nelson – Trafalgar* (Buenos Aires: Escuela de Guerra Navale, 1940).
99. Felipe Bosch, *Guillermo Brown: Biografia de un Almirante* (Buenos Aires: Alborada, 1966), p. 18.
100. Thomas Alexander Cochrane, Earl of Dundonald, *The Autobiography of a Seaman* (London: Richard Bentley & Son, 1890), p. 35.
101. Captain Juan José Fernández Parés, *Hombres de Mar, un estilo de vida* (Montevideo: Liga Marítima Uruguaya, 1990). See also, Kerr, *The Sailor's Nelson*, pp. 9–10; Lovette, *Naval Customs, Traditions, and Usage*, pp. 295–6.

Index

Compiled by Sue Carlton